Private International Law

By

Sir William Henry Rattigan

William S. Hein & Co., Inc.
Buffalo, New York
1996

Library of Congress Catalog Number 96-76320
ISBN 1-57588-083-0

Printed in the United States of America.

The quality of this reprint is equivalent to the quality of the original work.

This volume is printed on acid-free paper by
William S. Hein & Co., Inc.

PRIVATE INTERNATIONAL LAW.

BY

SIR WILLIAM HENRY RATTIGAN, LL.D.

OF LINCOLN'S INN, BARRISTER-AT-LAW;

VICE-CHANCELLOR OF THE UNIVERSITY OF THE PUNJAB.

Author of "The Science of Jurisprudence," "Roman Law of Persons," &c. &c.

LONDON:

STEVENS AND SONS, LIMITED,

119 & 120, CHANCERY LANE,

Law Publishers and Booksellers.

1895

LONDON:

PRINTED BY C. F. ROWORTH, GREAT NEW STREET, FETTER LANE—E.C.

PREFACE.

In a country like India, where the territory of the British Crown is at numerous points conterminous with the territory of independent Native States —which are reckoned at no less a number than 629, or, if the Burmese States are included, 688,— whose sovereignty within their own territorial limits is distinctly acknowledged by the Paramount Power and, as we shall see, has been judicially affirmed by the Judicial Committee of the Privy Council in a recent case,* the importance of the subject of Private International Law to the Indian law student cannot be denied. It is a subject, in fact, which not only possesses great theoretical interest for the Indian lawyer, but is one also which

* In the case of *Sirdar Gurdyal Singh* v. *H.H. The Raja of Faridkot,* (1894) App. Cas. 670.

very frequently demands his practical attention. It is, nevertheless, a subject upon which no text-book suitable to an Indian student exists at present, and this want has been particularly felt by those who were studying for a law degree at some one of our Indian Universities. The want, though perhaps not to the same extent, is probably also felt by English students, for such treatises as those of Westlake and Foote seem scarcely adapted for a college course, while those of Phillimore and Bar—the latter now made accessible to English readers by Mr. Gillespie's excellent translation—are clearly outside their range altogether. It has occurred to me, therefore, that there is an open field here which calls for labourers, and, although I would have been better pleased if some one more qualified and less occupied with the practical side of the profession than myself had been found to devote his leisure moments to its examination and elucidation, I have consented, at the express request of the leading members of the Faculty of Law of the Punjab University, and in the absence of others willing to undertake the task, to compile the following treatise, giving a brief historical introduction to the subject and stating the leading principles that are now generally accepted in the province of Private International Law, in language at once free from all ambiguity and simple in expression. In doing so I have carefully consulted all the leading treatises on the subject in English, German, French and Italian, and I have endeavoured to extract from them such rules as appeared to have gained more or less general recognition, not hesitating to adopt the very *ipsissima verba* of any writer of acknowledged merit whose language appeared to me to express a rule with such definiteness and clearness of expression that I could not myself hope to improve upon it. My special obligations are in this way due to Burge (but too little known to English students), Story, Westlake, and Phillimore amongst English writers; to Laurent, Calvo, Brocher, and Fœlix amongst French; Fiore, Fusinato, and Laghi amongst Italian; and last, but not least, to my old and honored friend Von Bar, amongst German Jurists. Remembering, however, that I was writing for English students, or rather for students who would require a more practical acquaintance with the English phase of questions of Private International Law than with that under any other system of law, particular care has been taken to give prominence to the views accepted by English authorities—which in every instance are quoted at the foot of the page, to enable the reader to refer to them, if necessary, for his own satisfaction.

W. H. R.

LAHORE,
March, 1895.

CONTENTS.

	PAGE
Preface	iii
List of Principal Authorities consulted	ix
Cases cited	xi

CHAPTER I.

Growth and general Theory of Private International Law 1

CHAPTER II.

Nationality and Domicil 15

CHAPTER III.

Law of Persons, and herein of Status and Capacity, Law of the Family, and of Artificial and Conventional Persons 47

CHAPTER IV.

Law of Things 80

CHAPTER V.

Law of Obligations, and herein of Contracts, Torts, and the Forms of Legal Transactions 99

CHAPTER VI.

Immaterial Rights, and herein of Copyright, Patents, and Trade-Marks 163

CHAPTER VII.

Law of Procedure, and herein of Foreign Judgments.. 188

PRINCIPAL AUTHORITIES CONSULTED.

Addison, *Law of Contracts.* 9th ed. 1892.

Anson, *Principles of the English Law of Contracts.* 7th ed. 1893.

Austin, *Lectures on Jurisprudence.* By Campbell. 2 vols. 1885.

Bar, *The Theory and Practice of Private International Law.* 2nd ed. Translated by E. R. Gillespie. 1892.

Banning, *Concise Treatise on the Statute Law of the Limitations of Actions.* 2nd ed. 1892.

Beach-Lawrence's *Wheaton's International Law.* 1861.

Bluntschli (J. C.), *Das moderne Völkerrecht der civilisirten Staaten als Rechtsbuch dargestellt.* 3rd ed. 1878.

Boullenois, *Traité et de la Personnalité et de la Réalité des Lois, Coûtumes, ou Statuts.* 2 vol. Paris. 1766.

Brocher (Charles), *Nouveau Traité de Droit International Privé.* Geneva, Bâle, Lyons, Paris. 1876.

——— *Cours de Droit International Privé.* 3 vols. Paris and Geneva. 1882–1885.

Burge, *Commentaries on Colonial and Foreign Laws generally, and in their Conflict with each Other and with the Law of England.* 4 vols. London. 1838.

Calvo (Charles), *Le Droit International, théorique et pratique.* 5 vols. Paris and Berlin. 1887-1888.

Copinger, *The Law of Copyright.* 3rd ed. 1893.

Dicey, *The Law of Domicile as a Branch of the Law of England.* London. 1879.

Field (Dudley), *Outlines of an International Code.* 3rd ed. New York and London. 1876.

Fiore (Pasquale), *Diritto Internazionale Privato.* (*Leggi Civili*). 2 vols. Terza edizione. Torino. 1888-1889.

Fœlix, *Traité du Droit International Privé.* 4th ed. 2 vols. Paris. 1866.

Foote (J. A.), *Concise Treatise on Private International Jurisprudence,* based on decisions of English Courts. 2nd ed. London. 1890.

Fusinato (Guido), *Il Principio della Scuola Italiana nel Diritto Privato Internazionale.* Bologna. 1885.

——— *Questioni di Diritto Internazionale Privato.* Turin. 1884.

Hall, *International Law.* 3rd ed. 1890.

——— *Treatise on the Foreign Powers and Jurisdiction of the British Crown.* Oxford. 1894.

Halleck, *International Law.* 3rd ed. 2 vols. 1893.

Heffter, *Das Europäische Völkerrecht der Gegenwart.* Berlin. 1882 and 1888.

Von Holtzendorff (Fr.), *Handbuch des Völkerrechts.* 4 vols. Berlin and Hamburg. 1885-1889.

Laghi (Ferdinando), *Il Diritto Internazionale Privato.* Vol. I. Bologna. 1888.

Laurent (E.), *Le Droit Civil Internationale.* 8 vols. Brussels and Paris.

Lorimer (James), *The Institutes of the Law of Nations.* 2 vols. 1883-1884.

Maine, *Lectures on International Law.* New ed. 1890.

Von Martens (F.), *Völkerrecht, das internationale Recht der civilisirten Nationen.* 2 vols. Berlin. 1883-1886.

Martens (G. F.), *Précis du Droit des Gens modernes de l'Europe.* 2 vols. Paris. 1864.

Merlin, *Répertoire Universale et Raisonné de Jurisprudence.* 3rd ed. Paris. 1887.

Pardessus, *Cours de Droit Commercial.* 3rd ed. Paris. 1826.

Pernice, *Geschichte des Römischen Rechts.*

Phillimore (R.), *Commentaries on International Law.* 4 vols. 1879-1889.

Piggott, *Foreign Judgments.* 2nd ed. 1884, and Supplement, 1886.

Pollock (F.), *Principles of Contract at Law and in Equity.* 5th ed. 1889.

Pothier, *Œuvres.* 11 vols.

Puchta (G. F.), *Institutionen des Römischen Rechts.* 3 vols.

Pulszky (Augustus), *The Theory of Law and Civil Society.* London. 1888.

Savigny (F.), *Geschichte des Römischen Rechts im Mittelalter.* 2nd ed. 1834.

——— *System des heutigen Römischen Rechts.* Vol. VIII., and English translation by Guthrie. 2nd ed. 1880.

Seuffert (L.), *Civil-Processordnung für das Deutsche Reich, erläutert.* 4th ed. 1889.

Smith, *Leading Cases in various Branches of the Law.* 9th ed. 2 vols. 1887.

Stephen, *Commentaries on the Law of England.* 11th ed. 1890.

Story (Jos.), *Commentaries on the Conflict of Laws.* 8th ed. Boston. 1883.

Taylor, *On the Law of Evidence.* 8th ed. 2 vols. 1885.

Thicknesse, *Digest of the Law of Husband and Wife.* 1884.

Vattel (E.), *Le Droit des Gens,* and English translation.

Vico, *Diritto Universale.*

Walker, *Science of International Law.* London. 1893.

Westlake (John), *Treatise on Private International Law.* 2nd ed. London. 1890.

Wharton (F.), *Digest of International Law.* 2nd ed. 3 vols. Washington. 1887.

Wheaton, by Beach-Lawrence, 1861; also ed. by Boyd, 1880.

Woolsey, *Introduction to Study of International Law.* 5th ed. 1888.

CASES CITED.

A.

PAGE

Abdallah v. Rickards 34
Abdul Messih v. Farra 32
Abouloff v. Oppenheim........ 234
Acutt, Blaine & Co. v. The Colonial Marine Insurance Co. . 234
Agnes Otto, The 161
Albion Insurance Co. v. Mills .. 143
Alivon v. Furnival............ 192
Allen v. Kemble 122, 208
Alliance Bank of Simla v. Cary 114, 196, 199
Alves v. Hodgson 130
Amalia, The 157
Andros v. Andros 70
Anglo-African Steamship Co., Re 215
Anstruther v. Adair 137
——— v. Chalmer 138
Antelope, The................ 114
Apollinaris Company's Trade Marks, The 179
Ardaseer Cursetjee v. Perozeboye 60
Armstrong v. Stokes 144
Atkinson v. Anderson 71
Att.-Gen. v. Alexander 46, 77
——— v. Mill.............. 112
——— v. Rowe 37
Atul Kisto Bose v. Lyon & Co. . 204
Augusta v. Chilian 161

B.

Bababhat v. Narharbhat 197
Bain v. Whitehaven and Furness Junction Railway 195
Banco de Portugal, Ex parte .. 92
——— v. Waddell .. 91
Bank of Australasia v. Harding 223
——— v. Nias....194, 223, 238
Baron de Bode's Case 218
Batthyany v. Walford 82

PAGE

Bayley v. Edwardes 244
Beavan v. Hastings 98
Becket v. McCarthy 224, 230
Bell v. Kennedy 43
Bempde v. Johnstone 35
Benham v. Mornington........ 128
Bent v. Young 82
Benton v. Horeau 132
Bertram v. Duhamel 116
Bethell, In re 60
Betts' Patent, Re 174
Biggs v. Lawrence............ 112
Birtwhistle v. Vardill..69, 73, 74, 84
Blake v. Smith 234
Blakes, Ex parte 91
Bloxam v. Favre 26
Boissière v. Brockner.......... 225
Boucher v. Lawson 113
Boucicault v. Delafield 168
Bourgeise, Re................ 21
Bowes, In re, Strathmore v. Vane...................... 199
Boyer v. Dively 62
Bradlaugh v. De Rin.......... 191
Brandon, Re 215
Branley v. S. E. Ry. Co.....75, 115
Bremer v. Freeman 86, 217
Brent v. Chapman 200
Brickwood v. Miller 93
Briggs v. Briggs 67
Brinkley v. Att.-Gen. 61
Bristowe v. Sequeville 113, 130, 131, 132
British Linen Co. v. Drummond 114
Brocklesbury v. Temperance Permanent Building Society. 145
Brook v. Brook 54, 58, 60
Brown v. Fitz Brown's Executors.............. 60
——— v. Gracey 216
——— v. Smith 35
Bruce's Case 38
Bullock v. Caird............75, 194

PAGE
Burke, Reg. *v.* 21
Burnand *v.* Rodocanachi 127
Buseck, In the Goods of 26
Busfield, Re.................. 215

C.

Calcutta Jute Mills Co. *v.* Nicholson 77
Caldwell *v.* Van Vlissengen.... 176
Californian Fig Syrup Co., In re 177
Callander *v.* Dittrich 242
Cammell *v.* Sewell 85
Campbell *v.* Dent 111
——— *v.* Liffman 115
Carron Iron Co. *v.* Maclaren .. 44
Casey *v.* Arnott 214
Cash *v.* Kennion.............. 116
Cassell *v.* Stiff................ 168
Castrique *v.* Imrie..85, 86, 234, 238, 243, 244
Cattarina Chiazzare 245
Cesena Sulphur Co. *v.* Nicholson 46, 77
Chamberlain *v.* Napier 119, 137
Chappel *v.* Purdey............ 168
Charkieh, The 79
Chartered Bank of India *v.* Netherlands India Steam Navigation Co. 152
City Bank *v.* Barrow.......... 85
City of Mecca, The 221
Clegg *v.* Levy 130, 133
Cochrane *v.* Paul 246
Collier *v.* Rivaz 86
Collins *v.* Brown......181, 182, 183
——— Co. *v.* Reeves ..76, 181, 182
Collis *v.* Hector 64
Combrinck & Co. *v.* De Kock ..178, 181
Commercial Bank of India, Re . 78
——————— S. Australia, Re .. 78
——————— Tasmania *v.* Jones . 106
Concha *v.* Murrietta 217
Connor *v.* Bellamy............ 106
Cooper *v.* Cooper 54, 55
——— *v.* Waldegrave 116
Cope *v.* Doherty.............. 156
Copin *v.* Adamson 46
Cox *v.* Mitchell 245
Craigie *v.* Lewin 35, 36
Crompton *v.* Bearcroft 58
Crookenden *v.* Fuller.......... 42
Cunningham, Ex parte........ 38

D.

PAGE
Dagleish *v.* Hodgson.......... 243
Dale *v.* Dumbarton Glass Co. .. 133
Dalhousie *v.* M'Donall 72
Dalrymple *v.* Dalrymple 216
Daly's Settlement, In re 40
De Bonneval *v.* De Bonneval .. 37
De Boulay *v.* De Boulay 180
De Cosse Brissac *v.* Rathbone.. 225
De Greuchy *v.* Wills 126
Delaurier *v.* Wyllie 143
De la Vega *v.* Vienna 208
Delta, The 246
Densham's Trade Mark, The .. 179
Dessilla *v.* Fels.. ....212, 213
Dever, Ex parte 92, 137
Di Sora *v.* Phillips............ 136
Doglioni *v.* Crispin 84
Dolphin *v.* Robins 40
Don *v.* Lippmann 196, 201, 206, 224, 230
Dost Ali Khan, In the Goods of 217
Doulson *v.* Matthews 152
Duchess of Kingston's Case.... 235
Duke of Brunswick *v.* King of Hanover 79
Duncan *v.* Campbell 136

E.

Earl of Lytton's Case 164
——— Stair *v.* Head 137, 138
Eclipse, The, and Saxonia 159
Ellis *v.* M'Henry 200
Emperor of Austria *v.* Day 194
Enohin *v.* Wyllie 84, 86, 138
Erichsen *v.* Last.............. 77
Esposito *v.* Bowden 111
Ewin, In re.................. 84
Ewing *v.* Orr-Ewing 86

F.

Fairbank, In re 94
Farina, In re 183
Fenton *v.* Livingstone 73, 74
Fergusson *v.* Fyffe 116
Fisher *v.* Ogle 243
Flack *v.* Holm 207
Flad Oyen, The 243
Fourgeaud *v.* Comte de Santa Venia 56
Fowler *v.* Barstow 215
Français, The 43
Frants *v.* Malgass 61
Freke *v.* Lord Carbery....80, 82, 84

G.

PAGE

General Steam Navigation Co. *v.* Guillon 76, 189, 193
Gibbs *v.* Frement 122
Godard *v.* Gray 222, 238
Goetz *v.* Aders 218
Gold *v.* Canham 237
Goodman *v.* Goodman 72
Goodman's Trusts, In re 70
Grant *v.* Easton 222
Gray *v.* Diwan Lachman Das .. 107
Great Australian Co. *v.* Martin . 215
Great Northern Railway *v.* Laing 142
Greef *v.* Verreaux 54
Greer *v.* Poole 137
Grell *v.* Levy 111
Grierson *v.* Grierson 58
Grove, In re, Vaucher *v.* Solicitor to Treasury 72
Gudin's Case 239
Guier *v.* O'Daniel 36
Guy Mannering, The 161

H.

Haldane *v.* Eckford 34
Hall *v.* Oder 223
Halley, The.................. 161
Hamilton *v.* Dallas..........38, 41
Hamlyn & Co. *v.* Talisker Distillery 51, 55, 108, 111
Hanfstaengl *v.* Empire Palace..164, 169
——— *v.* Newnes........ 169
Harris *v.* Quine 197
Harrison *v.* Harrison 83
Harvie *v.* Farnie 40, 67, 68
Hawksford *v.* Giffard 222
Heath *v.* Sampson 37
Henderson *v.* Henderson ..233, 236, 237, 242
Hertz *v.* Riera 113
Hervey *v.* Engelbert 198
Hicks *v.* Powell 128
Higgins *v.* Scott.............. 199
Hitchins *v.* Hitchins 211
Hobbs *v.* Henning............ 243
Hodgson *v.* De Beauchesne ..37, 42
Hog *v.* Lashley 88
Holman *v.* Johnson 114, 131
Holthausen & Cie *v.* Comptoir d'Escompte de Paris 75
Holthausen, Ex parte 93
Hooper *v.* Gumm.... 85
Hope *v.* Hope 111
Horne *v.* Rouquette 118

PAGE

Houston *v.* Sligo 247
Huber *v.* Steiner..114, 130, 201, 208
Hullett *v.* King of Spain 79, 194
Hunter *v.* Potts 91
——— *v.* Stewart 242
Huntington *v.* Attrill 114
Hutton *v.* Bullock 144
Hyde *v.* Hyde................ 60
Hymen *v.* Hehn 246

I.

Imlay *v.* Ellefsen 208
Indian Chief, The 39, 43
Industrie, The 136
Ingate *v.* Austrian Lloyd's 75
Inhabitants of Granby *v.* Inhabitants of Amherst............ 36
Innes *v.* Mitchell 234

J.

Jacobs *v.* Credit Lyonnais 102, 106, 115, 119, 136
James *v.* Catherwood 131
Jeffreys *v.* Boosey 164, 165, 171, 172
Jollet *v.* Deponthieu 91
Jones *v.* Garcia del Rio 111
Jonge Classina 43
Jurado *v.* Gregory 221

K.

Kaye *v.* Sutherland 214
Kerslake *v.* Clark 142
King *v.* Brampton 59
—— *v.* Foxwell 43
King of Spain *v.* Machado 136
Kinloch *v.* Fullerton 98
Kirchner *v.* Venus 141
Knight, Ex parte 94

L.

Leather Cloth Co. *v.* American Leather Cloth Co. 178, 185
Lee *v.* Abdy 96
Leon, The 157
Leroux *v.* Brown..........128, 132
Le Sueur *v.* Le Sueur 40
Lever *v.* Fletcher 113
Levy *v.* Solomon.............. 73
Lightfoot *v.* Tennant.......... 112
Lindo *v.* Belisario 218
Linn *v.* Cassadinos............ 43
Liverpool Marine Credit Co. *v.* Hunter.................. 234
Lloyd *v.* Guibert 145, 159
Lloyd Generale Italiano, Re .. 78

PAGE

Lolley's Case 66
Lopez *v.* Burslem 196
Low *v.* Low.................. 40
Lynch *v.* Provisional Government of Paraguay 88
Lytton's, The Earl of, Case.... 166

M.

McCarthy *v.* Decaix 66
Macfarlane *v.* Norris.......... 208
McHenry *v.* Lewis 245, 246
Macnamara *v.* D'Everaux 111
Madrid & Valencia Ry. Co., Re 78
Maharaja Sir Partab Singh *v.* Provincial Bank of India 204
Maillac *v.* Maillac 58
Male *v.* Roberts 54
Mali Ivo, The................ 245
Maltass *v.* Maltass............ 39
Mandalay *v.* Morton 79
Marrett, In re 35, 39
Marsh *v.* Billings..........179, 181
Maspons y Hermano *v.* Mildred 143, 149
Maughan, Re 215
Melan *v.* Fitz James 207
Melbourne, Ex parte.......... 93
Messina *v.* Petrocochino 244
Meyer *v.* Ralli 239
Mildred *v.* Maspons 144
Missouri Steamship Co., Re.... 102
"Morocco Bound" Syndicate *v.* Harris 168
Mostyn *v.* Fabrigas........153, 204
Moul *v.* Grœnings 170
Moxham, The................ 153
Muir *v.* Collett 75
Munro *v.* Munro 42, 72
Munroe *v.* Douglas 38
Mutrie *v.* Binney 245

N.

Neal *v.* Cottingham 91
Nelson *v.* Bridport..........82, 217
Newby *v.* Van Oppert & Colt's Firearms Co...............44, 75
Niboyet *v.* Niboyet..........68, 69

O.

Ochsenbein *v.* Papelier 234, 235
Ogden *v.* Folliott 186
Oldenburg, Prince, In re 217
Oliver *v.* Oliver 165
Ommanney *v.* Bingham 35
Orléans, Re D' 37
Ostell *v.* Lepage 244

P.

PAGE

Padley *v.* Camphausen 215
Pardo *v.* Bingham 114, 196
Parlement Belge, The 78
Parnell *v.* Walter 218
Patience, In re 35
Pattison *v.* M'Vicar 239
Pechell *v.* Hilderley 89
Peninsular & Oriental SS. Co. *v.* Shand 101, 102, 115
Peruvian Guano Co. *v.* Bockwoldt 246
——— Ry. Co., Re 78
Phillips *v.* Eyre 153, 154
——— *v.* Hunter 91, 240
Pickering *v.* Stephenson 75
Pierson *v.* Garnet 139
Potinger *v.* Wightman 41
Potter & Co. *v.* Braco de Prata Printing Co. 177
——— *v.* Brown 51, 91
President, The 44
Prince P. G. Oldenburg, Re .. 217

Q.

Queen *v.* Doutre.............. 107

R.

Raffenel, In the Goods of...... 44
Reddaway *v.* Banham 178, 179
Reg. *v.* Burke................ 21
Repeater, The, *v.* The Braga .. 160
Republic of Costa Rica *v.* Erlanger 77
——— of Liberia *v.* Imperial Bank............ 77
——— of Peru *v.* Weguelin.. 77
Reuss *v.* Bos 78
Richards *v.* Goold 130
Robertson *v.* Burdekin 195
Robey *v.* Snaefell Mining Co... 214
Robinson *v.* Bland 101, 128, 141
Rogers, Ex parte 93
Rose Co. *v.* Miller 183
Rosses *v.* Thakur Sahib of Gondul 154
Rouquette *v.* Overmann ..120, 122, 208
Rousillon *v.* Rousillon 111, 224, 230, 232
Routledge *v.* Low 171
Royal Bank of Scotland *v.* Cuthbert 62
Ruckmaboye *v.* Mottichand..114, 197
Russell *v.* Smyth 222
Rutlam Case, The 46

S.

PAGE

Santos *v.* Illidge 51, 112, 115
Saunders *v.* Drake 139
Savage *v.* Hutchinson 210
Schauer *v.* I. C. & J. Field 168
Schibsby *v.* Westenholz ..222, 226, 230, 231, 232
Scott *v.* Att.-Gen. 40, 67
—— *v.* Beavan 116
—— *v.* Royal Wax Works 76
—— *v.* Seymour 154, 245
Scottish Providential Association *v.* Cohen 95
Seixo *v.* Provezende 180
Sharpe *v.* Crespin 38
Shaw *v.* Goold 67
Shelby *v.* Guy................ 200
Siegert *v.* Findlater 185
Sill *v.* Worsick.............84, 91
Simonin *v.* Maillac 54, 58
Singer Manufacturing Co. *v.* Wilson 180
Sirdar Gurdyal Singh *v.* The Raja of Faridkot ..106, 222, 225, 232
Sitaram *v.* Aheeree Heerahnee . 104
Skinner *v.* East India Co. 152
Smith *v.* Nicolls 223
Solomon *v.* Ross 91
Somerville *v.* Lord Somerville .. 38, 42, 43
Sottomayor *v.* De Barros..55, 57, 58
Southgate *v.* Montgomerie 237
Spears *v.* Hartley 199
State Fire Insurance Co., In re . 116
Stavert *v.* Stavert 68
Steel *v.* Lindsay 36
Stern, Re.................... 36
Stewart *v.* Gelot.............. 131
Strachan *v.* McDougle 96
Sujan Singh *v.* Gunga Ram.... 101
Susa, The 43
Sussex Peerage Case 216, 217

T.

Talleyrand *v.* Boulanger 207
Tarleton *v.* Tarleton 237
Taylor *v.* Barclay 111
——— *v.* Scott 95
Thames Sulphur Co. *v.* La Société des Métaux 46
Thomas *v.* Hamilton 214
Thompson *v.* Barclay 111
Thorburn *v.* Steward 64, 92
Thornton *v.* Thornton 245
Tootal's Trusts, In re........32, 38
Townsend *v.* Jemison.......... 200

PAGE

Tozier *v.* Hawkins 215
Treschow *v.* Bockelman 115
Trotter *v.* Trotter 140
Tulloch *v.* Hartley............ 196
Turner *v.* Thompson 67

U.

Udny *v.* Udny ..15, 33, 37, 38, 43, 48, 50, 55, 57
Union Bank of London *v.* Lenanton 27
United States of America *v.* Hamilton 90
United States of America *v.* Wagner..................77, 78
Urquhart *v.* Butterfield 36

V.

Valery *v.* Scott............131, 134
Vallée *v.* Dumergue 46
Van Gratten *v.* Digby 64
Vanquelin *v.* Bonard 233
Vaucher *v.* Solicitor to Treasury 72
Vega, De la, *v.* Vianna........ 208
Voinet *v.* Barrett 225

W.

Walter *v.* Wilter 236
Warrenden *v.* Warrenden 128
Warrender *v.* Warrender 60
Waterhouse *v.* Stanfield 128
Watson's Case 240
Wauchope *v.* Wauchope 39
Waymell *v.* Reed 112
Westman *v.* Aktiebolaget Mekaniska Snickarefabrik....76, 215
Whitehead *v.* Thompson 237
Wild Ranger, The............ 156
Williams *v.* Colonial Bank 85
———— *v.* Dormer 40
———— *v.* Jones 222
Wilson, Ex parte 92
Wood *v.* Chart 168
Wright's Trust, Re 73
Wynne *v.* Jackson............ 131

Y.

Yates *v.* Thomson 129, 141, 195
Yorkshire Tannery Co. *v.* Eglington Chemical Co. 215

Z.

Zollverein, The 158

PRIVATE INTERNATIONAL LAW.

CHAPTER I.

GROWTH AND GENERAL THEORY OF PRIVATE INTERNATIONAL LAW.

Interchange of traffic between subjects of different States the basis of Private International Law.

1. The existence of conterminous independent States naturally leads to an interchange of traffic between their respective subjects, and once this traffic commences, the necessity of recognizing some general rules by which the jural relations arising out of it can be satisfactorily regulated is immediately felt. To supply these rules is the direct object of what is known to European writers of the present day as Private International Law, which, as has been said by one of the ablest continental writers on the subject, "determines the applicability of the legal systems and the jurisdiction of the agencies—the courts and magistrates—of different States in private legal relations." [1]

Restrictive meaning of the term.

2. Understood in this restricted sense, the term Private International Law, although not free from objection, is, on the whole, as good as and, perhaps, better than any other that has hitherto been suggested to replace it. The term is not of course to be taken as implying that there anywhere exists a body of laws binding upon the civilized States of the world, originating out of and sanctioned by a real *communis consensus* of all such States. No such comity exists and never will exist. For the realisation of any system of organisation of

[1] Von Bar. See his *Theory and Practice of Private International Law*, 2nd ed., translated by G. R. Gillespie, page 1.

CHAP. I.

mankind, under which all nations would submit to the power of a common legislature, is, as Bluntschli says, a "beautiful dream of the idealists." Each State must be conceded an absolute power of prescribing what law shall or shall not prevail within its own boundaries. It is therefore perfectly free to every State to deny the applicability of any rule, however generally recognized by other States, within its own territorial limits. But while such a power is conceded in theory there is practically this check upon the arbitrary exercise of it, that a State which persistently and openly declined to be bound by principles which were universally observed by other civilized States in regulating the inter-jural relations between their citizens and foreigners, would very soon find itself cut away from the general family of sovereign States, and its citizens subjected to many disadvantages in their dealings with the citizens of other States. For this reason there has sprung up a kind of customary law, partly based on principles drawn from the Roman law,[1] which at one time claimed to regulate the whole known world, partly on the opinion of learned juristical writers, and partly also on treaties and conventions between some of the more powerful modern States, the scope and object of which is to determine the rules by which private rights between subjects of different States, which are to have an extra-territorial effect, are to be regulated.

Slow and gradual development of the rules constituting Private International Law.

3. Such a customary law, as it has already been indicated, has had a slow and, in some respects, a severely contested development. Before proceeding to discuss its final results, it will be interesting to sketch the process of this development, from a system which, in its earliest phase, while it looked upon a foreigner in Rome as an outlaw, nevertheless

[1] In one of his Cambridge Essays the late Sir H. Maine thus speaks of the influence of Roman Jurisprudence in this department of law: "We cannot possibly overstate the value of Roman Jurisprudence as a key to International Law." *Life and Speeches*, by Sir M. E. Grant-Duff, p. 18.

recognized that the religion, the State, and the law of the foreigner had the same validity in his own territory, and for the citizens who were subject to them, as the religion, the State, and the law of Rome had for the Romans, and which instructed the native Roman judge that he was not competent to pass a judgment so as to have an extra-territorial effect.[1]

Position of strangers or foreigners in ancient times.

4. In almost all nations of antiquity, the Hebrews forming a noble exception, man outside his own country was a barbarian, an enemy and a slave. Ancient philosophy, it is true, proclaimed hospitality towards, and the inviolability of the stranger, who was said to be under the protection of the gods, who would visit even more severely an injury done to him than a similar injury done to a citizen. But while Plato as a philosopher preached humanity towards the stranger, as a Greek he could only look upon the latter as a barbarian and a natural enemy. And although in the fervour of a magnanimous nature Alexander the Great proclaimed in an edict that all honest men, to whatever country they belonged, were brothers, and that delinquents alone were strangers, he was, in truth, proclaiming a glorious anachronism, for this noble sentiment was very far off from being admitted as an accepted principle in Greek legislation. So Cicero as a politician belied the doctrine of a common law of nature which he advocated as a teacher of philosophy. And to come to India, the Brahminical authors of the Code of Manu had no higher consideration for the *Melcha*, who spoke a foreign language, than to include them in the category of beasts inferior to the elephant and horse, and only superior to the lion and the tiger. It was the Hebrew legislator who alone in antiquity commanded the judge to deal justly between man and man—the brother or the stranger whoever he may be.[2] But at a later period in the history of Rome, when she

[1] *Digest*, 2, 1, 20.

[2] Deut. i. 16.

became the political and commercial centre of many dependent nationalities, the stranger from being a *hostis*, or enemy, came to be looked upon as a mere *peregrinus* or foreigner—a transition which we learn from Cicero[1] marked a great progress in political ideas, elevating the stranger from the position of an outlaw under the earlier law to that of a person who was permitted to enjoy such limited rights as could be shown to exist by an application of what was called the *jus gentium*, a system which Roman jurists elaborated as being in conformity with the approved usages of all nations with whom Rome lived in peaceable intercourse.[2] Those rights, however, which were strictly based upon the *jus civile*, such as the *connubium* (or civil marriage), the *commercium* (without which ownership of property in the strict or quiritarian sense—*dominium ex jure quiritium*—could not be acquired), and the political rights of voting in the assembly and of holding public offices, were as yet still withheld from the foreigner. But with the celebrated constitution of Caracalla, which, with the view of increasing the revenue from the impost on successions, accorded the full rights of citizenship to all the free subjects of the Empire, a unification of the law was the natural result, and the distinction between citizens and foreigners was obliterated. So long, however, as the distinction lasted, disputes between Roman citizens and *peregrini*, or foreigners belonging to a State which had friendship or a treaty relation with Rome, were determined by a special Court (*Recuperatores*), and it is in the institution of *recuperatio* that we trace the first outlines of a system of international justice. In process of time, as German and other tribes began more and more to settle on Roman soil, and even to acquire a mastery, the same system which had regulated the dealings between citizens and *peregrini* was now extended to them. It was a further

[1] De Officiis, I. 12. [2] *Gaius*, I. 1; *Inst.* 1, 2, 1.

development of the same system which in the early portion of the Middle Ages, under the name of "personal law," obtained a very general recognition. The underlying feature of this later development was to do as little violence as possible to national customs and usages. Thus there came to be observed in the same territory, and even in the same city, distinct laws and customs which gave occasion to the oft-quoted remark of Bishop Agobardas, that five persons might be found walking or sitting together each of whom was governed by his own laws.

Scope and operation of personal laws.

5. The "personal" law thus took no account of actual domicil; for the rule was that each man lived by the law of the nation to which he belonged by descent, and at this period in the history of legal institutions the law of the father's nation was the law which ruled. The wife, and for a time the widow also, lived by the law of the husband's nation. But by a capitulary of Lothair I., enacted for Italy, the widow fell back into the law in which she had been born. By force of this system the status and capacity of persons and the right of succession were regulated by the personal law. In the case of contracts, also, the personal law of the parties prevailed, and as no one could capriciously change his own rank, so it was forbidden to change the law under which he lived. Difficulties, however, naturally arose when persons belonging to different nationalities or tribes wished to conclude legal transactions with each other, or when a process was to be decided in which the parties belonged to different tribes. To meet the former case, the device was invented of requiring the parties to declare beforehand by what law they wished to be bound *quâ* obligations arising out of such contract. Declarations of this kind were called *professiones juris.* And in the case of a penal process, the law of the accused person, as a general rule, prevailed, except that crimes of a public character were punished according to the law of the

CHAP. I.

ruling nation. Lastly, in the case of a transference of rights from others, and especially where they affected landed property, the law of the seller was the basis of decision. The reason for this latter rule was that the transference was conceived as a renunciation by the lawful owner in favour of the person who was to acquire it. To the Indian student this system of personal laws is more particularly interesting, inasmuch as it is the system which, to a large extent, he sees in full force and vigour in his own country. Under the tolerant rule of the British Government, civil rights, with certain exceptions, are determined by the personal law of the parties. And thus the orthodox Hindu, the Jain, the Sikh, and the Muhammadan may be said to live each under his own written or customary law, guaranteed to him by solemn statutory declarations which constitute, it may be said, the charter of his liberties. So that what Montesquieu said of Europe in the Middle Ages may be said with equal truth of India of the present day, "the territory is one, and the nations are diverse."[1]

The Statute theory.

6. In Europe, however, as we reach the close of the Middle Ages, the system of personal laws disappears, and with the break up of the Carlovingian Empire another and a very different system comes into prominence. It is that of the territorial theory, which was the outcome of the division of Europe into innumerable feudal lordships. Under this political change every feudal lord became the proprietor and sovereign of his own territory, and everyone who planted his foot within that territory became subject to all the laws which prevailed within it. Thus, as Savigny remarks, feudal vassalage and bondage transformed every nation from a mass

[1] See Savigny's *History of the Roman Law* in the Middle Ages, Vol. I., p. 100; Laghi, *Il Diritto Internazionale Privato*, Vol. I., §§ 26 and 27, pp. 26—28; and Von Bar's *Theory and Practice of Private International Law*, 2nd ed., §§ 13, 14.

of clan communities into a mass of feudal followers and retainers, and this transformation produced the juridical revolution known as that of the territoriality of laws. Descent now went for nothing, and the customs and other rules of law were intended not so much for man as for the land. The spirit of exclusiveness which this system engendered made the lot of the stranger even more pitiable than it was under the earlier epochs to which we have already referred. The very air bore slavery on its wings. But the influence of Christianity, the rise of free Italian burghal-communities, and the increasing spread of commerce, which last, as Montesquieu[1] observes, was, and always will be, one of the greatest co-efficients of civilization and of pacific international relations, combined to produce that doctrine of the Glossators and Commentators upon the conflict of laws which has obtained a wide celebrity under the designation of the *Statute* theory.

Origin of the Statute theory.

7. To comprehend this theory it is necessary to keep in mind the multiplicity of laws which came into existence, as the result of the causes to which allusion has just been made. There was, first of all, the Roman law, which at this time had become the universal law of all Christian States. But by the side of this general common law, inasmuch as each State and many of the larger cities had independent Legislative powers, there were numerous local laws or statutes which had a certain territorial operation. Then, again, the Church, the bishops, universities, and colleges claimed to have the right of enacting laws within their own jurisdictions. It can readily be imagined that in presence of such a multiplicity of laws there were many occasions on which a conflict arose between the common law and the local statute law; between, again, the statute law and the law of the particular

[1] XX. 2.

CHAP. I.

city or commune; and lastly, between the statute law of different territories. To solve conflicts of this nature, the jurists devised the so-called *statute* theory, which has had the largest and most dominating influence in shaping the modern doctrines of the conflict of laws and statutes, and which still has powerful adherents in the ranks of the Italian school of writers on Private International Law.

General principles of this theory.

8. Thus, the Roman law being the universal law applicable to all persons, statutes enacted by territorial lords for their own dominions were regarded as an exception to the general law, and consequently in their application were restricted to persons and things subject, expressly or impliedly, to the sovereignty of the enacting authority. This led to the assertion of the principle which is adopted by all writers of the later Middle Ages as incontestable, that the lawgiver can lay down rules only for his own subjects, and only in relation to things within his territory. From this leading principle three subordinate rules were deduced: 1, that a statute which affected persons did not apply to foreigners; 2, that a statute which affected things (in practice held to apply only to immoveables) applied to foreigners, because things are subject to the power of the authority in whose territory they are; and 3, that a statute which affected persons followed the citizen wherever he was. But in the application of these general rules certain exceptions were recognised. Thus, a statute relating to the solemnity of Acts and the forms of procedure bound all foreigners; a statute favourable to a citizen did not accompany him into a foreign territory; and, in an indirect way, foreign statutes and contracts affecting things were allowed an extra-territorial application. There was obviously considerable scope here for forensic discussion, and it was a matter of dispute as to which laws were properly to be regarded as laws of the person, and which again laws that affected things, and consequently in what cases the law

of the domicile or the law of the place where the thing was situate was to be applied. It may hence be stated that at the close of the Middle Ages three distinct sets of rules had to be applied according as they affected the person, immoveable property, or an act. Domicil (*lex domicilii*) furnished the key to the appropriate law in the first case, the site or situation (*lex rei sitæ*) in the second, and the locality of the action (*locus regit actum*) in the third. In the case of moveables, their easy transport from place to place served to identify them with the person of the owner, and thus the maxim came to be recognized that *moveables follow the person* (*mobilia personam sequuntur*). The nomenclature adopted by writers of this period for the three sets of rules just mentioned was *statuta personalia*, *realia*, and *mixta*. A rule of law whose operation may extend outside the territory of the law-giver, or extra-territorially, is a *statutum personale;* one whose operation is confined strictly to the territory of the law-giver is called a *statutum reale;* while *statuta mixta* are those which regulate the form of acts, or persons and acts together.[1]

The achievements of Jurists of the Middle Ages not to be despised.

9. On the whole, therefore, it may be conceded that, however defective may have been the methods adopted by the jurists of this period, and however contradictory at times may be their respective views on certain points, the credit must at least be allowed to them of having laid the foundations of the modern doctrines of private international law. It was through them that we have acquired the true idea of the personality of law, the principle of the autonomy of the will of man in acts and contracts, the important rule concerning the locality of the action, and above all the fundamental maxim of international jurisprudence, that States are bound to apply certain foreign laws not by reason of mere utility or courtesy, as some later jurists have endeavoured to maintain,

[1] See my *Science of Jurisprudence*, 2nd ed., pp. 326, 327.

CHAP. I.

but in deference to the higher claims of justice and equity (*ex debito justitiæ vel æquitatis*). Their decisions may not always be supported by arguments which would commend themselves to us at the present day; and we may smile at the solution which the great Bartolus suggested to the inquiry whether a particular law which favoured the succession of the eldest son to immoveables, was a law which dealt with persons or things, that the question depended on whether the words of the law were "the eldest son succeeds," or "the immoveables pass to the eldest son." But with all their defects they were imbued with a right sense of equity and justice, and in practical results the three centuries which followed added little to what had already been attained during the Middle Ages.

Nineteenth Century doctrines.

10. Coming now to the present century, we still find, in the first half of it, the statute theory dominating the works of French, Italian, Spanish, American, and English writers. It is the view generally recognized by Fœlix in France, by Rocco in Italy, by Torres Campos in Spain, by Kent and Story in America, and by Burge in England. In each of these writers, as in the works of the older statutarists, we trace the same notion that the personality of laws is an exception to the principle of absolute territoriality, and that no State ought to recognize foreign laws which are prejudicial to its own interests or to those of its own citizens. Expediency, as the favourite principle of the utilitarian school, is to supply the rule of decision in exceptional cases, and the judge is to determine whether expediency calls for the application of the foreign or native law. It was the German School that first sought to abandon this theory of the statutarists and to establish in the nature of the jural relation itself the reason of the territoriality or extra-territoriality of laws. Wächter, Schäffner, Thibaut, Puchta and Savigny laboured in this direction, and although these writers were fully alive to the importance

of the rule that the judge must primarily decide in accordance with the laws of his own country, they refused to shut their eyes to the fact that a mere blind and unthinking application of native law alone would render any civilized intercourse with foreign countries an impossibility. But it is to Savigny that the credit is pre-eminently due of having established that great cardinal principle which is daily gaining ground, that all States stand together in a great community of law and trade, involving a friendly recognition—resting upon the nature of the subject, and not, therefore, merely capricious according to the idiosyncracies of the individual judge—of the legal systems of other countries in reference to those jural relations which in their nature belong to these systems. We thus get clear of that peculiarly insular, jealous, and one-sided theory of Comitas, characterised by Schäffner as a haphazard and unlawyer-like principle, which was advocated by Felix and others of the French, Belgian, and Italian schools as dependent upon a voluntary and friendly concession by the sovereign power out of regard to the mutual advantages of such a course, and realize as a starting point the idea of an international community of law which restricts all territorial laws, and defines their competency, not with reference to a mere conflict of legal systems, but in view of a harmonious combination of all. The weak point, however, in Savigny's general doctrine is, that owing to the far-reaching differences in the moral conceptions of different nations and States, there must be gaps in the international community of law, and it can never be expected that any individual system can hold out its hand to help in realizing within its territory a jural relation, which, from its own point of view, must be regarded as immoral.[1] This difficulty has been attempted to be met by a special treatment of

[1] Von Bar's *Theory and Practice of Private International Law*, 2nd ed., § 29, and page 65 of Gillespie's translation.

CHAP. I.

so-called *prohibitive* laws, in the presence of which international community of law is said to come to an end. But this is a mere device to escape from the inconvenient consequences of deductions which are really untenable. At the same time the influence of Savigny's principle is seen in the more recent English and American literature on the subject of international law, and particularly in the works of Phillimore, Westlake, Lorimer, Beach-Lawrence, and Wharton. We have here evidence of the fact, noticed by Von Bar, that the active intercourse with the continent of Europe has made itself felt in the jurisprudence of these countries, and particularly in that of England, which no longer to the same extent rests itself upon the pure positivism of Wheaton, Story, and Burge, for whom the enunciation of principles by foreign authors had at most only a historical or literary interest. The new Italian school, founded by Mancini, starts from Savigny's theory of the legal community of nations, but it differs from the latter in the manner in which this theory is worked out. Thus while Savigny would determine the limitation of territorial sovereignty by the "nature of the subject," the Italian jurisprudence would substitute for this limitation an abstract rule of universal application, which it derives by dividing all systems of law into two parts: one of which is a mere expression of personality, or (which is the same thing) of nationality, while the other takes its rise from public order, the necessary respect that must be had for the *whole* as distinguished from the *individual*, for public welfare and for public order. But this attempted division of law leads to as many practical difficulties as that of Savigny's division into prohibitive and non-prohibitive laws, and Fusinato and Laghi do not hesitate to condemn the expression "laws which concern public order," or "laws in opposition to public law or public order," as highly inappropriate and ambiguous. Fusinato at the same time has exposed himself to the criticism, which Professor Laghi,[1] among Italian, and Bar[2] among German writers, freely make against him, of having himself adopted a mere circumlocution to express the same concept. It is certainly difficult to appreciate the real distinction between "laws which concern public order" and (according to the terminology recommended by Fusinato) "laws which concern the political, economical, and moral order of the State," or "the political, social, and economical interests of the State." As Bar forcibly says, "The laws which deal with the equal or unequal division of an inheritance among the children of a deceased parent, or give him a more or less extensive power of dividing the estate which he leaves, have, as their obvious object, politico-economical interests as well. Indeed it is quite possible that these interests stand in the very first rank, since it is quite conceivable that statutory regulations of this kind were passed for the very object, it may be, of protecting the authority of the father, or of preventing too minute a subdivision of property as a general rule, and not merely to guard against the partition of particular estates. Again, no one, for instance, will doubt that the forms of acquiring property in land are exclusively determined by the *lex rei sitæ*, and even in cases which concern moveables this is now the prevailing opinion. Is there any better ground for speaking of moral or politico-economical interests in these cases than in those which deal with the regulation of succession?" In view of these objections, another writer of the new school, Brocher, suggests a division into *Internal Public Order* and *International Public Order*, which perhaps expresses in a more satisfactory manner the idea of those laws that stand in a hostile attitude to all foreign laws. But here again, as

[1] *Diritto Internazionale Privato*, I., § 141, p. 134.

[2] *Theory and Practice of Private International Law*, 2nd ed., § 30, and page 71 Gillespie's translation.

CHAP. I.

Professor Laghi points out,[1] Brocher has not completed his task, because he has given us no precise criteria for determining what laws are to be included in the category of laws affecting International Public Order. The fact is that no single phrase or formula can be expected to do more than to embody a general notion, which will still need precision by the help of other criteria and principles, for the determination of the particular jural relations which fall within the scope of the controversy. These matters of detail must here be reserved for the chapters which follow. For the present it is sufficient to have briefly traced the rise and development of the subject of Private International Law to a point at which it is possible to arrive at a true solution of the difficult questions involved in the inquiry, as to what extent the native law is bound to respect the foreign law, and the conditions under which the latter must always yield to the former?

[1] Page 128, *op. cit.*

CHAPTER II.

NATIONALITY AND DOMICIL.

Legal personality consists of a *political* and a *civil status*.

11. A double status is ascribed by European systems of law to every individual at his birth. The one is called his *political* status, by virtue of which he becomes a subject of some particular country, and the other his *civil* status, by virtue of which he becomes invested with certain municipal rights, and incurs certain obligations as a citizen. The former, as Lord Westbury lucidly explained in *Udny* v. *Udny*,[1] "may depend upon different laws in different countries, whereas the civil *status* is governed universally by one single principle, namely, that of domicil, which is the criterion established by law for the purpose of determining civil *status*. For it is on this basis that the personal rights of the party, that is to say, the law which determines his majority or minority, his marriage, succession, testacy or intestacy, must depend." Although, as we shall see, this *dictum* is expressed in somewhat too general terms to be accepted as completely accurate, yet, as a high exposition of the English doctrine on the subject, it is of course entitled to considerable weight. Adopting it for the present as such, we must hold that the *political status* is determined by a man's *nationality*, and his *civil status* by his *domicil;* and it accordingly becomes necessary to treat these two conditions, which together complete a man's legal personality, separately, so that the distinction may more effectively be impressed upon

[1] L. R. 1 H. L. Sc. 441.

CHAP. II.

the reader, as it will serve to explain certain important points of difference which would otherwise tend to confuse and bewilder him in trying to master questions of detail.

Political status or nationality, how determined.

12. Two theories have been held at different periods for fixing the nationality of the individual, that of descent (the principle of *jus sanguinis*) and that of birth (*jus soli*). The former is the theory favored by the Roman law, under which the son of a *civis Romanus* was himself a *civis Romanus* quite irrespective of the accident of the place of his birth; and it is one of the instances of the final triumph of Roman principles of jurisprudence that this is the theory which is now more and more largely recognized in Europe. Even in England, where the common law adhered to the other theory (that of the *jus soli*), the statute law, from the reign of Edward III. downwards to our own time, has repeatedly adopted that of descent.[1] It cannot, however, be said that the latter has completely set aside that of the place of birth, which is still recognized in England and in the United States as one of the modes by which the character of a citizen may be acquired. These modes may be briefly stated as follows: (1) by birth in Great Britain or the dominions of the Queen; (2) by descent, up to and including the second generation of descendants of a natural-born British subject who are born abroad; and (3) by naturalisation, denization, and resumption of British nationality. The English Naturalisation Act of 1870 (33 & 34 Vict. c. 14, s. 4) makes the further provision that, in the event of a conflict arising out of the application of the *jus soli*, there shall be an unlimited right of option, which may be exercised at any time after majority. In the United States the principle of descent is held to pass the right of citizenship from father to children, subject, however, to the limitation that no such right shall

[1] *Vide* 7 Anne, c. 5, s. 3; 4 Geo. II. c. 21; and 3 Geo. III. c. 21.

descend to the descendants of persons who have never resided in the United States.[1] On the other hand, the Republics of South America and Venezuela adhere to the theory of the place of birth, on the ground mainly that an exclusive recognition of the principle of descent would lead at times to abuse, by permitting families for generations to enjoy all the advantages of nationality while (by the device of not becoming naturalized) they would escape from the special burdens of citizens, such as military service, and because by invoking the protection of foreign powers they might, in certain circumstances, become a danger to the very State which had hospitably received them. Acting, apparently, upon these objections, it is noteworthy that the new French Naturalization Law (1889) enacts that children born in France of a father also born in France are French citizens, and are therefore subject (under the military law) to the military service imposed upon citizens. The enactment of this law, being in manifest conflict with the English statutes of Anne, George II., and George III. (which conferred a British nationality upon grandchildren born abroad of natural-born British subjects), occasioned some questions being asked in Parliament. But it was then declared by the Under-Secretary for Foreign Affairs (Sir James Fergusson), that the Government had been advised, no doubt quite correctly, that it had no proper ground of protest. Obviously the French Legislature had, at least, as much right to legislate as to the nationality of persons born within French territory, as the English Parliament had in the case of persons who

[1] *Rev. Stat.* § 1993. It must not be overlooked that in federated States a double nationality has to be considered, *first*, that which consists in the attachment to the federation as a whole, and *second*, the rights of citizenship in the several individual States, by the political union of which the federation is constituted. In such federations domestic legislation may require that the co-operation of the federal authority is necessary to confer citizenship. Cf. Wharton, § 173, p. 343.

CHAP. II. were descended from natural-born British subjects. But where the French law is wanting in consistency is this, that while it acts upon the *jus soli* in the case of children born in France of a father also born in France, it holds to the contrary rule of *jus sanguinis* in the case of a child born abroad of a French father, quite irrespective of whether the foreign State concerned concedes its nationality to the descendants of French parents born within its territorial limits, or not. The law of the German Empire (of the 1st June, 1870) affirms the principle of descent to the fullest extent, refusing to recognize adoption or domicil as conferring the status of a citizen. By this law the status of citizenship can only be acquired (1) by descent; (2) by legitimation; (3) by marriage; and (4) by reception, in the case of a citizen passing from one state of the empire to another; and (5) by naturalization, in the case of foreigners. The Italian Code (Art. 8) takes an uninterrupted domicil of the father for ten years in Italian territory in place of the birth of the father there. But according to Article 5 of the same Code, if the father has lost his nationality before the birth of the child, the child is still an Italian (subject to a right of declaring for a foreign nationality on attaining majority) if it is born in Italy and has its residence there. In cases in which the choice or determination of nationality is referred to the will of the individual, the French law, till the year 1889, may be said to have rigorously acted upon the principle that the declaration is pre-eminently a personal matter which the individual himself can only make. But by an enactment passed in that year (Art. 1) this principle has to a certain extent been surrendered, for the new law recognizes the possibility of the declaration in favour of French nationality being made on behalf of a minor by his father or (if the father is dead) by the mother, or by a tutor if duly authorized by a family council. This, however, is a question which is more directly connected with that of "option," which may now be considered in its relation to nationality. CHAP. II.

When option may be exercised.

13. Option, in its historical origin, is said to be simply a formal declaration of emigration, and in order to receive effect it is, strictly speaking, necessary for the person who exercises it to transfer his residence into the territory in favour of which he decides. This option may arise under various conditions, some of which may be here considered. Thus an occasion for its exercise arises when a territory is ceded by one State to another. Modern practice allows the individual inhabitants of the ceded territory the right, under certain conditions, to preserve the nationality of the State which has made the cession. A similar right is claimed by some writers for the inhabitants of a conquered or annexed territory, provided they leave it by a certain limit of time. Instances of the recognition of this right may be seen in the provisions of the Treaty of Vienna of the 30th October, 1866, in connection with the cession of Venice, and in the treaty concluded between France and Germany in 1871, in connection with Alsace. But the agreement between Germany and England, with reference to the cession of Heligoland by the latter to the former, embodied in 53 & 54 Vict. c. 32, is the most recent instance. By that agreement all natives of the island had the right of declaring for British nationality, personally or by their parents or guardians, before the 1st January, 1892. The question of option also presents itself in connection with the dependent members of a family, *i.e.*, wives and children under age. Such persons ordinarily follow the nationality of the husband or father. The American law introduces an exception to this generally accepted principle. For although a woman by marrying an American is deemed to become herself a citizen of the Union, in the converse case the principle does not hold good, and

CHAP. II.

thus the American wife of a foreigner does not necessarily lose her right of American citizenship. So again, according to French Jurisprudence, if a husband after marriage changes his nationality, the wife does not unconditionally, *i.e.*, irrespective of her own consent, adopt the husband's new nationality, although, if the wife does actually follow the husband, and the State in which the husband has become naturalized recognizes the possibility of this naturalization extending to the wife, it may be presumed that she has tacitly accepted the change. This view does not appear, however, to be shared by English, Scotch, American, or German Jurists. In the case of a divorce, the woman is generally acknowledged to acquire the power of altering her nationality at pleasure. The question of a widow's power of adopting a new nationality is in England regulated by statute. She is permitted to change her nationality under the provisions of 33 & 34 Vict. c. 14. By the same statute, every child who, during infancy, has become resident in the country where the father or mother is naturalized, and who has, according to the laws of such country, become naturalized therein, shall be deemed to be a subject of the State of which the father or mother has become a subject, and not a British subject. Again, it is provided that where the father, or mother being a widow, has obtained a certificate of re-admission to British nationality, every child of such father or mother who, during infancy, has become resident in the British dominions with such father or mother, shall be deemed to have resumed the position of a British subject to all intents. And lastly, where the father, or the mother being a widow, has obtained a certificate of naturalization in the United Kingdom, every child of such father or mother who, during infancy, has become resident with such father or mother in any part of the United Kingdom, shall be deemed to be a naturalized British subject. It will be noticed that this last provision is intended to apply to children born *before* the certificate of naturalization is obtained, and that such children do not acquire British nationality unless they reside with the naturalized parent in the United Kingdom. How far the same provision would apply to children born *after* the certificate of naturalization is obtained has not been decided, but the better opinion appears to favour an affirmative answer to this question. There is certainly nothing in the Act to give the power of transmitting nationality to descendants of persons naturalized under it, and this was the opinion of Kay, J., in *Re Bourgeise*.[1] But the point was expressly left undecided by the Court of Appeal as one of great difficulty.[2]

Acquisition of nationality by aliens.

14. The acquisition of British nationality by aliens is regulated by the Naturalization Act of 1870 (33 & 34 Vict. c. 14), sect. 7 of which provides as follows:—

"An alien[3] who, within such limited time before making the application hereinafter mentioned as may be allowed by one of her Majesty's principal Secretaries of State, either by general order or on any special occasion, has resided in the United Kingdom for a term of not less than five years, or has been in the service of the Crown for a term of not less than five years, and intends, when naturalized, either to reside in the United Kingdom, or to serve under the Crown, may apply to one of her Majesty's principal Secretaries of State for a certificate of naturalization.

[1] 41 Ch. D. (1888), at p. 316.

[2] *Ibid.* 319.

[3] An alien was defined by Bramwell, B., in *Reg.* v. *Burke*, 11 Cox, C. C. 138, as "a subject of a foreign State who has not been born within the allegiance of the Crown of this kingdom." Cf. also Burge, *Comment. on Colonial and Foreign Laws*, Vol. I. p. 705. But a "statutory alien" is a person who, being at the time a British subject, has voluntarily become naturalized in a foreign State. *Vide* s. 6, 33 & 34 Vict. c. 14. As to the mode in which a declaration of alienage may be made, see section 3 of the same Act.

CHAP. II.

"The applicant shall adduce in support of his application such evidence of his residence or service, and intention to reside or serve, as such Secretary of State may require. The said Secretary of State, if satisfied with the evidence adduced, shall take the case of the applicant into consideration, and may, with or without assigning any reason, give or withhold a certificate as he thinks most conducive to the public good, and no appeal shall lie from his decision, but such certificate shall not take effect until the applicant has taken the oath of allegiance."[1]

A fee for grant of the certificate and registration is levied under an order of the Home Secretary, and a list of persons to whom certificates of naturalization have been granted during each month in the year is published in the London Gazette early in the month following. In India, the naturalization of foreigners is regulated by Act XXX. of 1852, which so far differs from the English statute that the applicant need only "be settled in the territories, or residing within the same with intent to settle."

Most continental nations also require as a condition precedent to naturalization a residence in the country for a certain period. But Italy and the German Empire are notable exceptions to this practice. In France no regard is paid to any domicile but one authorized by the Government, and by the French Naturalization Law of 1889, a three years' authorized domicile in France antecedent to naturalization, with the alternative of an *actual residence* of ten years, is required. Employment in French service abroad is, however, held equivalent to residence in France. The law of Spain requires a residence of ten years with the intention of

[1] The form of oath prescribed by the Act is as follows:—

"I , do swear that I will be faithful and bear true allegiance to her Majesty Queen Victoria, her heirs and successors according to law.

"So help me God."

establishing a domicile. In the United States, a residence of five years within the United States, and of one year at least within the particular State where naturalization is effected, is necessary. Naturalization, moreover, is only effected after a *causæ cognitio* by a court of record, or by a circuit or district court of the United States, and the applicant must prove his previous residence to the satisfaction of one of these Courts, and take an oath to support the constitution of the United States and to renounce and abjure his native allegiance. And in connection with this subject, it must be carefully borne in mind that the question whether any person is naturalized in any particular State must be determined by the law of *that* State.

Effect of naturalization.

15. An alien to whom a certificate of naturalization has been granted is entitled, in the United Kingdom, to *all* political and other rights, powers, and privileges, and is, on the other hand, subject to all obligations, to which a natural-born British subject is entitled or subject in the United Kingdom, with this qualification, that he will not, when within the limits of the foreign State of which he was a subject previously to obtaining his certificate of naturalization, be deemed to be a British subject unless he has ceased to be a subject of that State in pursuance of the laws thereof, or in pursuance of a treaty to that effect. So, likewise, a "statutory alien" to whom a certificate of re-admission to British nationality had been granted—the procedure for obtaining which is the same as that prescribed for an application by an alien—resumes from the date of the certificate of re-admission, but not in respect of any previous transaction, his position as a British subject, with the same qualification as that already mentioned in the case of a naturalized alien.

CHAP. II.

Power of Governor of any British Possession to grant certificate and of Colonial Legislature to enact laws for imparting naturalization.

16. The jurisdiction conferred on the Secretary of State in the United Kingdom, in respect of the grant of a certificate of re-admission to British nationality, may be exercised, in the case of any "statutory alien" being in any British possession, by the Governor of such possession; and residence in such possession shall, in the case of such person, be deemed equivalent to residence in the United Kingdom. But apart from this prerogative jurisdiction, section 16 of the English Statute (33 & 34 Vict. c. 14) also declares that all laws, statutes, and ordinances duly made by the Legislature of any British possession for imparting to any person the privileges, or any of the privileges, of naturalization, shall, within the limits of such possession, have the authority of law, but shall be subject to be confirmed or disallowed by her Majesty in the same manner, and subject to the same rules in and subject to which her Majesty has power to confirm or disallow any other laws, statutes, or ordinances in that possession. The earliest exercise, perhaps, of such a power by Colonial Legislatures was that of Jamaica, in the reign of Charles II., and by that of Antigua, in the reign of Anne in 1702. It is noticeable that India is not expressly mentioned in the statute of 1870, but having regard to its very general language, it would no doubt control the operation of the Indian Act (30 of 1852) in the same manner as any colonial law authorizing naturalization. Under the Indian Act the applicant, as we have seen, is only required to be "settled in the territories or residing within the same with intent to settle"; and the naturalized person "within the territories" is to be deemed "a natural born subject of her Majesty as if he had been born within the said territories, and shall be entitled within the said territories to all rights, privileges, and capacities of a subject of her Majesty born within the said territories." (Section 8.)

Letters patent of denization may be granted by Crown.

17. Another partial, but very ancient mode of removing the disabilities of an alien is that of denization, which is recognized as far back as a statute of 22 Henry VIII. (c. 8), and may still be conferred by letters patent of the Sovereign as a high and incommunicable branch of the royal prerogative.[1] But although this right is still preserved to the Crown by section 13 of the Naturalization Act of 1870, it is rarely solicited by aliens, inasmuch as the privileges it confers are less complete than those acquired by naturalization. Thus, the restrictions imposed by the 12 & 13 Will. III. c. 2, that no person born out of the United Kingdom, although he be naturalized or made a denizen, except such as are born of English parents, is capable of being of the Privy Council, or a member of either House of Parliament, or enjoy any office or place of trust, either civil or military, or have any grant of lands, tenements, or hereditaments from the Crown to himself, or to any others in trust for him, are still operative as regards denizens, although impliedly repealed as regards persons naturalized by the provisions of section 7 of the Naturalization Act of 1870.[2] On the other hand, no previous residence is a necessary qualification for denization, as in the case of naturalization under the statute of 1870, and it is this circumstance which alone keeps it from becoming obsolete. But denization in England is not in France looked upon as sufficient to destroy French nationality, a decision which appears to overlook the fact that the letters patent which confer it distinctly constitute the recipient "a free denizen and liege subject," without any limitation of place.[3] In France, formerly, a somewhat similar distinction between what was called *simple* and *grande* naturalization existed. But this was abolished by a law of the 29th June, 1867. The

[1] Burge, *Comment. on Colonial and Foreign Laws*, Vol. I., p. 712.

[2] See paragraph 15, *ante*.

[3] Cogordon's *La Nationalité au point de vue des rapports internationaux*, pp. 164—181; Brocher, *Cours de Droit International Privé*, Vol. I., p. 224.

CHAP. II.

distinction still exists, however, in Italy and Belgium, and it is only the "grand" naturalization which confers complete political rights.

Status of aliens in the United Kingdom.

18. Aliens who have not been naturalized or made denizens by letters patent may now (since the Naturalization Act of 1870) hold both real and personal property in the United Kingdom in the same manner in all respects as a natural born British subject; and a title to any such property may be derived through, from, or in succession to a natural-born British subject. The Act, however, does not qualify an alien for any office or for any municipal, parliamentary, or other franchise, nor does it affect any estate or interest in real or personal property to which any person has or may become entitled, either mediately or immediately, in possession or expectancy, in pursuance of any disposition made before the passing of this Act, or in pursuance of any devolution by law on the death of any person dying before the passing of the Act. Inasmuch, also, as the Act declares that aliens shall only be entitled to such rights and privileges of a British subject as are expressly given to them in the Act, it has been held that the privileges, for instance, conferred on British subjects by Lord Kingsdown's Act (24 & 25 Vict. c. 114), of making a valid will according to the *lex loci*, the *lex domicilii*, or the *lex domicilii originis*, are not by virtue of it extended to aliens, although the words "dispose of" (used in sect. 2) are generally interpreted as including a disposition by will.[1] Section 14 of the Naturalization Act, 1870, also provides that nothing in the Act shall qualify an alien to be the owner of a British ship.[2] This provision does not, of course, prevent an alien purchasing a British ship, but immediately as he

[1] *Bloxam* v. *Favre*, 9 P. D. (1883), 130; *In the Goods of Buseck*, 6 P. D. (1881), 211.

[2] As to the conditions necessary to constitute a ship a British ship, see s. 1, Merchant Shipping Act, 1894 (57 & 58 Vict. c. 60).

effected such a purchase the vessel would cease to be a British vessel. The consequence is, that an assignment of a ship sold to a foreigner, to be delivered to him abroad, need not be by bill of sale and does not require registration.[1] An alien, moreover, cannot claim to be tried by a jury *de medietate linguæ*, but shall be triable in the same manner as if he were a natural-born subject.[2]

Formal determination of nationality.

19. Cases may, and not unfrequently do, arise in which the question of nationality is by no means free from doubt, and it is a matter of considerable practical importance to know how a doubt of this kind is to be solved. Viewed from the standpoint of domestic legislation, the English Naturalization Act, 1870, s. 7, provides that the Secretary of State may grant a special certificate of naturalization to any person with respect to whose nationality as a British subject a doubt exists, and he may specify in such certificate that the grant thereof is made for the purpose of quieting doubts as to the right of such person to be a British subject, and the grant of such a special certificate shall not be deemed to be any admission that the person to whom it was granted was not previously a British subject. Under the German law there is no means of determining nationality in cases of the above description so as to be recognized as authoritative everywhere. Thus it may happen that different officials may some of them affirm, others negative the nationality of the same individual, and it is said to be by no means rare for judicial decisions to contradict the views of administrative officials.[3] By French law the question of doubtful nationality can be determined judicially by a special process, the decision in which finally settles the point for all purposes,

[1] *Union Bank of London* v. *Lenanton*, 3 C. P. D. (1878), 243.

[2] Section 5.

[3] Bar, § 84, page 189, Gillespie's translation.

whether connected with matters of administration or of public law.[1]

Possibility of a plurality of nationalities, so far as the personal law is concerned.

20. By the Civil Law of Rome, as Cicero informs us, a person could not be a citizen of two States,[2] and the weight of authority in continental Europe is in the same direction. But although in the event of a conflict between two completely independent States, it would not be possible for any individual to show perfect loyalty except to one of them, and so in principle we must decide against the complete recognition of a double nationality, it is nevertheless possible, so far as matters of private right are concerned, that a plurality of nationalities may co-exist. Thus some nations, while admitting an alien to naturalization, do so with the reservation that he shall be deemed to retain his previous nationality when within the limits of the foreign State of which he was a subject previously to his naturalization, unless he has ceased to be a subject of that State in pursuance of the laws thereof, or in pursuance of a treaty to that effect. This is so expressly provided by sect. 7 of the English Naturalization Act, 1870. In such cases the sovereign rights of the country over members of its community when within its territorial limits cannot be affected by the existence of similar rights on the part of another State, so as to control its right to give or refuse sanction there to acts wherever done. So, again, a plurality of nationalities in this sense may co-exist with respect to owners of property whose properties, once subject to one and the same sovereignty, have, in consequence of changes of territory, fallen under separate sovereignties. Such persons have often secured to them by treaties special advantages, *e.g.*, facilities in obtaining passports, rights of free residence, &c. Thus it seems that within the spheres of their respective jurisdictions each of two rival States may

[1] Cogordon, page 381.

[2] *Pro Balbo*, c. ii.

give effect to its own claim of nationality. But as regards all other States the true test appears to be, apart from treaty obligations, to recognize the nationality of that State which the individual has himself last selected. This is the principle underlying the English statute, in accordance with which a person naturalized as an Englishman will be recognized as such everywhere, except only within the territory of that State from whose allegiance he has not been legally released, and it is also best in harmony with the prevailing theory of freedom of emigration.

Expatriation not universally recognized by European States.

21. The general recognition of this last-mentioned theory has also mainly contributed to the abandonment of that principle, once tenaciously held by England and most other European States, that no one could expatriate himself (*nemo potest exuere patriam*). In this matter, as in so many others, we have at last had to return to the old Roman rule which recognized that no one should be compelled against his will to change or to retain a nationality (*ne quis invitus civitate mutetur, neve in civitate maneat invitus*).[1] Roman reason has thus triumphed over the feudal theory of "once a subject, always a subject," bequeathed to us by the Middle Ages; and no European State—except Russia[2]—now acts upon that theory of indissoluble allegiance which was pronounced by Blackstone, "a principle of universal law."[3] It is curious to notice that while up to 1870 this latter theory was vigorously asserted in England, in the United States it was as vigorously denied, as inconsistent with the fundamental principles of that Government," and the counter theory was at length proclaimed, in

[1] Cicero, *Pro Balbo*, c. 13, § 31.

[2] Natural-born subjects in Russia can only be released from their allegiance by the will of the Emperor. But naturalized foreigners are even there allowed to revert to their former nationality by a simple declaration, provided they shall have first paid all public as well as private debts due within Russian dominions. Grotius. II. chap V

[3] 1 *Comment.* 370.

an Act of the 27th July, 1868, as a "natural and inherent right of all people indispensable to the enjoyment of the right of life, liberty, and the pursuit of happiness."[1] Two months before this American Act was passed (*i.e.*, in May, 1868) a Royal Commission had been appointed in England to inquire into the English laws of naturalization and allegiance, the outcome of whose labours was the Naturalization Act of 1870, by which the capacity of a British subject to renounce his allegiance was distinctly recognized and affirmed. Sect. 6, which deals with this subject, enacts that "any British subject who has at any time before, or may at any time after, the passing of this Act, when in any foreign State, and not under any disability, voluntarily become naturalized in such State, shall, from and after the time of his so having become naturalized in such foreign State, be deemed to have ceased to be a British subject and be regarded as an alien." A proviso to this section, however, enabled a British subject already naturalized abroad to retain his British nationality by making, if within her Majesty's dominions, a declaration in the presence of any judge or justice of the peace or other officer authorized by law to administer an oath, or if out of her Majesty's dominions, in the presence of any officer in the diplomatic or consular service of her Majesty, within two years of the passing of the Act. On the other hand, sect. 3 of the Act permits aliens who may have become naturalized British subjects, to resume the nationality of the State to which they originally belonged, by making a declaration of alienage in all cases where her Majesty has entered into a convention with any foreign State to the effect that the subjects or citizens of that State who have been naturalized as British subjects may divest themselves of their *status* as such subjects, and such convention has been notified by Order of her Majesty in Council. A

[1] Wharton, § 171, p. 309.

convention of this kind was made with the United States and forms a schedule to the amending statute (35 & 36 Vict. c. 39) of 1872. It follows that in the absence of a convention such as that contemplated by the statute, naturalized aliens remain British subjects, and it is possible, but not very likely, that political embarrassments might arise if such persons claimed the protection of the State whose allegiance they had resumed. The famous Bancroft treaties[1] between the United States and the North German Bund, Bavaria, Baden, Würtemburg, Hesse, Austria-Hungary, and lastly, with Denmark, may also be mentioned as applications of the same leading principle of freedom of emigration, which we have seen is the corner stone of the English Naturalization Act, 1870. The wording of some of these treaties has, indeed, given rise to much hostile criticism as evidencing imperfect drafting. But whatever defects may exist in this direction, it is generally conceded that in acknowledging, as they do, the extinction of a subsisting nationality by the acquisition of a new one, and that the claim of the original State for fulfilment of military duty is extinguished by a residence for a certain prolonged term in another country, these treaties proceed on proper and practical lines.

But one nationality does not cease to exist until another is acquired.

22. But the question whether the nationality of an individual has ceased is closely dependent on the further question whether he has established a nationality for himself in some other State. The general interests of international legal order, it has been justly said, imperatively demand that every one should belong to some particular State: "*que tout homme doit posséder une nationalité,*" as a French writer[2] tersely expresses it. It follows, therefore, in so far as the personal law of the individual depends on his nationality,

[1] So called after the United States minister at Berlin.

[2] Cogordon, p. 17. Cf. Brocher, *Nouveau Traité de Droit International Privé*, ch. iii. p. 165.

CHAP. II.

that his old nationality must of necessity remain in existence until a new one is acquired. And a further corollary from the same general principle is, that the State to which this nationality attaches is under an indissoluble obligation to receive the individual back again, if need be, for residential purposes. The modern practice in European States is in accordance with the view, that in spite of expatriation having taken place, every State will in the end find itself forced, notwithstanding protestations and appeals to its own legislative enactments, to receive back into its dominions persons who may have previously left, but who have not acquired a new nationality and who are indigent. Thus Russia, in 1878, was forced to take back the Saratow colonists who had emigrated to Brazil; and again, in 1883, the Jews who had emigrated to Austria and the United States.[1] Hence an indefeasible right of residence in the State is one of the chief claims involved in the idea of nationality. Another important indication is the capacity to fill public offices and enjoy political rights which carry with them some participation in the control of the State. The enjoyment of such rights by foreigners is occasionally permitted, but always as an exception. It is not, however, to be overlooked that in many States there are classes of subjects who are without political rights. So, again, mere subjection to the system of private law in any particular State, or enjoyment of diplomatic protection, cannot be regarded as distinctive signs of nationality. The former is the mere consequence of residence within the territorial limits of a particular State as a corresponding duty to the advantages of public order which each resident enjoys there, while the latter is at times extended by international comity to persons who can in no sense claim to be subjects, as, for instance, in the case of persons in the East

What the idea of nationality imports.

[1] Bar, § 55, note 7, Gillespie's translation, p. 138. Cf. *Tootal's Trusts*, 23 Ch. D. (1883), 532; and *Abdul Messih* v. *Farra*, 13 App. Cas. (1888), 431.

who are under the protection of the European Powers,[1] and, conversely, is refused to persons who are undoubtedly subjects but who have forfeited their claim to the exercise of it in their favour by some breach of the native law. On the other hand, a foreigner, although he may be called upon to contribute to the support of the law, and to enrol himself in bodies of men for purposes of internal police, can not, otherwise than voluntarily, be employed against a foreign enemy, or against insurgents in possession of belligerent rights. His duty to the State in which he resides does not, in short, extend beyond affording his legitimate aid towards the suppression of internal riot or disorder.

Topics of law to which the principle of nationality is rightly applied.

23. Before quitting the subject of nationality it is needful to indicate the particular topics of law to which the principle of nationality is to be applied. Speaking generally, it may be said that the law of nationality will decide questions of capacity, of succession, of family law, and of guardianship, in France, Austria, Italy, and in all countries in which the *Code Civil*, or some adaptation of it, constitutes the domestic law, as well as in the German cantons of Switzerland, and in Russia. But in Prussia, England, and America the principle of domicil determines the personal law upon which majority or minority, marriage, succession, testacy or intestacy must depend. Lord Westbury, therefore, went too far when he declared, in *Udny* v. *Udny*, that civil status "is governed *universally* by one specific principle," *i.e.*, that of domicil. As a fact, nationality, or the tie of natural allegiance, is

[1] Thus, foreign members of crews of British vessels are protected while in an Oriental port. But it is important to remember that punitive jurisdiction does not go with protective jurisdiction in this instance. British Courts can only exercise criminal jurisdiction over British subjects, and persons to whom the privileges of subjects have been regularly extended; they consequently have no power to try a foreign seaman belonging to a British ship for any offence committed within or without the territorial jurisdiction. He must be handed over to the consular authority of the nation of which he is subject. Hall's *Foreign Powers and Jurisdiction of the British Crown*, p. 142.

CHAP. II.

adopted in many legal systems as the determinant principle for both political as well as civil status, and the distinction insisted upon by Lord Westbury is only recognized within a small minority of European States. Indeed, it is the conviction of many able writers on international law, that the future will pronounce in favour of the principle of nationality.[1]

Domicil distinguished from nationality.

24. Passing now to the question of what constitutes a domicil in the proper sense, it is important to remember at the outset that there is a very real distinction, according to most modern systems, between domicil and nationality. This distinction rests principally on the fact that in order to constitute the former, an intention of *permanent* residence in a country is all that is required. It is not at all necessary, however, that this intention should be coupled with an intention to change one's nationality. To effect the latter, at least according to English statute law, the individual has to avail himself of statutory assistance, and to submit himself to a prescribed procedure. But it is open to him to change his domicil at pleasure, with no control outside his own will. His *patria* and his *domicilium* are thus, as Lord Westbury pointed out in *Udny* v. *Udny*,[2] two very different things, which must not be confounded.

What constitutes a voluntary domicil.

25. We owe much of the learning connected with, as well as the generally accepted definition of, domicil to the investigation of the Roman lawyers.[3] And this, notwithstanding that the question of domicil as between subjects of Rome and those of another kingdom had no practical bearing for the Roman jurists, owing to the universal character of the Roman Empire. But the question had an importance in connection with the duties and responsibilities of municipal office, often

[1] Cf. § 92 Bar, and note 20, p. 203 of Gillespie's translation.

[2] L. R. 1 H. L. Sc. 460. Cf. also *Haldane* v. *Eckford*, L. R. 8 Eq. (1869), 631; *Abdallah* v. *Rickards*, 4 T. L. R. (1888), 622.

[3] Cf. 203 Dig. 50, 16; 27 § 1 D. 50, 1.

of a very burdensome nature, which the law imposed upon every one who had his *domicilium* in a particular place, and also in connection with the assessment and payment of taxes. Hence it was that the subject was very fully considered by Roman jurists, and with that scientific acumen which distinguishes their treatment of all legal questions. From their point of view that place was to be regarded as a man's domicil which he has *freely chosen* for his permanent abode, and as the centre at once of his legal relations and his business: the place to which he has transferred his tabernacle and his main establishment (*larem rerumque ac fortunarum summum*[1]), and the place to which he always intends to return at the end of any temporary absence.[2] No specific period of residence is necessary, provided a fixed intention that it should be permanent is present,[3] and from a prolonged residence this intention (called the *animus remanendi*) may be assumed if the other facts are consistent with this view. But it has been held that a Scotchman who resided in England for the last twenty-two years of his life, *living in lodgings, hotels, and lodging-houses*, had *not* thereby lost his Scotch, nor acquired an English domicil.[4] In America, little, if any, stress seems to be laid on the mode of living, whether on rent at lodgings, or in the house of a friend. "The apparent or avowed inten-

[1] C. 10, 40, 7; D. 50, 16, 203.

[2] As Sir Herbert Jenner Fust said, in the Prerogative Court of Canterbury, in the case of *Craigie* v. *Lewin*, 3 Curteis' Ecclesiastical Reports (1843), p. 435:—"I admit all that has been said in this case, that length of time is not important; one day will be sufficient, provided the *animus* exists: if a person goes from one country to another, with the intention of remaining, that is sufficient; whatever time he may have lived there is not enough, unless there be an intention of remaining." Cf. Pothier, *Intro. Général aux Coutumes*, Tom. X., p. 2; *uno solo die constituitur domicilium, si de voluntate appareat*. The French Civil Code, Arts. 102 and 103, adopts the same definition.

[3] See the Lord Chancellor's judgment in *Ommaney* v. *Bingham* (1796), cited *Bempde* v. *Johnstone*, 3 Ves. (1796), 202; *Brown* v. *Smith*, 15 Beav. (1852), 444, 449; and *In re Marrett*, 36 Ch. D. (1887), 400.

[4] *In re Patience, Patience* v. *Main*, 29 Ch. D. (1885), 976.

CHAP. II.

tion," said President Rush, in *Guier* v. *O'Daniel*,[1] "of *constant* residence, not the manner of it, constitutes the domicil." So, also, in the English case of *Craigie* v. *Lewin*,[2] living in furnished lodgings was treated as affording no criterion of domicil. On the other hand, mere temporary absences will not destroy a domicil which has once been established with reference to the criteria involved in the general definition. Nor, again, will a mere change of intention to retain the domicil so long as actual residence continues. Thus, where a British-born subject had acquired a domicil at Hamburg, a subsequent declaration in a will made by him in England while on a temporary visit, that it had not been his intention to renounce his domicil of origin as an Englishman, was held inoperative against the foreign domicil in fact.[3] So that it appears, to constitute domicil according to its true notion, there must be residence with the intention of remaining (*animus manendi*). But to retain a domicil once acquired there must be either actual continued residence originating with such intention, although the intention may no longer exist; or the intention to preserve the domicil must be retained although the actual residence has ceased. From this definition it seems to follow that mere residence, as a student, whose family residence was elsewhere, will not constitute domicil in a legal sense, and it was so decided by the Roman jurists,[4] and in 1881 by the Court of Session in Scotland.[5] There is also a similar decision in the American reports.[6]

[1] 1 Binney's Rep. p. 349, note.

[2] 3 Curteis' Eccl. Rep. (1843), p. 447.

[3] *Re Stern*, 28 L. J. Exch. 22; *S. C.* 3 H. & N. 594.

[4] L. 2, C. 10, 40. According to the *Epistola Hadriani*, however, a ten years' residence as a student was sufficient to establish a domicil.

[5] *Steel* v. *Lindsay*, 9 Ct. Sess. Rep., 4th Series, 160. See also *Urquhart* v. *Butterfield*, 37 Ch. D. (1887), 379.

[6] *The Inhabitants of Granby* v. *Inhabitants of Amherst*, 7 Massachusetts Reports, 1.

Domicil of necessity.

26. But in addition to a domicil of choice most systems also recognize what may be termed a domicil of necessity. This was ascribed by Roman law to a public official at the seat of his service, to the soldier at the place of his garrison, and to persons in dependent positions in a family at the place of domicil of the head. Involuntary exile (*relegatio*), if perpetual, also gave a necessary domicil at the place of relegation, and both in France[1] and in England,[2] persons deported or transported for life as the result of a criminal sentence are held to lose their domicil of origin. But persons merely incarcerated in prison for a limited period stand on a different footing. The requisite *animus* is clearly wanting in their case, and they are classed with persons absent on a long voyage, who are deemed to retain their domicil despite their temporary absence.[3] So in the case of political refugees, so long as their absence from their own country is involuntary, the English Courts refuse to consider it, *per se*, as involving a change of domicil.[4] In the case of persons holding public offices in a foreign country the question seems to depend on whether the office is one that is at variance with the supposition that the person filling it will continue to hold it for an indefinite period. If the circumstances negative such a supposition there will be no change of domicil. Thus a person whose domicil of origin was English, and who resided in England till his appointment as Chief Justice of the Island of Ceylon, was held not to lose his English domicil by residing in Ceylon as Chief Justice, and dying there after four years' service in that office.[5] So mere residence in London occasioned by par-

[1] Merlin, *Rép. de Jur. Domicile*, IV.

[2] Per Lord Westbury in *Udny* v. *Udny*, L. R. 1 H. L. Sc. (1869), 458; Phillimore, § 191, Vol. IV.; Dicey, p. 129.

[3] Phillimore, § 190; *Hodgson* v. *De Beauchesne*, 12 Moo. P. C. (1858), 285.

[4] *De Bonneval* v. *De Bonneval*, Curt. (1838), 856; *Heath* v. *Sampson*, 14 Beav. (1851), 441; *Re d'Orléans*, 28 L. J. P. (1859), 129.

[5] *Attorney-General* v. *Rowe*, 1 Hurls. & Colt. Exch. Rep. 31.

CHAP. II. liamentary duties affords no proof of domicil.[1] Nor will acceptance of an ambassadorial or consular office in a particular place found a domicil there,[2] nor, on the other hand, dissolve a domicil already established there.[3] As a general rule, however, unless the service is such as to indicate from the first that it will only be temporary, the official will *de facto* have the centre of his activity at the place of his service. It was in accordance with this rule that officials of the late East India Company who took up their residence for an indefinite period in India were held to have acquired a domicil there. This was so decided in *Bruce's case*,[4] and again in *Munroe* v. *Douglas*.[5] Since these cases, which in many quarters have been pronounced to be anomalous and exceptional,[6] were decided, India has passed under the direct government of the Queen-Empress, and from the date of the passing of the Indian Succession Act (1865), officials can no longer be said, as in the days of the East India Company, to expatriate themselves by accepting office, for instance, in Her Majesty's civil or military service.[7] But as entering the former service necessarily involves a foreign residence for an indefinite period for those members of it who are English born, and since the place of a man's home, or main establishment, decides the place of domicil, it would seem that the principle on which *Bruce's case*, and that of *Munroe* v. *Douglas*, were decided would still be applicable, although the East India Company has ceased to exist, to those cases where an Anglo-Indian domicil had been acquired *before* the

[1] *Somerville* v. *Lord Somerville*, 5 Ves. Rep. (1801), 750. Cf. also *Hamilton* v. *Dallas*, 1 Ch. D. (1875), 257.

[2] See the case of *Udny* v. *Udny*, L. R. 1 Scotch & Div. App. 441.

[3] Cf. *Sharpe* v. *Crespin*, L. R. 1 P. & M. (1869), 611.

[4] 2 Bosanquet & Puller's Reports (1790), 230.

[5] 5 Maddock's Reports (1820), 379.

[6] Per Chitty, J., in *Re Tootal's Trusts*, 23 Ch. D. (1883), at p. 537; per Lindley, L.J., in *Ex parte Cunningham*, 13 Q. B. D. at p. 425.

[7] § 10, Expl., Act X. of 1865.

Indian Succession Act of 1865 came into force.[1] A possible reason for the contrary view may, perhaps, be found in that "immiscible character" which, as Lord Stowell felicitously expressed it,[2] prevents Europeans generally from becoming incorporated to the full extent with the native population, or being admitted into the general body and mass of the native society, and which, as it was argued in *Maltass* v. *Maltass*,[3] would prevent the acquisition of a domicil there. But such an argument would have had as much practical force *before* as *after* the transfer of the government of India from the East India Company to that of the Crown, and, on the whole, the indefinite duration of the Indian service, and the fact of the Indian official's family usually residing with him, would, in the cases referred to, afford more cogent arguments in favour of an Indian domicil. So the French law fixes the domicil, in the case of an office conferred for the life of the holder and irrevocable, at the place where its functions are discharged, and admits of no proof to the contrary.[4] But where the office is of a temporary and revocable nature, the question whether the original domicil has been changed is one to be decided by the usual proof. Thus the office of "*grand-maître d'eaux et forêts*" was held, in the case of M. de Courteval, not to prevent the law of the original domicil from operating, mainly for the reason that the office was one which did not necessitate more than a visit of two or three months during the year to the Departement, and consequently did not involve a fixed residence.[5] A similar decision was given under the law of Holland with respect to a native of Amsterdam who resided at Smyrna as Dutch Consul, and upon the express ground that by accepting

[1] Phillimore, Vol. IV., § 162. Cf. also *Wauchope* v. *Wauchope*, 4 Rettie (1877), and *In re Marrett*, cited *supra*.

[2] *The Indian Chief*, 3 Robinson's Adm. Rep. (1801), pp. 28, 29.

[3] 1 Rob. Eccl. Rep. (1844), 81.

[4] Code Civil, Art. 109; Merlin, *Rép. de Jur. Domicile*, III.

[5] Cochin, *Œuvres*, IX., 124.

CHAP. II.

an office of this kind, which was only for a limited number of years, and not perpetual, no new domicil could be held to have been contracted.[1] But although an office may, in its nature, be of temporary duration, and the person may be removable at pleasure, yet if there are any circumstances indicating an intention to remain in the place, even if he were removed from the office, or if his employment ceased, the presumption that he had established his domicil in the latter place would rest on the same grounds as if the residence had been at first the object of his choice and not induced by his acceptance of the office.[2] The case of a married woman is another common example of a necessary domicil, for according to the jurisprudence of European countries, as well as under the Hindu and Muhammadan laws, she takes, on marriage, the domicil of her husband.[3] But where the wife has been divorced or judicially separated from her husband, and, it seems also, where the husband has abjured the realm, has deserted the wife, and established himself permanently in a foreign country, or where he has committed a crime for which he has been transported, the wife is considered entitled to acquire a distinct domicil for herself.[4] A mere separation *de facto*, however, not resulting from a decree of Court, will not of itself confer an independent domicil on a married woman by English law.[5] In the case of minors the domicil is that of the father, if alive, or that of the mother when the father is dead. An orphan during infancy follows the domicil of his guardian, in so far, at least, as the latter does not act with any fraudulent inten-

[1] *Nieuw Nederlands Advys Book*, Vol. I., p. 165.

[2] Burge, Vol. I., p. 52.

[3] *Turner* v. *Thompson*, 13 P. & D. (1888), 37, at page 41; *Harvie* v. *Farnie*, 8 App. Cas. (1882), 43.

[4] *Dolphin* v. *Robins*, 7 H. L. C. (1859), 390; *Le Sueur* v. *Le Sueur*, L. R. 1 P. & D. (1876), 139; *Williams* v. *Dormer*, 2 Rob. Eccl. (1851), 505; *Scott* v. *Att.-General*, 11 P. D. (1886), 128.

[5] *In re Daly's Settlement*, 25 Beav. (1858), 456, per Lord Romilly. Cf. *Low* v. *Low*, 19 Ct. of Sess. Rep. 4th Ser., 19th Nov. 1891.

tion so as to avail himself of some foreign rule of succession.[1] And in England and in the United States he can only change the domicil of the ward with the sanction of the Court which has supreme curatorial jurisdiction. Lastly, as regards succession to moveables, testate or intestate, the question of domicil is, in England, regulated by statutory law. By 24 & 25 Vict. c. 121, it is enacted, subject to conventions to be made with foreign States for its reciprocal application, that British subjects dying in a foreign country shall be deemed, for all purposes of testate or intestate succession as to moveables, to retain the domicil they possessed at the time of going to reside in such foreign country, unless they have resided in such foreign country for a year at least before their death, and shall have made a formal written declaration of an intention to become domiciled there. Similar provisions are made with respect to foreigners dying in Great Britain. The statute does not, however, come into operation except under an Order in Council of her Majesty after a convention has been made with the particular foreign State concerned for that purpose. This restriction on the operation of the Act is based on a high international principle that, apart from special conventions between particular States, the municipal laws of one country cannot, for *international* purposes, limit or enlarge the natural power of acquiring a domicil within the dominion of such laws. Thus, in *Hamilton* v. *Dallas*, it was contended that as Art. 13 of the French Civil Code prescribed certain conditions for the acquisition of domicil within its territories by foreigners, no domicil can be acquired for purposes of succession or testamentary disposition unless the conditions have been complied with. This contention was overruled by Bacon, V.C., who held that whether or not the 13th Article of the Code was intended to prevent the acquisi-

[1] *Potinger* v. *Wightman*, 3 Mer. (1817), 67.

CHAP. II.

tion of a domicil in France for the purposes of succession, "the fact that a foreigner can acquire a domicil *de facto* in France is not for a moment to be called in question. It requires no provision in the Code for that; it is a law paramount to the law of the Code, not provided against nor provided for in the Code, but a natural and national right, against which there is no interdiction or prohibition."[1] This reasoning does not, of course, mean that Courts of the enacting Legislature can ignore laws passed by it, but merely that Courts outside the limits of that Legislature are not bound to recognize such laws which profess to limit or enlarge the natural power of acquiring a domicil in deciding questions which private international law refers to domicil alone.

Possibility of double domicil.

27. That a man can have but one domicil for the purposes of succession is thoroughly settled in English jurisprudence.[2] But so far as there may be a question as to distinct jural relations of the same person, the possibility of a double domicil, recognized by the law of Rome,[3] does not appear to be denied,[4] at least by English lawyers. Thus, a person may have his commercial domicil in one place, while his domicil for purposes of succession may be in another. The former usually receives effect in questions arising during war, as to whether the ship or the wares of a person are to be regarded as belonging to the enemy, and the point for inquiry in such cases is whether in fact, or by presumption of fact, the goods come from the enemy's country, or are intended for his benefit.[5] Because, if a man carries on trade

[1] 1 Ch. D. (1875), 257.

[2] *Somerville* v. *Somerville*, 5 Ves. (1801), 756; *Crookenden* v. *Fuller*, 29 L. J. P. & M. (1859), 1; *Munro* v. *Munro*, 7 Cl. & F. (1840), 842; *Hodgson* v. *De Beauchesne*, 12 Moo. P. C. (1858), 285.

[3] *Dig*. 50, 1, 5, 6, § 2, and 27, § 2.

[4] Phillimore, § 51, Vol. IV.; Dicey, Ap. 61 *et seq*.

[5] Gillespie's translation of Bar, p. 120, note 40.

from a hostile port, as a merchant of that port, his property engaged in enterprises, which have originated from that port, will be regarded as in hostile ownership.[1] Indeed, the case of *Jonge Classina*[2] shows the possibility of having two commercial domicils, and it is sufficient to constitute a man a merchant of any place if he is there from time to time and acts as such. So the Scotch Courts have held that the *forum* of a travelling merchant who had no fixed place of residence was the place where he chanced to be for the time.[3] But the view of many French and Swiss jurists, notably Brocher[4] among the former, and Muheim among the latter, is against the possibility of a double domicil.

Can a man be without a domicil?

28. Another interesting question was raised by Roman jurists, as to whether a person can be without a domicil. They admitted the difficulty of answering the question in the affirmative, but cited the case of a person having abandoned his domicil and putting himself *in itinere* in order to seek a place wherein to establish himself, as showing the possibility of such a contingency arising in fact.[5] The English and American judges have solved the difficulty by holding that when a domicil of choice is abandoned, that of origin revives until a new one is completely fixed.[6] Mere

1 *The Indian Chief*, 3 C. Rob. (1801), 12; *The Portland, Ibid* (1800), 41; *The Susa*, 2 C. Rob. 255.

2 5 C. Rob. (1804), 297.

3 *Linn* v. *Cassadinos*, 9 Ct. of Session Rep., 4th Series, 849.

4 *Cours de droit international*, Vol. I., § 78, pp. 250, 251. Brocher is here speaking, however, of the general principle, and he does not deny that there may exist a plurality of domicils with reference to distinct jural relations. The French *Civil Code* (Arts. 102—104, 110, 111, 116) proclaims the unity of domicil, but see Art. 69 *Code proc. Civ.* Cf. also Calvo, *Le droit international*, II., § 681.

5 *Dig.* 50, 1, 27, § 2.

6 *Bell* v. *Kennedy*, L. R. 1 H. L. Sc. (1868), 307; *Udny* v. *Udny, Ibid.* 460; *Somerville* v. *Somerville*, 5 Vesey, 786; *King* v. *Foxwell*, L. R. 1 Ch. D. (1876), 518; *The Français*, 1 Gallison's (American) Repts. 467—469. Cochin (*Œuvres*, I., 184), in combatting the contention that a *comedian*, or travelling

CHAP. II.

abandonment thus divests all domicils except that of origin, and the latter reverts *in transitu*, and prevails until the party has acquired another. But abandonment, to have even the effect of destroying an acquired domicil, must be complete and evidenced by unequivocal overt acts, not merely consisting in an intention, residing, as Lord Stowell expresses it, secretly and undistinguishably in the breast of the party, and liable to be revoked every hour.[1] Thus, a French acquired domicil was held not completely abandoned by mere embarkation on a vessel bound for England, where the person was compelled by ill-health to reland, never, in fact, having quitted the French harbour.[2]

Domicil of juristic persons.

29. The possibility of having two commercial domicils has also been extended by the House of Lords to the case of corporations. "Places of business," said Lord Chancellor Lyndhurst in the leading case, "may, for the purposes of jurisdiction, be deemed the domicil."[3] It may be open to objection that the whole theory of domicil is dependent on the habits and relations of the natural man, and is thus inapplicable to the artificial creation known as a juristic person. But, as Bar forcibly points out, if States and nations are to walk in legal community with each other, they will, *de facto*, be forced to a mutual recognition of the juristic persons that are constituted or that have grown up in the territory of their neighbours, as possible objects of legal consideration.[4] And if this is true it equally follows that, for the purposes of justice, such juristic

player, was a person without a domicil, maintains that the domicil of birth would remain till it was superseded by the acquisition of another *animo permanendi*.

[1] *The President*, 5 Robinson's Adm. Reps. (1804), 279. Cf. Calvo, II., § 667.

[2] *In the Goods of Raffenel*, 32 L. J. P. & M. (1863), 203.

[3] *Carron Iron Co.* v. *Maclaren*, 5 H. of L. Cases (1855), 416, 449. See also *Newby* v. *Van Oppen and Colt's Patent Firearms Co.*, L. R. 7 Q. B. (1872), 293. Cf. Art. 69 of the French *Code proc. Civ.*; and Calvo, II., § 665.

[4] § 104, p. 228, Gillespie's translation.

persons must be permitted to have the right of suing and being sued. This position, however, involves the further necessity of attributing to them a domicil for the purpose of founding a proper *forum* or jurisdiction for the determination of suits in which they may be concerned as plaintiffs or defendants. The inexorable logic of the realities of human life and conduct demands, therefore, that juristic persons should in this matter be treated in like manner as natural persons, and a *persona standi in judicia* is now conceded to them by the jurisprudence of European countries, between many of whom conventions on the subject now exist.[1] Nor is it difficult to conceive in their case a centre of activity. In the case of such juristic persons as municipalities, churches, colleges, hospitals, and the like, they are by their very nature tied down to a particular locality, and thus there is a clear connection between the territory and the juristic person which at once fixes the centre of the latter's activity. It may not be as easy to assign the seat of this activity in the case of other juristic persons, such as corporations like railway, shipping, and other companies. But, as a rule, the question is found to be settled by the charter of their constitution or by special legislative enactment, and, failing this, a good practical rule is that embodied in sect. 19 of the German Code of Civil Procedure, which enacts that "unless some other seat is plainly discoverable, the place where the management of the concern is carried on is held to be the seat": that is to say, the central seat of activity or of the enterprise.[2] This is practically the rule adopted in the Code of Civil Procedure for India (Act XIV. of 1882),[3] which was also laid down by

[1] Cf. Lindley *on Company Law*, pp. 909, 914.

[2] Cf. Savigny, VIII. § 354, and a Belgian statute of 13th May, 1873, which runs as follows:—"Every society whose principal establishment is in Belgium, is subject to the law of Belgium, although the act of constitution may have been made in a foreign country."

[3] Section 17, Expln. II.

CHAP. II. the Privy Council in the celebrated *Rutlam case.*[1] So in the English case of the *Attorney-General* v. *Alexander*,[2] Amphlett, B., laid down the rule "that a corporation may be said to reside wherever it has its seat." And in a later decision, Huddleston, B., used similar language. "The artificial residence," he said, "which must be assigned to the artificial person, is *the place where the real business is carried on.*"[3] But the question where the "seat" or the "place of real business" is to be found can only be determined with reference to all the circumstances of the particular case. A corporation like an individual may, however, contract that it shall be dealt with as if it were domiciled in any specified country, and having so contracted, it will be held to its agreement, and service of a writ in the manner stipulated for by the contract will be considered valid.[4]

[1] 8 Moore's Ind. Appeals (1860), p. 291, at p. 307.

[2] L. R. 10 Ex. (1874), 33.

[3] *Cesena Sulphur Co.* v. *Nicholson,* L. R. 1 Ex. D. (1876), 454.

[4] *The Thames Sulphur Co.* v. *La Société des Métaux,* Times Law Rep. 1889, p. 118. Cf. as to natural persons *Copin* v. *Adamson,* L. R. 1 Ex. D. (1874), 17; *Vallée* v. *Dumergue,* 4 Exch. (1849), 290.

CHAPTER III.

LAW OF PERSONS, AND HEREIN OF STATUS AND CAPACITY, LAW OF THE FAMILY, AND OF ARTIFICIAL AND CONVENTIONAL PERSONS.

Scope of the chapter stated.

30. IN the preceding chapter we have considered the two ties by which a person, regarded merely as an individual human being, is bound to a particular territorial jurisdiction. We have now to consider the person as a legal entity clothed with jural relations, possessing a capacity for rights and a capacity for acting, and thus realising the complete idea of personality in a legal sense. Such a conception of personality is indispensable for general legal intercourse. But the rights and corresponding duties involved in this conception are so multiform in their nature that to attempt to generalise by subjecting them to a general treatment, which would embrace all those rules of law which admit of being so turned in expression as to treat of the incapacity of a person for some act, or for the exercise of some right, would only lead to confusion. It is more convenient to make each of these jural relations which have an importance from the point of view of private international law the subject of a separate inquiry.

Status, by what law determined.

31. When we speak of the *status* of a person in a legal sense we mean to refer to the aggregate of rights and duties which are attached to him either as a member of the community or as one of a class. It thus comprehends those personal conditions which affect a man's liberty, citizenship, and family, the *tria capita* of a full Roman citizen, and which, it has been

CHAP. III.

said, embrace those qualities which take effect either from birth, as citizenship, legitimacy, and illegitimacy; at a fixed time after birth, as minority or majority; or at an intermediate time after birth, as idiocy and lunacy, marriage and divorce.[1] All these qualities or conditions may be grouped together into two broad classes, the one relating to *political*, the other to *civil status*. We are not now concerned with the former, or *political* status, which we have already discussed under the topic of nationality. For our present purpose we have to do only with a man's *civil* status, that is to say with those civil qualities and capacities which Lord Westbury said,[2] using language which, as we have seen, although correct enough as an exponent of Anglo-American views on the subject is not quite accurate when examined with reference to other European systems, are governed universally by the single principle of domicil. In the enjoyment of these qualities and capacities the foreigner and the native subject now stand, speaking generally, on a footing of equality. It required, no doubt, a long and tangled course of evolution of legal ideas before this principle of equality was largely recognised. But modern practice and the statute law of the leading nations of Europe, excluding Russia, have now proclaimed and sanctified the noble doctrine that before the law the foreigner and the native subject are equal. It may be, indeed, that in certain respects foreigners are still treated in a manner which, at first sight, may seem to place them in a position of inequality as compared with native subjects. Thus they are frequently subject to foreigners' arrest (*Ausländer-arrest*) and to the obligation of finding security for costs.[3] But the inequality is here only apparent.

[1] Wheaton's *International Law*, § 84.

[2] *Udny* v. *Udny*, L. R. 1 H. L. (Sc.), 460.

[3] Bar, § 95, p. 210, Gillespie's trans.; Phillimore, § 385, Vol. IV.; and cf. §§ 380 and 549 Prov. of Act XIV. of 1882.

In reality such provisions are only intended to place both the native and foreign litigant on an equal footing, by imposing a reasonable check upon the facility which the foreigner enjoys of withdrawing himself from the jurisdiction of the tribunals, and thus enabling the native litigant to protect himself against the risk of legal process being in that way defeated. Now, it would involve a distinct encroachment upon this fundamental principle of modern international jurisprudence, if it were supposed that, as soon as a question about a foreigner was raised, the actual conditions which are recognised by the laws of the nationality of the foreigner, should be substituted for the conditions under which any proposition of law that touches legal capacity is applied to natives. Under this supposition, a man who, by the law of his nation could not acquire real property, would be equally incapacitated in the place where the property was situate, merely because he was a foreigner, although by the law of the latter place he laboured under no such disability. Hence, in dealing with those elements which go to constitute a man's civil status, the decision in any particular case is at once supplied, by remembering that only those laws which regulate the legal relation in question in other respects, have anything to do with the determination of this question.[1] In short, the question what law is applicable, is to be resolved just as if the foreign law did not exist at all; and what is to be regarded is whether the actual conditions are present which are essential to the application of some rule that increases or diminishes legal capacity, according to that system of law under which the question otherwise falls. Thus, if a man in his own country is declared incapable of succession, because he has given up some particular religious belief, such as Roman Catholicism for Protestantism, he may still take as

[1] Bar, § 147, p. 323, Gillespie's trans. See also § 137, p. 305, *Ibid.*

CHAP. III.

heir an estate in a country in which religious beliefs have no bearing upon the right of succession. It must be admitted, however, that very divergent theories have been propounded by juristical writers of different countries on this subject, and what adds to the difficulty of extracting any consistent doctrine from their works is, that each theory itself bristles with the exceptions by which it is surrounded. To the great Savigny belongs the credit of establishing amidst this general confusion of ideas the universal validity of the *lex domicilii*[1] [and by this expression is to be understood the law of the country in which the person has fixed his home, as distinguished from the *lex patriæ*, or law of the State to which he owes the allegiance of a subject, though this distinction is not always observed as it should be],[2] by pointing out that it is impossible to apply any other law than that local law to which the person belongs by residence to the various personal conditions and qualities by which his status is to be determined. And this is the rule to which Lord Westbury, in *Udny* v. *Udny*, gave the sanction of his great authority, and to the adoption of which English Courts are showing an increasing tendency.[3] It may, at all events, be said to be a rule generally recognized that the capacity, state, and condition of persons according to the law of their domicil will be regarded as to acts done, rights acquired, and contracts made, *in the place of their domicil, touching property situate there.*[4] The French law, however, stands by itself in providing that all questions of *status* and domicil, in the case of French subjects, even though domiciled abroad, shall be referred to French law, as the law of their nationality.[5] Nor must it be overlooked that even in those matters affecting status, where the personal laws of a foreigner do receive extra-territorial recognition, there is this underlying limita-

[1] *System*, Vol. VIII., § 362.

[2] Cf. Fœlix, § 27, and Art. 6 of the Italian Civil Code (*Codice Civile*).

[3] Westlake, pp. 45, 46.

[4] Story, § 101.

[5] Art. 3, Code Civil.

tion, which the adjudicating Court has to scrupulously observe—that this recognition will be refused whenever the enforcement of the foreign law would be opposed to the moral sense or political principles of the nation, or the doctrine of human rights,[1] or, expressed differently, would contravene some fundamental principle founded on considerations of public policy, and be prejudicial to the sovereignty or jurisdiction of the State from which that Court derived its powers, or would clash with the rights of the native subjects.[2] In such cases it is obvious one or other of the laws must give way; in which case, said Lord Ellenborough, "our own is entitled to the preference."[3] On the other hand, the doctrine of English and American jurisprudence in respect to contracts made abroad is, that, in the absence of an express declaration of the legislative will, they are not invalidated by prohibitions prescribed by the law of the forum where they are sought to be enforced.[4] Again, questions may arise out of a *status*, which cannot itself be recognized by the Courts of another nation, which, so far as they do not affect the mere personal capacity, may have to be decided according to the foreign law. Thus, the children of a polygamist Turk by a second or third wife, married by him in the lifetime of a living wife, would not be treated as bastards, in all respects, by Christian Courts; and it has even been asserted that a contract relating to the sale and purchase of slaves might be held legal, if legal in the domicil of the contracting parties.[5] From what has

[1] *The Opinions of Grotius*, by D. P. De Bruyn, 1894, pp. 74, 75; Westlake, § 215, p. 260; Nelson's *Selected Cases*, p. 261.

[2] Cf. the observations of Lord Herschell, L. C. in *Hamlyn & Co.* v. *Talisker Distillery*, Appeal Cases (1894), p. 209. So Burge writes: "But the *lex loci contractus* is not admitted when it violates the law of nature, public morals, or the policy or institutions of that State in which its validity is sought to be established." Vol. I., pp. 199—200.

[3] Cf. *Potter* v. *Brown*, 5 East's Reports (1804), 124—131; Foote, p. 45.

[4] Phillimore, § 676, Vol. IV.

[5] *The Opinions of Grotius*, by D. P. De Bruyn, p. 75. Cf. *Santos* v. *Illidge*, 29 L. J. C. P. (1860), 348; Pollock *On Contracts* (6th ed.), pp. 370—373.

been said it is apparent that, while the rule declaring that "the *status* of a person is determined by the law of his domicil"—understanding this last expression in the sense above indicated—is one very generally accepted in private international law, it is nevertheless open to many exceptions in its practical application. And we shall see, as we proceed, that many such exceptions exist in the treatment of questions affecting marriage and divorce, minority and majority. But it will be more convenient to treat each branch of these questions separately.

Distinction between prohibition and incapacity.

32. In dealing with questions affecting personal capacity the distinction, to which Mr. Foote,[1] following Bar,[2] has in England called attention, between a general prohibition and incapacity, must be remembered. The effect of such a prohibition by the laws of an individual State may be to impose some limitation on the exercise of a man's jural capacity in some particular direction. But inasmuch as he would not be affected thereby otherwise and more stringently than the other sane adults by whom he is surrounded, and who are in the same condition with respect to the prohibited act as himself, he cannot, strictly speaking, be said to labour under a personal incapacity differentiating his case from the normal condition of other persons. Thus the law may prohibit a marriage between persons standing towards each other in a given relationship, or a person from undertaking an obligation of a given character. Here we have a prohibition affecting not merely A. or B. as individuals, which would be a case of true personal incapacity, but all persons alike who were similarly conditioned to A. or B.

Effect of bankruptcy on jural capacity.

33. In the above connection it is also important to bear in mind that the bankruptcy laws of a State may, in a more or less degree, affect a person's jural capacity. The object of

[1] Page 46. [2] § 136, p. 304, Gillespie's translation.

these laws is to provide a procedure by way of a general execution of diligence against the whole estate of the bankrupt, for the purpose of due ranking and payment of all creditors. To this end the whole estate is laid under a general arrestment in favour of the whole body of creditors, and the bankrupt accordingly loses all power of alienation over property which is legally available for his creditors. But the loss of this power, which is necessary for the protection of the creditors, does not imply that in other respects the bankrupt will suffer any diminution in his general legal capacity, which, in fact, will remain undiminished. He will thus be able to take up or renounce a succession falling to him, though of course he cannot lay the bankrupt estate, which consists of his whole present property, under any obligations. And since from an international law point of view bankruptcy is not directly recognized as having any extra-territorial operation, even the withdrawal of the power of disposal from a bankrupt, which an adjudication of bankruptcy involves, does not extend to property belonging to him which is situated abroad. The bankrupt thus maintains his capacity of making perfectly valid conveyances of property so situated, so long as it is not withdrawn from him by a special decree of arrestment on the part of the foreign Court.[1]

The test of capacity to do an act, how judged.

34. By what law the capacity to do an act is to be tested is a point in regard to which, in English jurisprudence, it is extremely difficult, as we have already partially seen, to express a decided opinion. The older view appears to have been that the law of the place where an act is done, or a contract entered into, is the proper law to decide all questions of competency or incompetency. It has in support of it, so far as

[1] Bar, §§ 478, 479, pp. 1017 and 1019, Gillespie's translation.

CHAP. III.

ordinary mercantile contracts are concerned, the high authority of Lord Eldon, pronounced in a case which still stands un-overruled,[1] and of Sir Cresswell Cresswell,[2] amongst judges, and of Burge[3] and Storey[4] amongst juristical writers of England and America. Burge's argument in favour of this view is the most clearly and forcibly stated of any other on the same side. "This doctrine promotes," says that learned writer, whose extraordinary erudition has won the admiration of the most profound jurists of Europe,[5] "whilst that to which it is opposed is inconsistent with, those principles of mutual convenience which induce the recognition of foreign laws. The obstacles to commercial intercourse between the subjects of foreign States would be almost unsurmountable, if a party must pause to ascertain, not by any means within his reach, but by recourse to the law of the domicile of the person with whom he was dealing, whether the latter has attained the age of majority, and, consequently, whether he is competent to enter into a valid and binding contract. If the country in which the contract was litigated was also that in which it had been entered into, and if the party enforcing it were the subject of that country, it would be unjust, as well as unreasonable, to invoke the law of a foreign State for the benefit of the foreigner, and to deprive its own subjects of the benefit of the law of his own State." This view has also been adopted in the South African (British) Courts.[6] The tendency of more recent decisions of the English Court, at least in cases connected with contracts of marriage and other matrimonial contracts, is, however, in the opposite direction, and in *Cooper*

[1] *Male* v. *Roberts*, 3 Esp. (1800), 163.

[2] *Simonin* v. *Maillac*, 2 Sw. & Tr. (1860), 67, explained in *Brook* v. *Brook*, 9 H. L. C. (1861), 193.

[3] Vol. I., p. 132

[4] *Conflict of Laws*, § 103.

[5] See Bar, § 22, p. 46, Gillespie's translation.

[6] In *Greef* v. *Verreaux*, 1 Menz. 153, quoted in *The Opinions of Grotius*, by D. P. De Bruyn, pp. 78, 79.

v. *Cooper*[1] Lord Macnaghten, while admitting that in England the question was not finally settled, observed that the preponderance of opinion there as well as abroad seemed to be in favour of the law of the domicil.[2] It was, unfortunately, not necessary for the House of Lords in this case to deliver a definite ruling on the point, which would have, at all events, set the question at rest for English Courts. But in a still more recent decision the House of Lords has imported a new element into the decision of the question. The point in the case was whether Scotch or English law governed a certain arbitration clause in an agreement which was admittedly bad by Scotch law but good by English. The agreement had been executed in England, but one of the parties was a Scotch firm, and the place of performance was Scotland. The House of Lords held that English law applied, basing their decision upon the intention of the parties, as deducible from all the circumstances attending the contract.[3] So that, until the ultimate tribunal does determine the proper choice between the *lex domicilii* and the *lex loci contractus*, in the case of a conflict the dictum of the Appeal Court in *Sottomayor* v. *De Barros*[4] will probably be followed by all original Courts. It was there said to be "a well recognized principle of law" that the question of personal capacity to enter into any contract was to be decided by the law of domicil. "As in other contracts," said Lord Justice Cotton, "so in that of marriage, personal capacity must depend on the law of domicil." In *Cooper* v. *Cooper*, Lord Halsbury also stated his individual opinion that "the capacity to contract is regulated by the law of domicil."[5] And we have already seen that in *Udny* v. *Udny*, Lord Westbury used very emphatic language to

[1] 13 App. Cas. (1888), 88.
[2] *Ibid.* p. 108.
[3] *Hamlyn & Co.* v. *Talisker Distillery and Others*, (1894) App. Cas. 209.
[4] 3 P. D. (1877), 5; *S. C.*, 37 L. T. 415.
[5] 13 App. Cas. (1888), 99.

CHAP. III. enunciate the same doctrine. Two exceptions, however, have been engrafted on this general rule by a learned Scotch writer, Lord Fraser. Where a Scotchman has contracted with a foreigner, international law, he thinks, requires that a Court should deal fairly with both parties. Accordingly, in such cases the question for solution will be, did the Scotchman know the condition and status of the person with whom he contracted; did he use reasonable care and prudence; was he put upon his enquiry; and has he by his own neglect placed himself in a position of disadvantage? If he has acted prudently and with reasonable care, and if there was nothing in the appearance of the other party or the nature of the transaction to raise enquiry, justice requires that the *lex loci contractus* should govern the rights of the parties, and that the foreigner should not be able to shield himself by appealing to his own law of status, of which the other party was ignorant, and to which his attention was not directed.[1] The French law qualifies the general rule much in the same way, in favour of French creditors who have acted in good faith and without rashness. Thus, where a Cuban of twenty-two years of age, who by the law of his own country would not attain majority till twenty-five, whereas in France twenty-one is the age of majority, had accepted certain bills, and had stated thereon that he was domiciled in France, in a suit in which it appeared that the bank which discounted these bills, although it had not been in direct communication with the Cuban acceptor, had made inquiries from one of his creditors, who had been the medium between them, and had been assured of his full capacity, the plea of incapacity founded on Cuban law was repelled.[2] The other exception which Lord Fraser thinks the general rule in

[1] *Parent and Child*, pp. 570 *et seq.*

[2] *Fourgeaud* v. *Comte de Santa Venia*, Cour de Paris, 1879, Jour. VI., p. 488; Gillespie's translation of Bar, note F, p. 311.

favour of the *lex domicilii* admits of, relates to commercial obligations by a minor engaged in trade, and debts for board and lodging, which will bind a foreigner as much as a native, and upon the same grounds. But there is a third exception which may also be briefly stated here, and which rests on the distinction between capacity in the sense of having rights and acting lawfully, and a capacity to incur obligations by committing an illegal act. In the latter case the capacity is ruled by the law to which the illegal act is in itself subject, or, in other words, by the *lex loci actus*. This view, which is advocated by Bar,[1] is also in accordance with that followed in England, and accordingly no act can be treated as a wrong on the part of any defendant in whom it is not a wrong by the law of the country where it was done, whether that law did not regard him as a wrong-doer at the time, or whether he has since been enabled to justify it in that country by the enactment of an indemnity.[2]

Law applicable to marriage: (1) as regards essentials; (2) as regards outward formalities.

35. We have seen that both Lord Westbury (in *Udny* v. *Udny*) and Lord Justice Cotton (in *Sottomayor* v. *De Barros*) have placed marriage on the same footing as other contracts in regard to the application of the *lex domicilii*. But it is a contract completely *sui generis*, and unquestionably there is this peculiarity in marriage, that the status which results from it depends, in almost all countries, upon the intervention of public authority, applied by means of some ceremonial, civil or religious, by the due observance of which the tie is alone created. In considering, therefore, the question of capacity as applied to marriage, we must distinguish between the rules regulating the essentials of marriage —*i.e.*, the capacity of the contracting parties to enter into this permanent relation—and those which prescribe the external formalities which the parties must observe to secure the sanction

[1] Bar, p. 311, § 139, note (32), p. 309, Gillespie's translation.
[2] Westlake, § 196, p. 237, 3rd ed.

CHAP. III.

of the law to their contract. Now, the jurisprudence of the Continent of Europe,[1] as well as that of England, requires that matters affecting the former must be decided by the *lex domicilii.* The leading authorities on this point in England are *Brook* v. *Brook*[2] and *Sottomayor* v. *De Barros.*[3] In the former a marriage between persons, both of whom were domiciled in England, which was prohibited by English law, was declared invalid, although celebrated in a country (Denmark) by the law of which it was valid. So in the latter, a marriage contracted in England between first cousins who were natives of Portugal, and one of whom (the woman) was domiciled in England and the other (the man) in Portugal, was pronounced invalid on appeal on the ground that by the law of Portugal, which country was to be regarded as the place of the matrimonial domicil, such a marriage was not permitted, except under Papal dispensation, which had not been obtained, although by the law of England there was no legal objection to the marriage. On the other hand, the law of the United States holds that a marriage valid according to the *lex loci celebrationis* is valid everywhere.[4] The English Courts, however, will only apply this law with respect to the external formalities of marriage. Thus, in *Crompton* v. *Bearcroft,*[5] a Gretna Green marriage between persons domiciled in England was recognized, because only certain formalities prescribed by the English law, and not the essentials of marriage, had been evaded. In like manner, in *Simonin f. c. Maillac* v. *Maillac,*[6] the same principle was made the foundation for declaring a marriage valid which had been solemnized in England, in the manner prescribed by the law of England, between domiciled French

[1] Bar, § 157, pp. 343, 344, Gillespie's translation.
[2] 9 H. L. C. (1861), 193.
[3] 2 P. D. 81; 3 *Ibid.* (1877), 1.
[4] Wharton, §§ 126 *et seq.*
[5] Bull. N. P. (1767), 114; 2 Hagg. Cons. 443, 444. See also *Grierson* v. *Grierson* (1781), 2 Hagg. Cons. 86, 98, 99.
[6] 2 Sw. & Tr. (1860), 67.

subjects of the respective ages of twenty-one and twenty-nine, and which had been previously annulled by a French Court on the ground that it had been celebrated without the publication prescribed by the French law, and without the parties having sought or obtained the consent of their parents. It requires to be noted, however, that where by his personal law a party cannot marry *in any form without a certain consent*, the better opinion appears to be that consent, in such a case, will rank among the conditions of capacity, and not among the *forms* of marriage.[1] The same view holds good of a penal or religious incapacity for marriage according to a *lex loci actus*, where the direct effect of it is to prevent the marriage from ever having an inception. But English jurisprudence refuses to recognize the binding character of religious vows of celibacy as tending to the exclusion of a whole class of the population from the possibility of marriage.[2] An incapacity, moreover, of a purely artificial character enacted by the laws of a particular country with the view of depriving one or more persons of the right either of marrying or entering into any other relation permitted to other sane adults, has no claim to any international recognition.[3] And, again, with reference to the necessity of observing the requirements of the *lex loci* with respect to external formalities, this exception is recognized, that, within the lines of a British army serving abroad, the soldiers and British subjects accompanying the army are not subject to the foreign law, and therefore may marry with the forms of English law so far as it is possible to observe them.[4]

[1] Westlake, § 25, p. 59, 3rd ed.

[2] Westlake, § 22, p. 58.

[3] But see Bar, § 147, p. 324.

[4] *King* v. *Brampton* (1808), 10 East, 282. As regards marriages celebrated abroad in the chapel or house of a British ambassador, or British factory, see 4 Geo. 4, c. 91; and as to marriages solemnized on board one of her Majesty's vessels on a foreign station, see 42 & 43 Vict. c. 29.

CHAP. III.

Marriage, in view of above rules, to be understood in the sense of a monogamous marriage.

36. But marriage in the sense of the rules above stated is the voluntary union for life of one man and one woman, to the exclusion of all others. Hence Christian Courts will refuse to recognize or give effect to polygamous marriages, forbidden by Christian authorities, so far at least as the domestic law of their own State does not expressly command them to do otherwise with respect to non-Christian subjects within their own territorial jurisdiction. Thus, in *Hyde* v. *Hyde*,[1] Lord Penzance, following a dictum of Lord Brougham in *Warrender* v. *Warrender*,[2] pronounced a Mormon marriage to be null and void on account of the plurality of wives allowed by Mormon customs, a decision which can only be reconciled with that in *Brook* v. *Brook* by assuming that the latter, in applying the *lex domicilii*, meant to do so only in the case of a monogamous marriage in the Christian sense. So, in the case *In re Bethell*,[3] Mr. Justice Stirling followed the authority of Lord Penzance, and declared that a Baralong union, celebrated at Mafeking, in British Bechuanaland, between Christopher Bethell, a domiciled Englishman, and a girl of the Baralong tribe, in accordance with the forms which obtained among the Baralongs, was not such a one as an English Court could give effect to. And the same doctrine had been previously laid down by the Supreme Court of the Colony of the Cape of Good Hope in a case which was decided in 1860, in which the Court pronounced a marriage celebrated according to Muhammadan law to be null and void on the ground of its polygamous character.[4] A further application

[1] L. R. 1 P. & D. (1866), 130. Cf. *Ardaseer Cursetjee* v. *Perozeboye*, 10 Moore, P. C. (1866), 375, where the Privy Council held that Parsee marriages were not within the form of a charter extending the jurisdiction of the Ecclesiastical Court to her Majesty's subjects in India, "so far as the circumstances and occasions of the said people shall require."

[2] 2 Cl. & F. (1835), 531; 9 Bl. N. R. 112.

[3] 38 Ch. D. (1888), 220.

[4] *Brown* v. *Fritz Brown's Executors*, 3 S. 313.

of the doctrine is to be found in another Colonial case, where the Court held that a native is not entitled to damages from a person who has had carnal connection with his wife, to whom he was married according to native custom, which allows polygamy, inasmuch as the so-called marriage was merely concubinage, and not binding.[1] Of course, as far as polygamous marriages in India are concerned, the British Legislature in that country having expressly guaranteed to the native subjects the enjoyment of their own personal laws in regard to marriage and certain other matters, the domestic tribunals are bound to recognize these laws when dealing with the rights of native subjects within the limited sphere of their operation. All rules of private international law are to this extent liable to local restriction, and as it is the province of a Court to obey the law of its own *forum*, where that law prescribes the system of law to be administered within its territorial jurisdiction, every Court which owes obedience to it must be implicitly guided by its provisions. But from the point of view of private international law, since its maxims are based on the notion of a jural intercommunion between different legal systems, and there can be no such intercommunion in respect, at all events, to such a jural relation as marriage between a system admitting a polygamous union and a Christian monogamous system, it follows that a marriage of the former kind lies outside the sphere of its general rules. That this is the true reason why the *lex loci* in regard to polygamous marriages is ignored may be concluded from the fact that a monogamous marriage contracted with a non-Christian under the law of a non-Christian but monogamous country (*i.e.*, Japan) by a Christian domiciled in the United Kingdom will be recognized.[2] And the Courts of the United

[1] *Frants* v. *Malgass*, 5 Juta, 108, quoted by De Bruyn in his *Opinions of Grotius*, p. 86.

[2] *Brinkley* v. *Attorney-General*, 15 Prob. D. (1890), 76.

States have recognized the validity of a marriage celebrated between two Indians in Missouri according to Indian customs, under the superintendence of an agent of the United States Government.[1]

Effect of a foreign marriage on the property of the spouses.

37. It was laid down by Lord Meadowbank, in a Scotch case in 1814, that "the legal assignments of a marriage operate without regard to territory all the world over."[2] But this dictum is neither true of the Continental nor even of the English doctrine of the effect of marriage on property. It is by no means the case that Continental nations generally recognize marriage as operating as a legal assignment in the unqualified manner stated by Lord Meadowbank. On the contrary, in the majority of cases the fact is exactly the reverse.[3] And in regard to real property, the dictum is certainly not in harmony with the law of England, or with that of the United States, according to which the rights acquired by the spouses respectively at marriage in the immoveable property of the other are to be determined absolutely, independently of any contract, by the *lex rei sitæ*—that is to say, by the law of the place where the property is situate.[4] Indeed, as Burge truly remarks, there is a great diversity amongst the several systems of jurisprudence as to the disposition of the property of the husband and wife which the law makes, on the occasion and as the effect of their marriage.[5] Thus it may happen that the law of the country in which the parties were married may be at variance with that of the country in which either of them was domiciled before their marriage, or with

[1] *Boyer* v. *Dively*, 58 Miss. 510.

[2] *Royal Bank of Scotland* v. *Cuthbert*, 1 Rose, 481; 17 F. C. 79.

[3] Thus the French Civil Code (Art. 1401) only admits an assignment of moveable or personal property belonging to the husband or wife at the time of marriage; but not of the immoveables which were then existing. Cf. Burge, Vol. I., ch. VII., § 8, p. 599.

[4] Burge, Vol. I., ch. VII., § 8, p. 599.

[5] Sect. 1: Burge, Vol. I., pp. 599, 600.

that of the country in which they had subsequently acquired a domicil, or in which their property was situate. Where such a conflict arises it becomes necessary to ascertain by which of these systems of jurisprudence the rights of the married parties in the property of each other are governed.

Prevailing rules on the subject.

38. In determining this important question, the following rules will be found to best accord with English and American views[1] :—

(1) If there is an express contract between the intended spouses respecting their rights and property, present and future, the contract will govern, subject, as to its validity, to the same principles as would apply to any other contract made at any given place, and, as to its formal requisites, to the *lex loci actus*.

(2) If there is no express contract, the law of the matrimonial domicil—*i.e.*, that of the husband at the time of marriage—will regulate the rights of the husband and wife in the *moveable* property belonging to either of them at the time of marriage, or acquired by either of them during the marriage. The reason given by Grotius for this rule is that the marital power relates primarily to persons and only indirectly to property.[2]

(3) But in the absence of an express contract, the rights of the parties in *immoveable* property will be regulated by the *lex rei sitæ*.

In the British Colonial Courts of South Africa,[3] however, the operation of the *lex rei sitæ* is suspended by that of the matrimonial domicil, in accordance with the opinions of Savigny[4] and Phillimore,[5] and in the same Courts a sub-

[1] Story, *Conflict of Laws*, §§ 183—186; Westlake, §§ 35, 36, 37.
[2] *Opinions*, by D. P. De Bruyn, p. 139.
[3] Cf. *Opinions of Grotius*, by D. P. De Bruyn, pp. 89, 138—140.
[4] § 24; § 379, Vol. VIII.; Guthrie's translation, p. 242.
[5] § 445, Vol. IV.

CHAP. III.

sequent change of domicil does not introduce community in regard to immovable property acquired and situated in the colony which was not permitted by the law of the matrimonial domicil. Upon this latter point they adopt the reasoning of Voet,[1] that "removal of itself cannot alter the communion of goods once introduced, but in the new domicil that will remain which was introduced, and that will continue excluded which was first excluded, for removal cannot change the contracts made before marriage." But here again this dictum must be understood as subject to any positive prohibition by the law of the country where the property is situated, and whither the parties have removed. Thus, the law of South Africa (where the Placeat of the Emperor Charles V., of 1540, sect. 6, still obtains as a part of the Roman-Dutch law, which was introduced by the Dutch colonists upon their settling at the Cape of Good Hope in the year 1650)[2] will not allow the wife to claim any preference under a deed of hypothecation, granted to her by her husband at the time of marriage, in security of her marriage settlement over the concurrent creditors on his estate, and any preference given to her at the time when he contemplated the sequestration of his estate will be considered an undue preference in case of insolvency.[3]

It would appear, however, that according to English authorities, where the marriage takes place on the faith of an agreement that the husband shall transfer his domicil to another country, the law of the latter country will be held to govern the legality and operation of an express matrimonial contract as to property.[4] But where no such

[1] Voet *ad Pand.*, 23, 2, 87.

[2] *Thorburn* v. *Steward*, L. R. 3 P. C. C. 478. In the Cape Colony this Placeat has been repealed by Act XXI., 1875.

[3] *The Opinions of Grotius*, by D. P. De Bruyn, p. 90.

[4] *Colliss* v. *Hector* (1875), L. R. 19 Eq. 334. Cf. *Van Grutten* v. *Digby*, 31 Beav. (1862), 561 (*S. C.*, 32 L. J. Ch. 179), where an ante-nuptial deed

agreement exists, the law of the matrimonial domicil will govern (except as to immoveables) as stated above, even although another domicil may have been adopted between the date of the marriage and that when the property in question was acquired. This principle has also been incorporated in the Married Women's Property (Scotland) Act (1881), statute 44 & 45 Vict. c. 21. Sub-section 1 of section 1 of this statute runs as follows:—"Where a marriage is contracted after the passing of this Act, and the husband shall at the time of the marriage have his domicil in Scotland, *the whole moveable or personal estate of the wife, whether acquired before or during marriage, shall by operation of law be vested in the wife as her separate estate*, and shall not be subject to the *jus mariti*." Sub-section 5 then adds a proviso that "nothing herein contained shall exclude or abridge the power of settlement by ante-nuptial contract of marriage," thus giving effect to the first of the rules above enunciated.

The personal relations of the spouses, how regulated.

39. We have already had occasion to remark that marriage cannot be looked upon as a mere contract, although the entering into this relation may resemble a form of contract. So that while the existence of the relation itself may be the effect of a contract, yet its terms—that is to say, the personal relations of the spouses—lie outside the contractual freedom of the parties, who are not competent to agree that some only of the consequences of marriage shall apply to them, and not the rest. Thus in respect of measures of personal constraint which the husband can put in force upon his wife, or in respect of the duties which each of the spouses owes to the

in English form was executed in France. "I hold," said Romilly, M. R. (p. 567), "it to be the law of this country that if a foreigner and Englishwoman make an express contract previous to marriage, and if on the faith of that contract the marriage afterwards takes place, and if the contract relates to the regulation of property within the jurisdiction and subject to the law of this country, then and in that case this Court will administer the law on the subject as if the whole matter were to be regulated by English law."

CHAP. III.

other, the matter is regulated by law and not by agreement of parties. How that law is to be ascertained is a question as to which there is no general consensus of opinion. Thus the French Courts, after some earlier variance as to the application of the law of the husband's nationality or that of his domicil, have finally pronounced in favour of the latter.[1] According to Story, the matrimonial domicil, or, if that is not clear, the domicil of the husband, will rule.[2] By the law of England,[3] however, with which the law of Scotland coincides,[4] the conjugal rights which flow from a marriage (so far as they are of the description here referred to) must be decided by the law of the *forum*.

Test of jurisdiction to grant divorce.

40. The law of England regards divorce as operating as a change of *status*, and it was upon this principle that the older cases—of which *Lolly's*[5] and *McCarthy* v. *Decaix*[6] were the leading ones—laid down the peculiarly insular doctrine that a marriage celebrated in England could only be dissolved by English Courts and in conformity with English law. But it is to be observed that in *McCarthy* v. *Decaix* Lord Brougham, while feeling himself bound to follow *Lolly's Case*, clearly indicated his objection to that decision, and several other eminent judges in subsequent cases expressed their dissatisfaction with it and refused to treat it as a conclusive authority against a divorce granted in the domicil.[7] Finally, the validity of a foreign divorce came

[1] Guthrie's note at p. 380 of his translation of Bar. Cf. 2 Fiore, §§ 597—599, who argues in favour of the territorial law in respect to all measures of personal constraint against the wife.

[2] *Conflict of Laws*, § 198. [3] Westlake, § 33, p. 65. [4] Fraser, p. 1318.

[5] 1 Russ. & Ry. (1812), 237. [6] 2 Russ. & Ry. (1831), 614.

[7] Westlake, § 52, p. 86. It was with reference to these critisisms that the Indian legislature felt itself justified in assuming for Indian Courts jurisdiction to grant divorces, irrespective of the place of marriage, if the adultery was committed in India. See the interesting speech of the late Sir H. Maine, in presenting the Report of the Select Committee on the Indian Divorce Bill, on the 26th February, 1869. *Life and Speeches of Sir Henry Maine*, by Sir M. E. Grant-Duff, pp. 99—104.

up before the House of Lords in *Harvey* v. *Farnie*,[1] and the older doctrine was then departed from and the more reasonable doctrine was laid down, that a decision of a foreign Christian tribunal dissolving a marriage celebrated in England will be treated as valid if the parties were domiciled within the jurisdiction of that Court at the time of marriage, and continuously therefrom till the date of the decree by it (in other words, "from the beginning to the end of the transaction"), although the decree may proceed upon grounds that may not be known to the law of England as grounds for a divorce. It is, perhaps, not definitely settled whether any residence short of that necessary to constitute domicil will be deemed, in England, to confer jurisdiction upon a foreign Court to dissolve a marriage celebrated in England. Lords Chelmsford and Colonsay expressly reserved their opinion upon this point in *Shaw* v. *Gould*.[2] The English Courts[3] themselves, however, assume jurisdiction—

(a) When the husband, being either the petitioner or respondent, is domiciled in England, and this irrespective of the *locus delicti* or the place where the matrimonial offence complained of was committed; or

(b) When there is such actual residence on the part of the husband in England which, although insufficient to found domicil, negatives the suggestion that it was merely that of a traveller or visitor, or taken up with the intention of obtaining or facilitating the divorce, and in this case also irrespective of where the matrimonial offence was committed; or

(c) When there is such residence as is mentioned in the last preceding clause on the part of the wife, if she is the petitioner, and if she has been deserted by

[1] L. R. 8 App. Cas. (1882), 43. Cf. also *Scott* v. *Att.-Gen.* 11 P. D. (1886) 128; *Turner* v. *Thompson*, 13 P. D. (1888), 37; and *Briggs* v. *Briggs*, 5 P. D. (1880), 163.

[2] L. R. 3 E. & I. A. (1868), 55.

[3] Gillespie's translation of Bar, Note K. on sects. 173—180, pp. 399—403; Westlake, §§ 44—46.

CHAP. III.

the husband, or has been so treated by him as to justify her in living apart from him, and if up to the time she was so deserted or began to be so justified in living apart she had been domiciled or resident with her husband in England.

In America actual domicil is requisite to confer jurisdiction.[1] The jurisdiction formerly claimed by Scotch Courts by virtue of a residence of forty days by the defender coupled with citation there, and in other cases by virtue of a citation in Scotland and the fact of the commission of adultery there, has been distinctly abandoned.[2] At the present time the Scotch Courts adopt substantially the same grounds for founding jurisdiction as are recognized in England.

What law regulates sufficiency of grounds for divorce.

41. Assuming that a Court has jurisdiction with reference to the above rules to hear a suit for dissolution of marriage, the question remains: By what law is the sufficiency of the grounds alleged for the exercise of that jurisdiction to be determined? Here, at all events, principle as well as authority are in favour of the application of the law of the *forum*, which is also the rule adopted in England and Scotland both for granting divorces there and for recognizing the validity of foreign divorces.[3]

Test of jurisdiction in other matrimonial causes.

42. For the purpose of founding jurisdiction in other matrimonial causes, such as to decree judicial separation or restitution of conjugal rights, English Courts adopt substantially the same rules as regulate their jurisdiction to grant a divorce. This was expressly so stated by Brett, L. J., in *Niboyet* v. *Niboyet*.[4] But a distinction was drawn

[1] Story, *Conflict of Laws*, § 230 (a.); Bishop's *Law of Marriage and Divorce*, Vol. II. § 141. As regards South African decisions, see *Opinions of Grotius*, pp. 92, 93.

[2] *Stavert* v. *Stavert*, 9 Ct. of Sess. Rep., 4th Series, p. 519, where all the earlier authorities are reviewed.

[3] *Harvey* v. *Farnie*, L. R. 8 App. Cas. (1882), 43; Gillespie's translation of Bar, p. 400; and Westlake, § 52, p. 84, 3rd ed.

[4] 4 P. D. (1878), 1.

as regards suits for a declaration of nullity of marriage, or in respect of jactitation of marriage, in which jurisdiction is made to depend on the defendant's being resident in England, not temporarily as a traveller or a visitor, nor for the mere purposes of the suit. "How would it be possible," said Lord Justice James,[1] in *Niboyet* v. *Niboyet*, "to make domicil the test of jurisdiction in such a case? Suppose the alleged wife were the complainant, her domicil would depend on the very matter in controversy. If she was really married, her domicil would be the domicil of her husband; if not married, then it would be her own previous domicil."

Legitimacy and legitimation closely connected with marriage and divorce.

43. Closely connected with the subject of marriage and divorce is that of legitimacy, which necessarily depends on the validity of a pre-existing marriage, which often again involves the question of the validity of a divorce of one of the parties to it from a previous marriage. Now, as the law of some nations confers an *ex post facto* legitimacy on a person born out of wedlock, but whose parents have subsequently lawfully married, the subject of legitimacy further involves that of legitimation *per subsequens matrimonium*. But as the *status* in the latter case is determined by somewhat different considerations and rules to that in the former, it will be as well to consider each case separately.

Test of legitimacy.

44. As regards legitimacy, resulting as this *status* does from a lawful marriage—or, as Lord Brougham expressed it,[2] legitimacy *sub modo*, legitimacy and being born in wedlock—it follows that since the validity of the latter, as regards essentials, depends on the personal law or *lex domicilii* of the husband at the date of marriage, so that of the former must equally depend upon the *lex domicilii* of the child's father, or the law under which the child was born. The view of English jurisprudence on this point was very clearly stated by Lord Justice

[1] At p. 9.

[2] *Birtwhistle* v. *Vardill*, 7 Cl. & Fin. (1840), at p. 954.

CHAP. III.

James *In re Goodman's Trusts.*[1] "What is the rule," he asks, "which the English law adopts and applies to a non-English child?" and he proceeds to answer it in the following lucid manner. "This is a question," he says, "of international comity and international law. According to that law as recognized, and that comity as practised, in all other civilized communities, the *status* of a person, his legitimacy or illegitimacy, is to be determined everywhere by the law of the country of his origin—the law under which he was born.[2] It appears to me that it would require a great force of argument derived from legal principles, or great weight of authority clear and distinct, to justify us in holding that our country stands aloof from the rest of the civilized world. . . . And as the law applies universally to persons of all countries, races, and religions whatsoever, the proper law to be applied in determining kindred is the universal law, the international law, adopted by the comity of States. The child of a man would be his child so ascertained and so determined." In a still later case the principle of the law was stated by Kay, J., in equally clear terms: "By international law, as recognized in this country, those children are legitimate whose legitimacy is established by the law of the father's domicil."[3] Hence the offspring of a polygamous marriage, which itself would not be treated in England as valid, would nevertheless, it would seem, be legitimate, if the law of the State of the father's foreign domicil attributed to such offspring the *status* of legitimacy in the same sense as the English law. But the exact point does not appear to have as yet arisen, and the conclusion is here stated only as a deduction from the authorities which have already been quoted. Polygamy, in fact, as Bar argues,[4] is, in the supposed case, only the remote foundation of a claim, which in other respects does not come into conflict with

[1] 17 Ch. D. (1881), at pp. 296—298.

[2] *I.e.* domicil of origin, not the law of the *place* of birth.

[3] *Andros* v. *Andros*, 24 Ch. D. (1883), 637.

[4] § 36, p. 96, Gillespie's translation.

our legal system; it is a condition precedent to the process for asserting that claim. Polygamy exists and did exist in the foreigner's country, and the decisions of our judges cannot touch it. It is different where direct effect is sought to be given to the operation of a polygamous marriage, as where the assistance of our Courts is applied for to constrain a woman who has escaped from the harem of a Mussulman to continue her polygamous marriage. Such assistance would undoubtedly be refused if repugnant to the law of the Court.[1] It is necessary, moreover, to remember that some personal laws—*e.g.*, the Muhammadan law, as well as the law of some of the Continental States, notably Italy[2]—give a right of succession to children who have merely been so *recognized* or *acknowledged* by the father in his lifetime. And it is necessary to distinguish such cases from that of *legitimacy* in the correct sense. For although in a country where the law sanctioned such a recognition such children would succeed *as legitimate*, the law of England would refuse to acknowledge them as such, and consequently, in the case of an intestacy, they would have no right of succession to property in England, and even in the case of a will in their favour the succession duty on the real estate would be realized in England as if the children were strangers in blood to their putative father.[3] Again, where the capacity of a woman to remarry depends on the validity of a divorce, the jurisdiction for which is not deemed in England to have been internationally competent, the children of the remarriage will be deemed illegitimate in England, notwithstanding that the remarriage is deemed to be valid in the place where it was celebrated, and by the personal law of the new husband.[4]

45. Where the personal law permits legitimation by subse- Test of legitimation.

[1] Bar, § 96, p. 97, and see particularly note 6 on that page.
[2] *Codice Civile*, Lib. III. § 744.
[3] *Atkinson* v. *Anderson*, 21 Ch. D. (1882), 100.
[4] Westlake, § 53, p. 89, and authorities there cited.

CHAP. III.

quent marriage, that is to say, attaches this consequence to the subsequent marriage between the parents of the child, the primary important question is, as put by Lord Cottenham in a Scotch case, "Can the legitimation of the child be effected in the country in which the father is domiciled at his birth?"[1] If it cannot, the child obviously cannot acquire a capacity for legitimation.[2] But this rule only prevails where there has been no change in the father's domicil between the dates of the birth of the child and the subsequent marriage. It is true that Lord Brougham in the combined judgment in *Dalhousie* v. *M'Donall*, and *Munro* v. *Munro*, indicated his opinion (coinciding with that of Savigny in this respect)[3] that if the domicil was not the same at both periods, that of the father at the time of marriage should give the rule. But as the domicil at both periods was the same in those cases, the point did not actually arise, and Lord Brougham's opinion was merely *obiter*. Subsequent cases have now established that, if the father's domicil has changed between the periods of birth and marriage, the law of that domicil at *both* periods must admit of legitimation in order to confer the *status* of legitimacy. "The domicil at birth," said Lord Justice Cotton in the leading case,[4] "must give a capacity to the child of being made legitimate; but then the domicil at the time of the marriage, which gives the *status*, must be domicil in a country which attributes to marriage that effect." So that on the one hand illegitimacy by the law of the father's domicil at birth attaches to the child once and for ever, while the sanction of the law of the father's domicil at the date of marriage is so far essential that, without it, the child cannot

[1] *Dalhousie* v. *M'Donall*, 7 Cl. & F. (1840), 817; and *Munro* v. *Munro*, 7 Cl. & F. (1840) 842, both cases having been argued in the House of Lords together.

[2] *Wright's Trusts*, 2 K. & J. (1856), 595; *Goodman* v. *Goodman*, 3 Giff. (1862), 643; *Re Grove, Vaucher* v. *Solicitor to Treasury*, 40 Ch. D. (1888), 216.

[3] System, Vol. VIII., p. 380; Guthrie's translation, p. 250.

[4] *In re Grove, Vaucher* v. *Solicitor to Treasury*, 40 Ch. D. (1888), at p. 233.

acquire the status of legitimacy. A child validly legitimated in this sense is treated as a "child" under the English Statute of Distributions and for the purposes of the Legacy and Succession Duty Acts, as also in the construction of wills. But no such legitimated child would have any title—as we shall see *post*[1]—to succeed *ab intestato* to land in England.[2] For in deciding upon the title to real estate, the *lex loci rei sitæ* must always prevail.[3] Again, legitimation by the fact of a subsequent marriage between the parents of a child born in a country politically foreign, will not cause the child to be naturalized thereby, under 4 Geo. II. c. 21, so as to hold British land, although the father was a natural-born British subject. Nor will it be possible to substitute for the above double test of legitimation the laws or customs of a religious sect to which the parents of the child may belong. Thus in a case where all the parties, including the child, whose legitimation was in issue, were Jews domiciled in England, and it was sought to prove that the rules of their religion, which they recognised as binding laws amongst themselves, authorised legitimation by a subsequent marriage, it was held that the contention was untenable, inasmuch as neither a religious sect nor any other self-constituted body can be permitted to set up a special personal law within the domain of a State, which would be tantamount to the assertion of an *imperium in imperio*, a claim that could not be tolerated for a moment.[4] In this case the law of the domicil being the English law, and not permitting legitimation by subsequent

[1] See para. 51, p. 87.

[2] *Birtwhistle* v. *Vardill*, 5 B. & C. (1826), 438; 2 Cl. & Fin. (1830), 571.

[3] Per Lord Brougham in *Fenton* v. *Livingstone*, 5 Jur. N. S. (1859), 1183. The reason for this seems to be that, to inherit land, it is not enough to be the issue of married parents, but it is also necessary to be the issue of parents who would have been married if they had gone through the ceremony of marriage in the country where the land lies, and the issue must have been born in such wedlock.

[4] *Levy* v. *Solomon* (1877), quoted in Foote, p. 66.

CHAP. III.

marriage, effect had to be given to it, not with reference to any presumed intention of the parties to abide by it by electing an English domicil, but because the interests of the general body of the inhabitants of the country required its adoption. It is also necessary here to repeat the principle which has already been more than once impressed upon the student of international law, that personal *status* does not follow a man everywhere, if its consequences are absolutely repugnant to the law of the country where he goes, and where it is sought to introduce them.[1] Thus no effect will be given to the *lex domicilii* in favour of legitimation by a subsequent marriage, if its acceptance involves the recognition within the domain of another State of a marriage which the law of that State regards as incestuous.[2] In such a case our legal system and our Courts will not lend themselves to the direct realization of legal relations or claims which would be regarded by our law as absolutely untenable.[3]

Capacity of juristic persons, how determined.

46. We have now said all that is necessary on the subject of the *status* and *capacity* of natural persons. But besides these persons, who claim a legal recognition as individuals simply by reason of belonging to the great family of the human race, there are certain intangible, artificial creations to which the law ascribes a juristic personality, investing them with rights and exacting duties from them, which have still to be considered. We have already discussed the rules for determining the domicil of such juristic persons,[4] and in regard to their capacity for the acquisition of rights and for acting, the analogy between them and natural persons will generally be found to supply the rules applicable in each case. Thus, if a foreign corporation is permitted in its artificial character to enter into jural relations with outside parties, all

[1] Per Littledale, J., in *Birtwhistle* v. *Vardill*, 5 B. & C. 455.
[2] *Fenton* v. *Livingstone*, 5 Jur., N. S. 1183.
[3] Bar, § 36, p. 96, Gillespie's translation.
[4] *Vide* para. 29; *ante*.

such dealings must stand on the same footing as those of natural persons. On the same condition such a corporation may sue, and be sued, in its corporate name; but the earliest direct precedent in England for admitting foreign corporations to *defend* an action at law in their corporate capacity is, perhaps, that of *Newby* v. *Van Oppen*.[1] There was certainly no such precedent up to 1858.[2] It is now, however, an established rule of private international law that a corporation duly created according to the laws of one State may sue, and be sued, in its corporate name in the Courts of other States.[3] And the right to sue extends, in the case of a foreign corporation, to all actions founded upon a contract entered into within the jurisdiction of the *forum*, provided the contract is one which is warranted by the constitution of the corporation, and is not illegal by the law of the *forum*.[4] The nature of its constitution, and whether it has a corporate right to sue and be sued—in other words, its judicial capacity —is determined by the law of its domicil.[5] And thus, also, the liabilities of members of foreign corporations will, in England, be determined by the law of the country in which they were formed. Accordingly, where by the law of that country the corporation, and not the individuals who make up the cor-

[1] L. R. 7 Q. B. (1872), 293; Story's *Conflict of Laws*, § 565, p. 780, note (1). Cf. Chapter 29 of the *Civil Procedure Code for India*.

[2] *Per* Williams, J., in *Ingate* v. *Austrian Lloyd's*, 4 C. B. N. S. 709.

[3] Lindley *on Company Law*, p. 909; Westlake, § 305.

[4] *Ibid*. p. 910.

[5] Cf. the Scotch case of *Muir* v. *Collett* (1862), 24 Ct. of Sess. Rep., 2nd Ser., p. 1119. But see the English case of *Bullock* v. *Caird*, L. R. 10 Q. B. (1875), 276; and cf. *Branley* v. *S.-E. Rail. Co.*, 12 C. B., N. S. p. 70. So in a Turkish company managed in England, it was held that the law which governed it was the Turkish law. *Pickering* v. *Stephenson*, L. R. 14 Eq. (1872), 322. The German Courts have followed the same principle of determining the jural capacity of a juristic person by the law of the domicil. *Holthausen & Cie* v. *Comptoir d'Escompte de Paris*, Appeal Court of Köln, 28 April, 1877, Jour. V. 629. And French jurisprudence acknowledges no distinction between an individual and a "moral" (juristic) person in matters of title to sue and defend. Cf. Brocher, *Cours de Droit International*, I. p. 201.

CHAP. III.

poration, are liable in damages for delicts, or *quasi* delicts, committed in the course of carrying on the business of the corporation, an English Court will protect a shareholder against whom, as an individual, proceedings are taken.[1]

More recently conventions have been entered into between the British Government and various foreign countries, such as France (15th May, 1862), Belgium (8th December, 1862), Italy (26th November, 1867), Germany (27th March, 1874), and Spain (1883), which distinctly provide that "joint-stock companies and other associations, commercial, industrial and financial, constituted in conformity with the laws in force in either of the two contracting States, may exercise in the dominions of the other *all* their rights, including that of appearing before tribunals for the purpose of bringing an action or of defending themselves, with the sole condition in exercising such rights of always conforming themselves to the laws and customs in force in the said dominions."[2] And the analogy between a natural person and an artificial person has been further applied in the interpretation of the rules under the Judicature Acts for the service of writs of summons, or notice thereof, out of jurisdiction,[3] and, in regard to the exercise of personal rights, such as that of a trade-mark.[4] So also the limits of the jural capacity of an artificial person, for instance, to hold land in England, are determined much in the same way as in the case of a natural person with reference to a double qualification—namely, first by the general powers defined by its constitution (that is to say, by the law of its domicil), and secondly, by the special restraints, if any,

[1] *General Steam Navigation Co.* v. *Guillon*, 11 M. & W. (1843), 877.

[2] See the Convention with Spain, published in the *London Gazette* of the 5th February, 1883, at p. 643.

[3] *Scott* v. *Royal Wax Candle Co.*, L. R. 1 Q. B. D. (1876), 404; *Westman* v. *Aktiebolaget Mekaniska Snickarefabrik*, 1 Ex. D. (1876), 237.

[4] *Collins Co.* v. *Brown*, 3 K. & J. (1857), 423; and *Collins Co.* v. *Reeves*, 4 Jur. N. S. (1858), 865.

imposed by the law of the country where such powers are proposed to be exercised (that is, in the case of land, by the *lex loci rei sitæ*). Again, just as a natural person residing abroad would be, so a foreign corporation is only liable to income tax on the profits arising from the business carried on by it in England, and not on its entire profits.[1] But an English, Scotch, or Irish corporation is liable, as a "person residing within the United Kingdom," to income tax on its entire profits, notwithstanding that all its business is carried on abroad, and that subsequently to its incorporation it has been registered abroad.[2] Foreign corporations, moreover, when once they have become litigants in an English court, occupy the same position as natural individual persons, and their peculiar nature is not allowed to deprive their opponent of any of the ordinary rights incidental to litigation.[3] Accordingly Order XXXI. r. 5, of the Schedule to the Judicature Acts provides that if any party to an action be a body corporate or any other body of persons, empowered by law to sue or be sued, whether in its own name or in the name of any officer or other person, any opposite party may apply at Chambers for an order allowing him to deliver interrogatories to any member or officer of such corporation or body of persons, and an order may thereupon be made. The same rule has been applied to the case of a foreign republic, and if the juristic person happens to be a plaintiff, all proceedings may be stayed until a proper person is named on its behalf to give discovery.[4] A company which is domiciled in England (that is to say, which derives its incorporation or other legal

[1] *Att.-Gen.* v. *Alexander* L. R. 10 Exch. (1874), 20; *Erichsen* v. *Last* 7 Q. B. D. (1881), 12.

[2] *Cesena Sulphur Co., Ltd.* v. *Nicholson*, and *Calcutta Jute Mills Co., Ltd.* v. *Nicholson*, 1 Ex. D. (1876), 428.

[3] Foote, *Private Inter. Jurisp.*, 2nd ed., p. 121.

[4] *Republic of Costa Rica* v. *Erlanger*, 1 Ch. D. (1875), 171; *Republic of Liberia* v. *Imperial Bank*, L. R. 16 Eq. (1873), 179; 9 Ch. 569; *Republic of Peru* v. *Weguelin*, L. R. 7 C. P. 352; 20 Eq. (1875), 140; *United States of America* v. *Wagner*, L. R. 2 Ch. (1867), 582, 589.

CHAP. III.

existence from the law of England), is subject to be wound up in England wherever it may be, and, if all its business is abroad, that is deemed to be only an additional reason for winding it up.[1] But if the company is domiciled out of the United Kingdom, it is subject to winding-up proceedings in England if it has an office there,[2] but not otherwise, even though it may carry on business there by means of agents.[3] And an order for winding-up of a company domiciled in England carries all the moveable and immoveable property in any part of the British dominions.[4] Nor will the pending of a foreign liquidation affect the jurisdiction to make such an order, although, in making it, the Court will endeavour to pay due regard to the order of the foreign Court, so as to make its own proceedings auxiliary to those of the latter.[5]

Position of the Sovereign in monarchical States.

47. We have seen that Republican States occupy a position in the matter of suing and being sued in their international name analogous to that of foreign corporations. But in monarchical governments it is the Sovereign, and not the State, of which he is the political head, that is recognised in foreign Courts and in diplomatic intercourse.[6] The Sovereign, therefore, not only represents the State in respect of the public property and *choses in action* of the nation, but as an individual he may have private rights of his own. In the former case he is treated as a corporation sole, and no proceeding *in rem* against the public property of a foreign Sovereign or sovereign State will be permitted;[7] in the latter, as a private

[1] *Re Madrid and Valencia Rail. Co.*, 3 De G. & S. (1849), 127; *Re Peruvian Railways Co., Ltd.*, L. R. 2 Ch. App. (1867), 617; *Reuss* v. *Bos*, L. R. 5 E. & I. A. (1871), 176.

[2] *Re Commercial Bank of India*, L. R. 6 Eq. (1868), 517; *Re Commercial Bank of South Australia*, 33 Ch. D. (1886), 174.

[3] *Re Lloyd Generale Italiano*, 29 Ch. D. (1885), 219.

[4] Westlake, §§ 137, 138, p. 154, 3rd ed.

[5] *In re Commercial Bank of S. Australia*, 33 Ch. D. (1886), 174.

[6] See Lord Cairns's judgment in *United States of America* v. *Wagner*, L. R. 2 Ch. 593.

[7] *The Parlement Belge*, 5 P. D. 197, 217.

person, with certain privileges, among which is that of not being liable to be sued unless he has waived his privilege, expressly or impliedly, by voluntary submission to the jurisdiction or otherwise; as, for instance, by himself suing as a plaintiff, or by carrying on trade as a private individual,[1] or by acquiring immoveable property within the jurisdiction.[2] Upon these points, so far as sovereign princes in India are concerned, the Code of Civil Procedure of 1882 (Act XIV.) contains the following provisions:—

"Sect. 433.—(1) Any (sovereign) Prince or (ruling) Chief, and any Ambassador or Envoy of any Foreign State, may, with the consent of the Governor-General in Council, certified by the signature of one of the secretaries to the Government of India (but not without such consent), be sued in any competent Court.

"(2) Such consent may be given with respect to a specified suit, or to several specified suits, or with respect to all suits of any specified class or classes, and may specify, in the case of any suit or class of suits, the Court in which the Prince, Chief, Ambassador, or Envoy may be sued; but it shall not be given unless the Prince, Chief, Ambassador, or Envoy—

"(a) has instituted a suit in the Court against the person desiring to sue him, or

"(b) by himself or another trader within the local limits of the jurisdiction of the Court, or

"(c) is in possession of immoveable property situate within those limits, and is to be sued with reference to such possession or for money charged on that property.

"(3) No such Prince, Chief, Ambassador, or Envoy shall be arrested under this Code, and, except with the consent of the Governor-General in Council, certified as aforesaid, no decree shall be executed against the property of any such Prince, Chief, Ambassador, or Envoy.

* * * * * *

"(5) A person may, as a tenant of immoveable property, sue without such consent as is mentioned in this section, a Prince, Chief, Ambassador, or Envoy from whom he holds or claims to hold the property."

"Sect. 434.—A sovereign Prince or ruling Chief may sue, and shall be sued, in the name of his State: Provided that in giving the consent referred to in the last foregoing section the Governor-General in Council or local Government, as the case may be, may direct that any such Prince or Chief shall be sued in the name of an agent or in any other names."

---

[1] *Hullett* v. *King of Spain*, 1 Cl. & F. 354; *Duke of Brunswick* v. *King of Hanover*, 6 Beav. 1, 51; *Mandalay* v. *Morton*, 1 B. C. C. 47a.

[2] Dana's Wheaton, § 103; *The Charkieh*, L. R. 4 A. & E. 97.

CHAPTER IV.

LAW OF THINGS.

CHAP. IV.

General classification.

48. THE jurisprudence of Continental Europe, following that of the old Civil Law, knows no other classification of things except that of *mobilia* and *immobilia*. But the English law rejects this classification, and substitutes for it that of *real* and *personal* estate, a distinction which becomes still more peculiar to itself by the special meaning it attaches to the term "personal estate." As commonly understood in international jurisprudence, this term would be restricted to *moveables* of every description. But in English law it receives a wider interpretation, and is held to include leaseholds for years, which one would ordinarily classify under the head of immoveable property[1]: for land, as Lord Selborne observed in a well-known case,[2] whether held for a chattel interest or for a freehold interest, is, as a matter of fact, immoveable and not moveable.

Different theories as to the proper law by which rights in things are determined.

49. Three different theories as to the law which is to govern property of either description internationally have been adopted by juristical writers. There is, first of all, the theory that, while rights in immoveables are to be determined by the *lex rei sitæ*, rights in moveables are to be determined by the *lex domicilii* of a person—the person being the owner. This theory rests on the fiction that moveables in a legal sense must be deemed to be at the place where the person has his

[1] Jarman *on Wills*, Vol. I., p. 4, n.

[2] *Freke* v. *Lord Carbery*, L. R. 16 Eq. 461.

domicil, because since it is in the absolute power of the owner to take them from one place to another, it must be purely accidental where they may actually be at any given time, and in this condition of uncertainty the only safe rule to act upon is to give effect to the maxim *mobilia ossibus inhærent*, or *mobilia sequuntur personam*. But this theory is open to the double objection that it is, in the first place, altogether illogical to attempt to determine disputed rights in moveables by the law of the domicil of one of the parties concerned, for the title can only be settled by the decision itself, and to invoke the law of the owner's domicil in order to arrive at that decision, is to proceed in a "vicious circle," which obviously leads to no practical result; and, in the next place, as the owner's domicil may often be widely removed from the place where the moveable in dispute is *in fact*, it would seem to be unreasonable, in such a case at all events, to decide who is the owner of the thing with reference to a law which cannot give the possession of that thing. The second theory is to restrict the application of the maxim *mobilia sequuntur personam* to cases of "general or universal assignments" resulting by operation of law—as, for instance, in the case of transmission of moveables on death, bankruptcy, and marriage—and to apply the *lex loci rei sitæ* to all cases of "particular assignments" arising out of alienations *inter vivos*: that is to say, the distinction is drawn between the cases in which a man's moveable property is considered as an entirety, grouped round his person as a centre, and those in which the articles which compose it are separately considered. This is, in substance, the theory advocated by Fœlix, Demolombe, Aubry, Rau, and Brocher,[1] and more recently by Foote and Westlake in England.[2] And the third theory is to apply the *lex loci*

[1] Bar, § 222, p. 491, Gillespie's translation; Brocher, I. § 48, p. 122; Calvo, II., § 711, p. 209.

[2] Foote, p. 226, 2nd ed.; Westlake, p. 168.

rei sitæ to moveables as well as immoveables. This is the theory advocated by Grotius,[1] Fiore,[2] and Asser-Rivier, and, with certain modifications, is practically adopted by Bar as supplying the only true law that can be applied, and resting upon the intolerable inconvenience of any other doctrine.[3]

But general consensus in favour of *lex situs* governing all questions relating to immoveables.

50. In regard, however, to immoveables, the rule universally accepted in all civilised countries is, that all questions concerning property of this description, including the forms of conveying it, are decided by the *lex situs;* and, in like manner, what does and what does not fall within the character of real or immoveable estate must also be decided by the same law.[4] So also, speaking generally, the incidents which arise in connection with such property are to be referred to the *lex situs.*[5] Thus, for instance, the liability for deterioration or waste is to be decided and measured by this law;[6] and since no action can be brought in a British Court to interfere with the possession of immoveable property, except in the *forum* of the *situs,*[7] the rules of limitation and prescription applied to immoveables must necessarily be determined with reference to the same law, which, *ex hypothesi*, is that of the *forum.* But in the possible case where a Court has incidentally to inquire into the title to foreign land (*e.g.* in administering and enforcing personal equities), and the local

1 *Opinions of Grotius*, by De Bruyn, p. 293 (N. P. 386).

2 Fiore, I., § 91, pp. 118—120; Bar, p. 491, Gillespie's translation.

3 Bar, § 226, p. 499, Gillespie's translation; and § 227, p. 500.

4 Story, *Conflict of Laws*, § 447, cited with approval by Lord Selborne in *Freke* v. *Lord Carbery*, L. R. 16 Eq. (1873), 461.

5 *Nelson* v. *Bridport*, 8 Beav. (1848), 547, 570.

6 *Batthyany* v. *Walford*, 36 Ch. D. (1887), 269.

7 *Vide* sect. 19 of Act XIV. of 1882 (*The Code of Civil Procedure for India*). But where accounts can be more conveniently and satisfactorily taken in England, a bill for the redemption of a mortgage of foreign land has not only been entertained, but an injunction granted in support of it against a proceeding to foreclose the mortgage in the *forum sitûs.* (Westlake, § 174, p. 197, 3rd ed.) And, in such a bill, the *lex sitûs* is the law to be applied. *Bent* v. *Young* (1838), 9 Sim. p. 190.

law of limitation is intended only to regulate procedure, and neither confers or takes away a title, there might arise a conflict between the *jus fori* and the *lex situs*, and in such a case the former would, of course, govern the procedure of the Court. Indeed, it is the opinion of Mr. Dana[1] that it is impossible, in international law, to be governed by indirect operations of a law on real property, and that as ordinary statutes of limitation are simply intended as rules of repose, resting on the policy of the State, it seems reasonable that any State may apply them to all suits in which the aid of its tribunals is invoked, whether the thing is within or without the territory of the State, and is moveable or immoveable, corporeal or incorporeal. Lastly, in connection with the operation of the *lex situs* upon immoveable estate, it is this law which determines the liability of such estate, apart from any equitable considerations, for the debts of the owner. "It is admitted," said Lord Selborne, in *Harrison* v. *Harrison*,[2] "as I understand, that the burden of liability to debt, so far as relates to real estate, can only be created by the *lex loci rei sitæ*." So again, all questions concerning restraint on the alienation or disposition of immoveables are to be decided by the *lex situs*, whether the restraint be general or special, or whether the restraint be total or limited to a certain proportion of the value.[3] And when a security is given on immoveables for a debt, which is also personally due, as in the case of a Scotch heritable bond, the *lex situs* of the immoveables decides whether the debt is to be considered an alienation of so much of the value of the immoveables on which it is secured, or as a mere debt with collateral security.[4] The rights of husband and wife in and to the English immoveables of either, are

[1] Wheaton on *Int. Law*, § 143, n.
[2] L. R. 8 Ch. (1872), 342.
[3] Westlake, § 165, p. 191, 3rd ed.
[4] *Ibid.* § 160, p. 190.

CHAP. IV.

regulated by English law as the *lex situs*, and on principle the *lex situs* must prevail when the situation of the immoveables is foreign, whatever the matrimonial domicil.

Prevailing theory in England and the United States of America in regard to moveables, and exceptions to the same.

51. Of the theories above explained in § 49, the second is the one which may be said to have the largest support in England as regards moveables. Property of this description is said to have "no locality," a phrase which is explained by Lord Loughborough as meaning, not that personal property has no visible locality, "but that it is subject to that law which governs the person of the owner,"[1] that is to say, the law of the place of his domicil.[2] With respect to the disposition of it, with respect to the transmission of it, either by succession or the act of the party, it follows, said Lord Loughborough in the same case, the law of the person. The proposition thus enunciated by Lord Loughborough is claimed by him to be "not only of the law of England, but of every country in the world where law has the semblance of science." The same proposition has been laid down by eminent English and American judges in several other cases, with, as Story says,[3] "unbroken confidence and general unanimity." For instance, by Abbott, C. J., in *Birtwhistle* v. *Vardill*[4]: "Personal property has no locality;" by Bayley, B., in *In re Ewin*[5]: "The rule is, that personal property follows the person, and is not in any respect to be regulated by the *lex situs*. . . . Wherever the domicil of the proprietor is, there the property is to be considered as situate;" and by no one more distinctly than by Lord Selborne in a case which has already been cited.[6] "The maxim of the law of the civilised world," said his lordship, "is, *mobilia sequuntur personam*, and is

[1] *Sill* v. *Worsick* (1791), 1 H. Bl. 690.

[2] Story, *Conflict of Laws*, § 377; *Doglioni* v. *Crispin* (1866), L. R. 1 H. L. 301; *Enohin* v. *Wylie*, 10 H. L. C. (1862), 1; S. C. 31 L. J. 402 Ch.

[3] *Conflict of Laws*, § 380.

[4] 5 B. & C. (1826), 451.

[5] 1 C. & J. (1830), 156.

[6] *Freke* v. *Lord Carbery*, L. R. 16 Eq. 466.

founded on the nature of things. When *mobilia* are in places other than that of the person to whom they belong, their accidental *situs* is disregarded, and they are held to go along with the custom." But, however general may be the language in which the rule *mobilia sequuntur personam* has been laid down in these cases, there are other English and American decisions, whose authority cannot now be questioned, which have undoubtedly restricted the application of that rule by engrafting certain exceptions upon it. Indeed, Mr. Bigelow points out that the exceptions to the maxim have become so numerous that it cannot safely be invoked for the decision of any but the simplest cases at the present day. Thus the cases reported as *Cammell* v. *Sewell*,[2] *Castrique* v. *Imrie*,[3] *Hooper* v. *Gumm*,[4] and *Williams* v. *Colonial Bank*,[5] may be said to have established the doctrine in regard to the transfer of moveables *inter vivos* or of any less real interest in them (such as pledge or lien)[6] that, "if personal property is disposed of in a manner binding according to the law of the country where it is, that disposition is binding everywhere." And the title so acquired by operation of the *lex situs* prevails notwithstanding that it may be imperfect by the law of the former owner's domicil, and although the property be afterwards brought within the territorial jurisdiction of that law. Following out this doctrine, the

[1] Note (a) to § 383, Story's *Conflict of Laws*, p. 543, 8th edit.

[2] 3 H. & N. (1860), 138; 5 Ibid. 745; 27 L. J. Exch. 447; 29 L. J. Ex. 350.

[3] L. R. 4 H. L. (1870), 414, and at p. 429.

[4] L. R. 2 Ch. App. (1867) 282.

[5] 38 Ch. D. (1888) 388, affirmed by H. of Lds. (12 May, 1890) 15 App. Cas. 267.

[6] Thus in the case of *The City Bank* v. *Barrow* (1880), 5 Ap. Cas. 664, to which Lord Selborne was a party, Lord Blackburn said:—"The pledge upon which the defendants claim was made in Canada, in respect of goods *then in Canada*. I take it, therefore, that there is no doubt that the validity of the pledge depends upon the Canadian law;" and this was the law which, throughout the case, was applied by all the judges and noble lords who took part in the decision.

CHAP. IV. property in a moveable will be held in England to be such as the judgment *in rem* (*i.e.*, a judgment which disposes of the thing itself, and not merely of the interests which any parties have in it) of a Court within the jurisdiction of which the moveable is situate has decided it to be.[1] As Blackburn, J., delivering the opinion of the judges in *Castrique* v. *Imrie*,[2] said: "The inquiry is, first, whether the subject-matter was so situated as to be within the lawful control of the State under the authority of which the Court sits; and, secondly, whether the sovereign authority of that State has conferred on the Court jurisdiction to decide as to the disposition of the thing, and the Court has acted within its jurisdiction. If these conditions are fulfilled, the adjudication is conclusive against all the world." In practice, however, except in Admiralty cases, the procedure in English Courts is *in personam*, and not *in rem*. On the other hand, the distribution of moveable personal estate in the hands of executors or administrators is regulated generally by the law of the domicil of the deceased, and so also the law of the testator's domicil at the time of his death, if there has been no change of domicil since the execution of the will, or that of the domicil at time of execution if there has,[3] and that of an intestate at the time of his death,[4] have respectively supreme authority, in the former case, in all matters connected with the capacity of the testator, the formalities, execution, construction, and effect of a will of moveable personal property, and, in the latter, in all matters connected with the succession to, and distribution of, his personal estate. But when the right of succession has once been ascertained, the rights resulting therefrom belong to, and follow the person of, the living successor, not of the dead testator, or predecessor.[5] And as regards the matri-

[1] Westlake, § 149, p. 177.

[2] L. R. 4 E. & I. A. 429.

[3] 24 & 25 Vict. c. 114, § 3.

[4] *Enohin* v. *Wylie*, 10 H. L. C. 1; *Bremer* v. *Freeman*, 10 Moo. P. C. (1857), 312; and *Collier* v. *Rivaz*, 2 Curt. (1841), 855.

[5] Per Lord Selborne in *Ewing* v. *Orr-Ewing* (1885), 10 App. Cas. (Sc.) 502.

monial law, it is settled that, in the absence of express contract, the law of the matrimonial domicil will determine the respective rights of the spouses in the moveable property belonging to either of them at the time of marriage, or acquired by either of them during marriage, but you will go to the *lex rei sitæ* to ascertain what the character of the property is.[1] It must, however, be remembered that, as pointed out in a previous paragraph,[2] the legitimacy of legatees, as well as of next of kin, is referred by English law to the law of the domicil of their father at the time of their birth; and in cases of legitimation *per subsequens matrimonium* the legitimation must be valid both by the law of the father's domicil at the time of birth and at the time of the subsequent marriage. According to the Continental view, the validity of a will is tested either by the law of the domicil or by the law of the place where it was made, in accordance with the maxim *locus regit actum* (the place governs the act); and thus a change of the testator's domicil after execution of the will and before his death is immaterial, whereas the English Courts formerly had recourse in all cases, whether in case of a will of a foreigner or of a British subject, to the law of the testator's domicil at the time of his death.

Effect of change of domicil on validity of will under old law.

51A. And by this last expression was understood the *law of the place of domicil as it existed at the time of the testator's death*, and thus any change in that law subsequent to his death, in the case of a foreigner, will have no retrospective effect given to it with respect to personal property in England.

[1] Westlake, §§ 36 and 167; Bar, § 229, and note 4, pp. 506, 507. Laurent argues that the matrimonial law, so far as it affects the property of the spouses, depends entirely on their will, and that the matrimonial domicil is only one of the circumstances from which this will is to be ascertained: § 201, Vol. V., p. 431, *Droit Civil Inter.*; cf. also § 213, Vol. III., p. 413, *Ibid.* According to Fiore, the rights of the spouses in the property belonging to them are to be regulated by the common law of the State of which the husband was a citizen at the time of marriage: Vol. II., § 638, p. 142.

[2] *Vide ante*, § 45, p. 73.

CHAP. IV.

This was decided in a case where a domiciled Paraguayan died in Paraguay leaving personal property in England, and after his death all his property wherever situate became by a change in the Paraguayan law the property of the nation of Paraguay, and his will became by the same change in the law absolutely invalid, Lord Penzance in refusing to give any retrospective effect to this alteration in the Paraguayan law and in maintaining the right of the legatees under the will, made the following important observations. "The question is," said his lordship, "in what sense does the English law adopt the law of the domicil? Does it adopt the law of the domicil as it stands at the time of the death, or does it undertake to adopt and give effect to all retrospective changes that the legislative authority of the foreign country may make in that law? No authority has been cited for this latter proposition, and in principle it appears both inconvenient and unjust. Inconvenient, for letters of administration or probate might be granted in this country which this Court might afterwards be called upon, in conformity with the change of law in the foreign country, to revoke. Unjust, because those entitled to the succession might, before any change, have acted directly or indirectly upon the existing state of things, and find their interests seriously compromised by the altered law. As, therefore, I can find no warrant in authority or principle for a more extended proposition, I must hold myself to the adoption and application of this proposition, *that the law of the place of domicil as it existed at the time of the death* ought to regulate the succession to the deceased in this case."[1] And any attempt on the part of the testator to evade the express provisions of that law will be futile.

Thus, in *Hog* v. *Lashley*,[2] where the personalty referred to in the will was locally situate in England, it was held that

[1] *Lynch* v. *Provisional Govt. of Paraguay*, L. R. 2 P. & D. (1871), 268.
[2] 6 Bro. P. C. (1792), 577; 3 Hagg. Eccl. 415.

a Scotch testator could not exclude his children from the *legitim* or share in it given imperatively by the Scotch law, and which was beyond his disposing power. Nevertheless the doctrine that a will valid by the law of the testator's domicil at the time of execution will be invalidated by a subsequent change of domicil if not in accordance with the law of the *last* domicil, which is also the doctrine adopted in America,[1] is open to serious objection, and, as Savigny[2] long ago pointed out, is not justifiable in principle. Phillimore[3] pronounces it fraught with obvious and many inconveniences, and it is satisfactory to find that English legislation has distinctly departed from it.[4]

Provisions of Lord Kingsdown's Act, as to proper law governing validity of wills of personal estate.

51B. Accordingly, in connection with the effect of a change of domicil on a will of personal estate made *out* of the United Kingdom by a *British* subject, wherever domiciled at the time of making or of death, Lord Kingsdown's Act (24 & 25 Vict. c. 114) now enacts that such a will may be admitted to probate if it was executed in compliance with the forms prescribed *either* by the *lex loci actûs*, the *lex domicilii* at the *time of its execution*, or the *lex domicilii originis* of the testator. And as regards any will of personal estate made *within* the United Kingdom by a *British* subject, the statute also enacts that the will should be admitted to probate if it was executed in compliance with the forms required by the laws for the time being in force in that part of the kingdom where it was made. In neither case will any subsequent change of domicil of the testator be deemed to revoke or to invalidate or to affect the construction of any will or other testamentary instrument. But with reference to the alternative tests of validity offered by the statute, it has been held by Lord Penzance[5] that only one can be adopted in each case, so that

[1] Story, § 473; *Nation* v. *Coon*, 10 Miss. Repts. 513.
[2] *System*, Vol. VIII., § 381. [3] Vol. IV., § 865.
[4] 24 & 25 Vict. c. 114, §§ 2—4.
[5] *Pechell* v. *Hilderley*, L. R. 1 P. & D. (1869), 673.

it is not competent for those who seek to set up a testamentary paper to endeavour to secure the advantages of two conflicting jurisdictions.

Certain classes of moveables have a distinctive international character, which regulates law applicable to them.

52. There are, however, certain moveables which have a special international character attached to them, and this character will govern the law applicable to them. Thus on the open sea a ship is part of the territory of the country to which she belongs, and accordingly, in so far as the ship and the cargo in her are concerned, the *lex rei sitæ* will prevail.[1] But the waters of havens where the tide ebbs and flows are not properly, as was held by Story in an American case, the high seas, unless those waters are *without* low water mark.[2] So also with respect to "literary and artistic works" in those countries which have adopted the Convention of Berne,[3] of 1885, as, for instance, England under the sanction of the International Copyright Act, 1886 (49 & 50 Vict. c. 33), the enjoyment of all rights in a work of this kind is subject to the fulfilment of the conditions and formalities prescribed by the law of the country in which the work had its origin; and the enjoyment cannot last longer in the other countries of the union than the period for which protection is allowed to it in the country of origin. The country where the first publication took place, or, if this publication took place simultaneously in several countries of the union, that country among those whose law gives the shortest period of protection, is held to be the country of origin.

1 Bar, § 228, note 11, p. 503; Westlake, § 154, p. 185, 3rd ed.

2 *United States* v. *Hamilton* (1816), 1 Mason, 152.

3 A full translation of this Convention will be found in Scrutton *on Copyright*, and an abstract of it is given in Bar, p. 762, Gillespie's translation. See also the Order in Council of the 28th November, 1887, at pages 6703—6707 of the *London Gazette* of the 2nd December, 1887, embodying a translation of the Convention entered into between Her Majesty the Queen and the Governments of Belgium, France, Germany, Hayti, Italy, Spain, Switzerland; and Order of 10th August, 1888, extending the provisions of the same Convention to the Grand Duchy of Luxemburg, published in the *London Gazette* for 1888, p. 4345.

Effect of bankruptcy on personal estate of the debtor.

53. The effect of bankruptcy as operating as an assignment of the bankrupt's property needs to be next considered. The English notion regards bankruptcy as operating as a universal assignment to trustees or assignees for the benefit of the creditors of all the personal chattels of the bankrupt wherever situate,[1] and, so far as an English adjudication of bankruptcy is concerned, irrespective of the bankrupt's actual domicil.[2] To give an English Court jurisdiction to make an adjudication it is sufficient if the debtor is domiciled in England, *or*, within a year before the date of the petition, has ordinarily resided or had a dwelling-house or place of business in England. The English statute also regards the actual situation of personal chattels as immaterial, making, in fact, the efficacy of a bankruptcy depend on the rule of *mobilia sequuntur personam.* And the English Courts will accordingly concede to a foreign bankruptcy the same universal effect that the English law claims for bankruptcies declared by itself, allowing it to operate as an assignment of the debtor's personal estate situate in England, including *choses in action.*[3]

Formerly indeed the title of the foreign assignee to the debtor's *choses in action*, so as to sue upon them in his own name, depended upon the assignability of the obligation which it was sought to enforce. But by the Judicature Act of 1873, s. 25, sub-s. 6, it was enacted that *any* absolute assignment (not purporting to be by way of charge only) by writing under the hand of the assignor of *any* debt or other legal *chose in action*, of which express notice in writing shall have been given to the debtor's trustee, or other person from

[1] *Phillips* v. *Hunter*, 2 H. Bl. (1795), 402; *Still* v. *Worsick*, 1 H. Bl. (1791), 665; *Neal* v. *Cottingham*, *ibid.* (1764), 132, n; *Hunter* v. *Potts*, 4 T. R. (1791), 182; *Ex parte Blakes*, 1 Cox, 398.

[2] Bankruptcy Act of 1883, sect. 6 (1).

[3] *Solomons* v. *Ross*, 1 H. Bl. (1764), 131, n.; *Jollet* v. *Deponthieu*, *ibid.* (1769), 132, n.; *Potter* v. *Brown*, 5 East (1804), 124; *Banco de Portugal* v. *Waddell* (1880), 5 App. Cas. 161, at p. 169.

CHAP. IV. whom the assignor would have been entitled to receive or claim such debt or *chose in action*, shall be, and be deemed to have been, effectual in law (subject to prior equities) to pass and transfer the legal right to such debt or *chose in action* from the date of such notice, and all legal or other remedies for the same. So that since this statute assignees under a foreign bankruptcy by procuring from the bankrupt such a written assignment as the statute requires, and giving the required notice to the garnishee, could obtain a clear title to sue in their own names for *choses in action* of the bankruptcy in England. As regards the actual distribution of assets, and the priority of creditors, these are matters which must be determined by the law of the country where the bankruptcy has been adjudicated and the distribution ordered[1]—in other words, by the law of the *forum*, or the *lex loci concursus*. But as equality of distribution is the great aim of all bankruptcy proceedings,[2] where the property of the same debtor is being simultaneously administered in bankruptcy both in England and abroad, a creditor who has received a dividend in the foreign bankruptcy is not entitled to receive anything in the English one until all the creditors have been made equal. Nor will this principle of equality under the law of the English *forum* be departed from even where the creditor may have been entitled to priority by the law of the foreign bankruptcy.[3] But where a person is adjudicated a bankrupt in England, and he has partners residing abroad who are not bankrupt, a creditor who has succeeded in partly recovering his debt from the latter will still be entitled to share *pari passu* with the other creditors in the dividends under the English bankruptcy, for the reason that in such a case "equality of dis-

1 *Thorburn* v. *Steward* (1871), L. R. 3 P. C. 478; *Ex parte Melbourn* (1870), L. R. 6 Ch. App. 64; *Ex parte Dever* (1887), 18 Q. B. D. 660.

2 *Opinions of Grotius* by D. P. De Bruyn, p. 100.

3 *Ex parte Wilson* (1872), L. R. 7 Ch. App. 490; *Ex parte Banco de Portugal* (1879), 11 Ch. D. 317, confirmed on appeal, 5 App. Cas. 161.

tribution," as the judge said, "cannot possibly be attained."[1] The law of the bankruptcy, that is of England in an English bankruptcy, governs also the mode in which the trustees hold whatever foreign property of the bankrupt they obtain, and they accordingly hold it subject to all equities against the bankrupt which are not impeachable under the bankrupt laws themselves. So that if the bankrupt had entered into a binding contract to give security on it there will be a good security as against the trustees, though the security has not been completed by the law of the place where the property is situate or recoverable.[2]

Bankruptcy proceedings will not *per se* convey perfected title to trustee in case of foreign immoveables.

54. As regards the effect of bankruptcy on real estate, inasmuch as sect. 168 of the Bankruptcy Act, 1883 (46 & 47 Vict. c. 52), enacts that "property" is to include "money, goods, things in action, land, and every description of property, whether real or personal, and whether situate in England or elsewhere," an English bankruptcy would appear to carry all the real or immoveable (as well as the personal or moveable) property of the bankrupt in any part, at least, of the British dominions.[3] But this does not mean in such an absolute sense as to ignore the requirements, if any, of the local law in order to perfect a title with respect to real property situate within the territorial limits of that law. On the contrary, there seems to be no doubt that, in principle, to render the assignment of the real estate complete, the forms prescribed by the *lex rei sitæ* must be complied with. Thus, an English bankruptcy, although passing immoveable property in a British colony, will not supersede the necessity of registration to complete the title prescribed by the law of that colony.[4] And as regards land in a foreign country as distinguished from colonial land, it is clear that the only way an

[1] *Brickwood* v. *Miller* (1817), 3 Mer. 279.

[2] *Ex parte Holthausen* (1874), L. R. 9 Ch. App. 722.

[3] Westlake, § 137, p. 154.

[4] Per Jessel, M.R., in *Ex parte Rogers* (1881), 16 Ch. D. 666; cf. also *Opinions of Grotius*, pp. 101—106.

CHAP. IV.

English Court exercising jurisdiction in bankruptcy could reach such land, would be by exercising its compulsory powers under sect. 24 of the Act of 1883, and compelling the bankrupt to execute a valid conveyance of it to the trustee. In like manner, no foreign bankruptcy will of itself pass land in England to a trustee or assignee, and the foreign Court will also have to exercise such compulsory powers as it possesses, in order to compel the bankrupt to transfer the English land for the benefit of his creditors.[1] So far, however, as Courts having jurisdiction in bankruptcy in England, Scotland, and Ireland, and other "British" Courts are concerned, sect. 118 of the Bankruptcy Act of 1883 provides that "they shall severally act in aid of, and be auxiliary to, each other; and an order of the Court seeking aid, with a request to another of the said Courts to exercise, in regard to the matters directed by the order, such jurisdiction as either the Court which made the request, or the Court to which the request is made, could exercise in regard to similar matters within their respective jurisdictions." It is not explained by the Legislature what is the true meaning intended to be given by the term "British Courts" in the above section. It has, indeed, been applied in one case as justifying an order being made in England in aid of the Cape of Good Hope Court of Bankruptcy.[2] But the better opinion appears to be that sect. 118 of the English Act was only intended for Scotch, Irish, and English Courts, and also for such other British Courts as are not under legislatures of their own.[3]

Law applicable to transfer of *choses in action*.

55. Allusion has been made in the last two preceding paragraphs to bankruptcy operating as an assignment of the debtor's *choses in action*, and we have seen that in England since the passing of the Judicature Act of 1873, such assignments can

[1] *Vide* Bar, § 479, pp. 1018—1021, Gillespie's translation.
[2] *In re Fairbank, Ex parte Knight* (1887), 4 Morell, 50.
[3] See Foote, *P. I. Jurisprudence*, 2nd ed., p. 212.

only be made in writing, and written notice of the fact is also required to be given to the debtor. But the question by what law the validity of an ordinary assignment of a *chose in action* is to be decided has received no authoritative determination. By Roman law the assignment of a right of action was merely in its form a mandate to sue, but in its results it was the same as a real transfer of the right.[1] The law of Scotland holds to the view that the law of the place of assignment determines its validity, on the principle of the maxim *locus regit actum*. Thus where an obligation had been assigned in England, by a deed which would have availed to transfer it in Scotland, the country where the main contract was to be performed, it was held that the assignee could not sue upon it in Scotland, because the claim was one which the law of England pronounced to be incapable of being assigned or transferred.[2] So in another case[3] the law of the place of assignation of a policy of life insurance was held to determine the validity of the transfer. Lord M'Laren explained the reasons on which this rule was founded as follows: "The assignment of the right of credit in the policy is a new contract, distinct as regards its nature, mode of constitution and the law that regulates it, from the contract constituted by the policy itself, and the validity of the assignment will, in general, be determined by the *lex loci contractus*—that is, according to the law of the country in which the transaction is made or the security given." In a similar assignment of a right of credit in an English policy made in favour of the assignor's wife, which was not permitted by the law of the place of assignment, Day and Wills, JJ., held that the assignment was void, basing this decision on the application of the law of the place to which

[1] Cf. Arndt's *Pandekten*, § 254, note 4.

[2] *Taylor* v. *Scott* (1847), 9 Ct. of Sess. Reps. 2nd Series, 1504.

[3] *Scottish Provident Association* v. *Cohen* (1888), 16 Ct. of Sess. Reps., 4th Series, p. 112.

CHAP. IV. the contract truly belongs.[1] But it would seem that neither the Scotch nor the English Courts have consistently followed any single principle. Thus, on the one hand, the Scotch Courts have preferred the claim of an attaching creditor in Scotland to that of an assignee whose assignment, although valid by the *lex loci contractus*, had not been intimated to the debtor in Scotland.[2] The ground on which these decisions proceed is, that the question is not one of rights but of the remedies which these rights confer upon their holders, and that such a question must be determined by the law of the country in which the competition arises and the remedy is sought. This reasoning is to some extent supported by the doctrine advocated by Bar, one of the greatest of living writers on private international law. He regards the right to enforce payment (the *jus exigendi*) as an independent transaction, which must be transferred in accordance with the law that regulates it, and so long as the debtor has not actually paid the assignee, if the assignment is not complete by the local law by reason of non-intimation to the debtor, it is ineffectual against an attaching creditor who has meanwhile arrested payment.[3] But if, as Bar himself would appear to admit, and as the Scotch Courts would also seem to concede, the validity of the assignment itself is good, whether regard be had, according to Bar's view, to the law which determines the obligation generally, or to the law of the place of assignment, as the Scotch Courts require, the question between the assignee and the attaching creditor would not seem to be one relating to remedies but to rights. If, then, by the application of the proper law the assignment itself has validly conveyed to B. the debt which C. owes to A., there is nothing left for a creditor of A. to attach in the hands of C., and his diligence cannot be rightly deemed to secure him a remedy

[1] *Lee* v. *Abdy* (1886), 17 Q. B. D. 309.

[2] See the case of *Strachan* v. *McDougle* (1835), 13 Ct. of Sess. Rep., 1st Series, 954. Cf. also Bell's *Comment.* II., p. 18.

[3] §§ 274, 275, pp. 601—603; Gillespie's translation.

which would destroy B.'s previously acquired right. The unsoundness of the contrary view cannot be more forcibly demonstrated than it was by Lord Rutherford in a Scotch case: "If the right," said the learned lord, "be complete by the law of the country which must regulate the transfer, it seems impossible to maintain that, as a matter of remedy, something further must be done which the law of Scotland requires for completion of the right in the case only of transfers that are regulated by that law." On the other hand, the jurisprudence of England and that of the United States has wavered between the exclusive adoption of the law of the creditor's domicil in accordance with the principle of *mobilia personam sequuntur*, and that of the law of what has been termed the *situs* of the obligation, which, generally speaking, is deemed to be that of the debtor. But it will often happen that there will be more than one *forum* in which a right of action can be enforced at the same time, whether by reason of the debtor's domicil or even transient presence, or because it is the court of the *locus solutionis* or *locus celebrationis*.[1] It is, therefore, difficult to fix the true *situs* of a *chose in action* at the time of the assignment, and it is only in a purely metaphorical sense that one can speak of its *situs* at all. In this conflict of authority an English writer cannot be expected to propound any very clear doctrine, but if one may venture to express an individual opinion on the subject in hand, it would appear to be the sounder principle to apply to an assignment of a *chose in action* the same law by which the original obligation is governed in regard to its nature and incidents. For, as Bar correctly states the proposition,[2] the question whether an obligation has been validly transferred, is identical with the question whether an obligation still subsists for the advantage of the former creditor, or whether another person

[1] Cf. Foote, *P. I. Jurisprudence*, 2nd ed., p. 247.

[2] Bar, § 274, p. 601, Gillespie's translation.

CHAP. IV.

can claim the advantages for himself. The assignee, in fact, stands in the shoes of the original creditor, and the law which rules the obligation generally (as between him and the debtor) ought also to decide between the debtor and the substituted creditor, whether the assignment is good or bad—in other words, whether the obligation was assignable at all, and, if so, under what restrictions or limitations.

Principles governing transmission of contract obligations to heirs.

56. As regards the question whether a contract obligation descends to heirs, the general principle appears to be that the heir never undertakes more than what is fixed by the law under which he takes the succession. But according to Bar[1] there is this further principle to be observed, that before the obligation can bind the heir, this effect must also be attributed to it by the law to which the obligation is in itself subject. It has been ruled in Scotland, however, that the question whether a foreign obligation, *e.g.* a promissory note, will affect the heir of the debtor, must be determined, not by the foreign law, which frees the heir, but by the law of Scotland, the place in which the inheritance is situated, and by the laws of which it must be taken up.[2] In England a foreign heir who has accepted the succession without benefit of inventory may probably be sued on the personal obligation he has thereby assumed towards the creditors of the deceased.[3]

1 *Private Inter. Law*, § 283, p. 627, Gillespie's translation.

2 *Kinloch* v. *Fullerton*, House of Lords, 1 Pat. App. (1739), 265.

3 *Beavan* v. *Hastings*, 2 K. & J. (1856), 724.

CHAPTER V.

LAW OF OBLIGATIONS, AND HEREIN OF CONTRACTS, TORTS, AND THE FORMS OF LEGAL TRANSACTIONS.

Aspects under which obligations resting on contract may be best considered internationally.

57. Obligations arising out of or resting on contract have to be considered internationally not only with reference to their intrinsic validity and effects, but also with reference to their formalities and their interpretation. And it is under each of these aspects that it will be most convenient to consider the particular territorial law by which the parties must be held to be governed. Because it is impossible to adopt any theory which would furnish a rule to be applied generally to those numerous questions which Courts have to determine when parties to contractual engagements come to litigate concerning their rights, or liabilities arising therefrom. By adhering to the mode of treatment suggested we avoid the necessity of formulating any general rule regulating the law to be applied when one or both of the parties to a contract happens or happen to belong to a different nation from that of the *forum*, or when the contract has been entered into or is to be fulfilled extra-territorially. But although any attempt to formulate such a rule would be futile, and would be found in practice to be subject to numerous exceptions, some account of the theories which have prevailed amongst juristical writers on private international law in connection with the subject of the present chapter may be useful, not only as a historical study, but equally so from the more practical point of view of illustrating the difficulty and

CHAP. V.

danger of all attempts of the kind here referred to, and which, for our own part, we wish to avoid.

Prevailing theories regulative of law to be applied, examined, and criticised.

58. It is obvious that in case of a jural relation arising out of contract the local laws which may compete for consideration may be, *first*, the *jus fori*, or law of the place where the action is raised; *second*, the *lex loci contractus*, or law of the place where the contract was made or had its origin; *third*, the *lex loci solutionis*, or law of the place of performance; *fourth*, the *lex domicilii* of the creditor; and *fifth*, the *lex domicilii* of the debtor. And, as might have been expected, each of these competing laws has found favour with individual jurists and has been elevated into a regulative principle. But there are fatal objections to the universal application of each of them, though in the case of some of them there are far more weighty reasons in their favour than in that of the others. Thus, those who would adopt the *jus fori* are forced to reject all foreign law whatsoever, and to leave the judge no other guide except the law of his own state. Such a theory no doubt cuts the root of all controversy by the application of a simple process. But the objection to it is that it is subversive of all international comity, and would destroy all extra-territorial trade for the nation which ventured to adopt it, thus reducing it to a position of isolation which would be intolerable in the present condition of commercial development. The place where the contract was made or had its origin is not, indeed, open to the same serious objections, and has received, and still maintains, a large measure of support, more especially in the Franco-Italian systems. The fundamental basis of this theory, or at least of its most recent phase, under the influence of Fiore and Laurent, rests on the intention or autonomy, as it is called, of the parties, and a presumed "voluntary subjection" to a particular law, namely the *lex loci contractus*. It has also found some favour with English judges, and is nowhere more

forcibly advocated than by Lord Justice Turner, in delivering the judgment of the Privy Council in *The Peninsular and Oriental Steam Navigation Co.* v. *Shand*.[1] "The general rule," it is there said, "is that the law of the country where a contract is made governs, as to the nature, the obligation, and the interpretation of it. The parties to a contract are either the subjects of the Power there ruling, or, as temporary residents, owe it a temporary allegiance: in either case equally they must be understood to submit to the law there prevailing, and agree to its action upon their contract. It is, of course, immaterial that such agreement is not expressed in terms; it is equally an agreement in fact, presumed *de jure*, and a foreign Court interpreting or enforcing it on any contrary rule defeats the intention of the parties, as well as neglects to observe the recognised comity of nations." But notwithstanding the definitiveness of this language and the authority of the tribunal which committed itself to this ruling, it cannot be said, at the present time, to have settled any rigid rule for the guidance of English Courts. In the first place, the judgment itself proceeds, after speaking of the doctrine embodied in the passage already quoted as establishing a "general rule," to point out that "there are no doubt exceptions and limitations on its applicability." It is obvious, for instance, that, proceeding as the rule does upon the *presumed* intention of the parties to submit to the law of the place of contract, that presumption must necessarily give way where a contrary intention can be established, not only with reference to the express terms of the contract, but indirectly and impliedly with reference to the nature of the contract. Thus in *Robinson* v. *Bland*,[2] where the question was as to the lawfulness of the consideration for a bill of exchange drawn by one person

[1] 3 Moo. P. C. (1865), N. S. 290. See also *Sujan Singh* v. *Gunga Ram*, decided by the same tribunal in 1881, reported in the I. L. R. VIII. Calcutta Series, 337.

[2] Burr. (1760), p. 1078.

CHAP. V. in one country on himself in another, and there was no circumstance from which to draw an inference favouring a view to a law other than that of the place of contract (which was against a recovery on the bill), except the mention of the place the bill was drawn on, Lord Mansfield in applying the *lex solutionis*, or law of the place of fulfilment, declared that "the law of the place (*i. e.*, of contract) can never be the rule where the transaction is entered into with an express view to the law of another country as the rule by which it is to be governed." And in cases [1] decided subsequently to that of the *Peninsular and Oriental Steam Navigation Co.* v. *Shand*, although stress has been laid on the intention of the parties as regulating the choice of a law, no such rigid general rule as that laid down by the Privy Council judgment has been adhered to or affirmed. Nor on principle can this general rule be based on the *presumed* intention of parties—for it is surely stretching a presumption beyond its legitimate bounds to attribute, for instance, to two Frenchmen in England, who happen to make a contract there which they intend to fulfil in Paris, an intention to be bound by the law of England, of which they are, perhaps, wholly ignorant. The rule would also be inapplicable to a case where the contract was concluded between foreigners of different countries who did not meet, for the question in what place the contract in such a case was legally concluded could only be determined by a rule of positive law, and we would thus find ourselves landed in a circle of this kind, that, until the place of contract was ascertained, the law governing it could not be determined; and yet to ascertain the place we would have to apply a certain rule of positive law, which *ex hypothesi* could not for the moment be determined.[2] Next we have the theory which

[1] *Jacobs* v. *Crédit Lyonnais* (1884), 12 Q. B. D. 589; and *Re Missouri Steamship Co.* (1888), 42 Ch. D. 321.

[2] Cf. *Cowan* v. *O'Connor* (1888), 20 Q. B. D. 640, as to the English law in such a case, or sect. 4 of the Indian Contract Act as to the Indian law.

selects the place of performance as regulative of the law to be applied. This is the theory which, under the influence of Savigny's great authority, is the favourite one with German jurists, and which has been affirmed by the Court of the Empire[1] as most in accordance with prevailing practice. It is the common principle which Savigny deduces from all the various cases which he groups together as founding jurisdiction,[2] or the Roman *forum contractus*; and it is the principle which the law of civil procedure (s. 29), enacted in 1876 for the German Empire, adopts as the proper alternative to the *forum rei*. And whether the place for fulfilment is expressly fixed by the contract or depends upon a tacit expectation, a voluntary submission to the law of this *forum* is to be assumed. But here, again, it is surely just as arbitrary an assumption to make that the parties have had the law of the place of performance in view as it is to infer that they have contemplated exclusively the law of the place where the contract was made, a theory which we have already rejected as unsound. As V. Martens pertinently asks, "If two Russians have concluded a contract in Russia, the performance of which is to take place in England, why are we to hold that they have fixed their thoughts on the law of England, and not on that of Russia?" Again, suppose there are several places of fulfilment, as where, for instance, a joint stock company appoints different places for the payment of the interest or the repayment of principal on its debenture debts. Can it be held that it has thereby submitted itself to a plurality of laws as regards the substance of its obligations? The old German Court of Commerce in 1878 decided in the negative, and if we are guided by considerations of reason, we must admit quite correctly.[1] Moreover, too much stress appears to be laid by the advocates of this as well as the preceding

1 Bar, § 249, note 10, p. 541, Gillespie's translation.

2 *System*, Vol. VIII., § 370, and pp. 160—164 of Guthrie's translation.

theory on the intention or autonomy of the parties. It may of course be readily conceded that in contracts between private persons considerable scope is necessarily left to the free action of the parties. They can, as it is said, "choose their circumstances," and in this way *indirectly* the law that is to govern. But it would be contrary to all principle to allow parties to choose as they please the territorial law which shall apply to their respective obligations, a matter which is never *directly* dependent upon their will. Thus with reference to the particular circumstances of a contract, we may say that this or that law is to govern the relations of the parties, guided by rules and considerations which lie altogether outside the sphere of their free action. But to say this, is not the same thing as to say that it is left to the autonomy of the parties, by any capricious declaration they may choose to make, to determine what law shall regulate their contract.[1] Foote, indeed, still argues to the contrary. According to him the parties should in theory be able to contract themselves out of or into any law they please, and the only question for a tribunal called upon to enforce the contract should be—By what law did the parties intend that their rights should be defined and governed? But then he tells us in the same breath that this theory is based on the assumption "that the parties entering into the contract are of full capacity to do so by *every* law, and that *no* law *is transgressed or intended to be transgressed* by the subject-matter of their agreement." A theory, however, which is thus qualified scarcely deserves the name, and to speak of the intention of the parties as "absolutely unfettered," when both as regards the question of their capacity and the legality of the

[1] Bar, § 247, p. 537, Gillespie's translation. Cf. *Sitaram* v. *Aheerce Heerahnee* (1873), where it was held by the Bengal High Court that parties could not contract between themselves to avoid a marriage on the happening of any event that they may think fit to fix upon: 11 Beng. Law Reports, 129.

subject-matter of the contract that intention is distinctly controlled, is as reasonable as if a man who was placed within an area surrounded by four high walls was said to be "unfettered" in his freedom of action. The very qualification which he adds removes the possibility of conflict between the foreign and the local law precisely in regard to those questions where such a conflict produces the greatest difficulty, and in the absence of such a conflict the *intention* of the parties is of no consequence.[1] The whole theory, in fact, rests on a fiction, which is as contrary to principle as it is often opposed to the actual but unexpressed intentions of the parties, as, for instance, in all probability in the illustration given by V. Martens. We may, therefore, pass on to the consideration of the fourth and fifth theories, which may be conveniently discussed together, as each of them depends on the application of the personal law of one of the parties. The former recognises the personal law of the creditor as governing the contract, while the latter gives the preference to the personal law of the debtor. Now, as the inception of a contract depends upon the will of *both* parties, the objection may be raised against either theory that in recognising the personal law of only *one* of the parties as the leading and exclusive principle, it gives undue weight to the will of that party in regard to matters which, if they are to be dependent on the will of the parties at all, ought only to be regulated by the *concurrent* will of *both* parties (*duorum plurimum in idem placitum consensus*). At the same time there would certainly appear to be more reason why a preference should be shown to the personal law of the debtor than to that of the creditor. The former is undoubtedly more closely bound up with the whole legal transaction than the latter. The person of the debtor, for instance, cannot be changed without substituting an entirely new obligation for

1 *Private Inter. Juris.*, 2nd ed., p. 336. A reference to his book will show that he does not attempt to meet the counter-criticisms.

CHAP. V. that of the old one,[1] but the person of the creditor may, as we have seen, be varied without involving this consequence. The performance of the obligation depends, moreover, mainly on the act of the debtor, and it is the *forum* of the latter, as we shall see, which, as a general rule, gives jurisdiction in accordance with the well-known maxim of the law, *actor sequitur forum rei.*[2] It is the domicil of the debtor, again, which, in the absence of any express stipulation to the contrary, is generally regarded as the place of performance. And, speaking generally, the condition of the defendant is more usually favoured (*conditio defendentis potior est*). So that in a choice between the personal law of either party, there is more authority in the generally accepted principles of jurisprudence for an election in favour of that of the defendant. But even here it is impossible to adopt the latter theory without large limitations and restrictions. Thus in the matter of the rate of interest, the law of the defendant's domicil will not prevent the award of a higher rate of interest stipulated for in the contract than it sanctions, if that rate is valid by the law of the place where the contract was made.[3] Generally speaking, however, the law of that country with which the original contract has most real connection will also regulate the rate of interest.[4]

Again, the contract upon which a plaintiff sues may be one which, although valid by the *lex domicilii* of the defendant, is not enforceable by some particular rule of the personal law of the former affecting his professional *status*, if it is by virtue of that *status* that the plaintiff seeks to enforce his claim. Thus, a barrister's right to sue and recover pay-

[1] See sect. 62, illust. (a), of the Indian Contract Act. Cf. also *Commercial Bank of Tasmania* v. *Jones*, (1893) App. Cas. 313.

[2] See the judgment of the Privy Council in *Sirdar Gurdyal Singh* v. *The Raja of Faridkot*, (1894) App. Cas. 670.

[3] Stephen's *Commentaries*, Vol. II., p. 82.

[4] *Connor* v. *Bellamy* (1742), 2 Atk. 382. Cf. also *Jacobs* v. *Crédit Lyonnais*, 12 Q. B. D. 589.

ment for his services depends on the law affecting his bar, and not on that of the place where he is retained or of that where his services are to be performed, or, as may be added, on that of the accidental domicil of the defendant.[1] This decision may be justified on the principle that if the object of some particular rule of law (here that of the barrister's bar) can only be attained by leaving the *lex loci contractus* or the *lex loci solutionis* entirely out of the question, the judge must not hesitate to apply the rule accordingly.[2] So also the duty, as well as the expediency, of upholding, wherever it is possible, *bonâ fide* transactions with the subjects of other States, which Phillimore calls the first principle of private international law,[3] places another limitation on the application of the law of the debtor's domicil as one of a universal and exclusive character. Accordingly, where the application of the law recognised at the domicil of the debtor would do violence to *bona fides*, while other local laws would indubitably support it, then the latter and not the former is the law which, by the unanimous voice of all systems of legislation, must decide.[4] It is thus apparent that the personal law of neither of the parties can be raised to the position of an exclusive rule. And we thus reach the final conclusion which applies to all the theories we have examined alike, that it is not possible upon the basis of any one of them to decide all conceivable cases. Large exceptions must be admitted in the application of each of them. It is not surprising, therefore, that a writer even of Mr. Westlake's accuracy and research is not able to formulate a more general rule than the following: "Under these circumstances," he says, "it may probably be said with truth that the law by which to determine the

[1] *Queen* v. *Doutre* (1884), 9 App. Cas. 745. See also the same principle affirmed by the Chief Court of the Panjab: *Arthur Gray* v. *Diwan Lachman Das*, March, 1895.

[2] Bar, § 253, p. 553, Gillespie's translation.

[3] § 705. [4] Bar, § 251, p. 548, Gillespie's translation.

intrinsic validity and effects of a contract will be selected in England on *substantial considerations*, the preference being given to the country with which *the transaction has the most real connection*, and not to the law of the place of contract as such."[1] A rule which cannot be expressed in more definite terms than this may be said to be hardly entitled to be called a rule at all. But, unfortunately, it does not seem possible, as far as the view adopted by English Courts is concerned, to improve upon it, for we find that very much the same language was still more recently judicially employed in the House of Lords in *Hamlyn* v. *Talisker Distillery*.[2] In that case, a contract was entered into between an English and a Scotch firm, signed in London but to be performed in Scotland, containing an arbitration clause which was valid by English law but invalid by Scotch law, and the question arose by what law the clause was to be governed. The Scotch Court of Session held that the law of Scotland applied, inasmuch as that country was the *locus solutionis*, and that the reference to unnamed arbitrators was consequently invalid. On appeal, however, to the House of Lords, this decision was reversed, and it was held that as the language of the arbitration clause clearly indicated that the parties intended that the rights under it should be determined by the law of England, where the contract was made and where one of the parties resided, that was the law which had to be applied to test the validity of the clause. Lord Herschell, L.C., in disposing of the points, made the following important observations: "Where a contract," he said, "is entered into between parties residing in different places, where different systems of law prevail, it is a question, as it appears to me, in each case, with reference to what law the parties contracted, and according to what law it was their intention that their rights, either under the

[1] *Private Inter. Law*, sect. 212, p. 258.

[2] (1894) App. Cas. 202, at pp. 207, 208, and pp. 212, 213.

whole or any part of the contract, should be determined. In considering what law is to govern, no doubt the *lex loci solutionis* is a matter of great importance. The *lex loci contractus* is also of importance. In the present case, the place of the contract was different from the place of its performance. It is not necessary to enter upon the inquiry, which was a good deal discussed at the bar, to which of these considerations the greatest weight is to be attributed —namely, the place where the contract was made, or the place where it is to be performed. *In my view they are both matters which must be taken into consideration, but neither of them is, of itself, conclusive, and still less is it conclusive, as it appears to me, as to the particular law which was intended to govern particular parts of the contract between the parties.* In this case, as in all such cases, the whole of the contract must be looked at and the rights under it must be regulated by the intention of the parties as appearing from the contract. *It is perfectly competent to those who, under such circumstances as I have indicated, are entering into a contract, to indicate by the terms which they employ, which system of law they intend to be applied to the construction of the contract and to the determination of the rights arising out of it.*" Lord Watson used similar language. "When two parties," he said, "living under different systems of law enter into a personal contract, which of these systems must be applied to its construction depends upon their mutual intention, either as expressed in their contract, or as derivable by fair implication from its terms. In the absence of any other clear expression of their intention, it is necessary and legitimate to take into account the circumstances attendant upon the making of the contract and the cause of performing its stipulations contemplated by the parties: and amongst these considerations the *locus contractus* and the *locus solutionis* have always been regarded as of importance, although English and Scotch decisions differ in regard to the relative weight which ought to be attributed

CHAP. V.

to them when the place of contracting is in one *forum*, and the place of performance in another. In the present case it does not appear to me to be necessary to discuss the relative value of these considerations, because, in my opinion, the clause of reference is expressed in terms which clearly indicate that the parties had in contemplation and agreed that it should be interpreted according to the rules of English law."

In the face of these observations, whose importance fully justifies their being quoted *in extenso*, it were vain, even if it were possible, which is not the case, to attempt to construct a single theory for universal application.

The difficulty, in fact, of doing so would, as we have seen, be insuperable, and it arises from the very complex nature of the subject with which any such theory would have to deal. Covering, as the endless multiplicity of relations of obligation do, the whole vast region of trade and private enterprise, which the underlying principle of freedom of contract only bounds by the limits of human activity and ingenuity, the law of obligations, in an international sense, cannot possibly be constructed on the lines of a single principle. It will be found in practice expedient, with reference to "substantial considerations"—to employ Mr. Westlake's phrase—to subject an obligation in certain respects to the law of the place where the parties declared their intention, while in other respects the application of the law of the place of performance as regards certain conditions of performance, or the law of the place where the action is brought, may be most suitable, and most in harmony with the presumed intention of the parties. We can no more hope to reduce the complexity we have to cope with within the limits of *any* given rule than we can expect any one particular positive law to exhaustively provide a hard and fast rule for every conceivable case which may arise for decision. But, nevertheless, it is possible to construct a *set of rules* upon general legal principles which will furnish a guide for the determination of the law applicable in some of the most important relations of obligation, where the parties themselves have left the matter in doubt, and, for the rest, analogical reasoning must accomplish the task of solution. More than this cannot be attempted, but this much we may venture to try, with special reference to English jurisprudence.

58. In the first place, then, there are certain preliminary rules which have received general recognition. *Thus, contracts which would have the effect of destroying international comity will not be enforced.* Upon this principle a British Court will refuse to recognise a contract having for its object to revolutionize a friendly country, or to supply funds to an insurgent Government not recognized by the sovereign of these realms—a fact of which a Court must take judicial cognisance.[1] *Again, a claim which the law of the forum regards as opposed to a fundamental principle of domestic jurisprudence, founded on considerations of public policy, or* contra bonos mores *in the sense of that law, is inadmissible.*[2] Thus contracts in undue restraint of trade,[3] or impeachable on the ground of champerty if affecting English litigation,[4] or between husband and wife with the view of facilitating proceedings in England for divorce,[5] have not been enforced. *Contracts that are directed to anything that is legally impossible, or that is forbidden by the law of the forum, will also not be enforced.* Thus, to contract for a right in an immoveable which is unknown to the *lex rei sitæ*,[6] or to create a charitable trust contrary to the

Certain preliminary rules stated.

1 *Jones* v. *Garcia del Rio* (1823), T. & R. 297; *Taylor* v. *Barclay* (1828), 2 Sim. 213; *Thompson* v. *Barclay* (1828), 6 L. J. Ch. 93; *Macnamara* v. *D'Everaux* (1824), 3 L. J. Ch. 156; *Esposito* v. *Bowden* (1857), 27 L. J. Q. B. 17, Exch. Ch.

2 *Hamlyn & Co.* v. *Talisker Distillery*, (1894) App. Cas. 209, 214.

3 *Rousillon* v. *Rousillon* (1880), 14 Ch. D. at p. 369.

4 *Grell* v. *Levy* (1864), 16 C. B. N. S. 76.

5 *Hope* v. *Hope* (1857), 8 D. M. G. 731.

6 Bar, § 248, p. 539, Gillespie's translation. Cf. *Campbell* v. *Dent* (1838), 2 Moo. P. C. 292.

CHAP. V.

provisions of the Mortmain Act,[1] or to smuggle goods into a country in violation of the laws of that country.[2] In this connection it must be added that according to the view of the majority of the judges in the Exchequer Chamber in *Santos* v. *Illidge*,[3] which was an action by a Brazillian against British subjects for non-delivery of slaves sold by them *in Brazil*, which the defendants could lawfully perform *there*, there was nothing in the English statutes forbidding the purchase, sale, or barter of slaves (5 Geo. IV. c. 113; 6 & 7 Vict. c. 98), to prohibit such a contract by a British subject *in a country where the possession and sale of slaves is lawful.* It is to be observed that the learned judges who adopted this view did so expressly on what they considered to be the right interpretation of the English statute law. And upon this interpretation the decision does not conflict with the rule stated in the text. But there is no doubt that if the British statutes had distinctly prohibited the sale of slaves *anywhere* (or, as it was said in the Court of Common Pleas, "all over the world") by a British subject, there could have been no recovery upon the contract in an English Court. Inasmuch, however, as it was held the prohibition had not this extended effect, and as the contract for the sale of slaves was not *per se* so iniquitous as to be unenforceable, the decision was clearly supportable in principle.

So again, *contracts that are illegal by the law of the place of performance are void everywhere.* Because, as Bar explains the rule, if we were to admit such contracts to have binding force, we should be doing violence to the law of the other State, which seems entitled, by virtue of its territorial sovereignty, to refuse to allow certain transactions within its

[1] *Att.-Gen.* v. *Mill* (1827), 3 Russ. 328.

[2] *Waymell* v. *Reed* (1794), 5 T. R. 599; *Lightfoot* v. *Tennant*, 1 B. & P. 551; *Biggs* v. *Lawrence* (1789), 3 T. R. 454.

[3] (1859) 6 C. B. N. S. 841; and in appeal (1860), 8 C. B. N. S. 861.

own territory.[1] Thus in *Hertz* v. *Riera*,[2] where an agreement had been made in Spain between a merchant and an officer of the Spanish Government, which the fiduciary position of the latter rendered void by Spanish law, and Spain was also the country of performance, the contract was not one that could be recovered upon in England even if the allegation that it had been renewed and repeated out of the Spanish dominions had been proved, which was not the case. But in England and in the United States a singular exception has been admitted in the application of the rule last mentioned.

It is said that the obligations of revenue laws have less claim to respect than any other legal commands: indeed Pardessus affirms that, in so far as customs duties go, States live in a kind of war with one another. And thus it has been held *that an act declared illegal by a foreign revenue law as the law of the intended place of performance is not illegal at all, but can be validly contracted for in England.* Accordingly, a contract made in England to defraud the revenue laws of Portugal, was supported by Lord Hardwicke.[3] Ever since his time it was held to be settled, or at least considered to be settled, that, in a British Court, we cannot take notice of the revenue laws of a foreign State. "It would be productive of prodigious inconvenience," said Pollock, C. B., in *Bristowe* v. *Sequeville*, "if, in every case in which an instrument was executed in a foreign country, we were to receive in evidence what the law of that country was, in order to ascertain whether the instrument was or was not valid." [4] It is difficult, however, while admitting the inconvenience referred to by Chief Baron Pollock, to approve altogether of the policy

[1] § 248, p. 539, Gillespie's translation, and § 255, p. 557.

[2] (1840), 11 Sim. 318.

[3] *Boucher* v. *Lawson* (1735), Cas. temp. Hardwicke, 85—89. Cf. also *Lever* v. *Fletcher* (1780), Park on *Marine Insurance*, 506, 8th ed.

[4] (1850), 5 Exch. Reps. at p. 278; *S. C.*, 19 L. J. Exch. 289.

CHAP. V.

of these decisions, and though the doctrine is stated here on the strength of the latter, it is by no means certain that these decisions would be implicitly followed at the present day.[1] Lord Mansfield certainly states the practice in regard to this doctrine too broadly when he says, "No country ever takes notice of the revenue laws of another."[2] Analogous to this doctrine is that so tersely expressed in the rule stated by Chief Justice Marshall in *The Antelope*,[3] that "*the Courts of no country execute the penal laws of another.*" But a proceeding, in order to come within the scope of the latter rule, must be in the nature of a suit *in favour of the State whose law has been infringed*, and accordingly a suit for a penalty may be enforced by a private individual in his own interest.[4] Lastly, in regard to the extinction of obligations, two leading principles are recognised: *first* that *an English Court will not enforce an obligation after it has been barred by the English Statute of Limitations, notwithstanding that it has not been barred according to its proper law;*[5] *and conversely, that an English Court will permit an action to be brought on a contract so long as the obligation resulting from it is not barred by the English law, notwithstanding that the obligation which in fact resulted from it has become barred according to its proper law.*[6]

Law governing the intrinsic validity and effects of a contract.

60. Having disposed of the preliminary rules which all contracts have to satisfy, we may now proceed to consider the law applicable to other questions connected with contractual

1 Cf. Westlake, § 213, p. 258, 3rd ed.; 3 Kent, *Comm.* 266, 267; Story, *Conflict of Laws*, § 257; and Bar, § 255, p. 557, Gillespie's translation, and note at p. 559. Pothier condemned the doctrine as thoroughly false (*Œuvres*, Vol. V., *Assur.* § 58, p. 286. Paris, 1861 ed.)

2 In *Holman* v. *Johnson* (1775), Cowp. 343.

3 10 Wheaton, 123.

4 *Huntington* v. *Attrill*, (1893) App. Cas. 150, at pp. 156—161.

5 *British Linen Co.* v. *Drummond* (1830), 10 B. & C. 903; *Pardo* v. *Bingham*, (1868), L. R. 6 Eq. 485; *Ruckmaboye* v. *Mottichand* (1853), 5 Moore, I. App. 234; *Campbell* v. *Liffman* (1837), 5 C. & F. 1.

6 *Huber* v. *Steiner* (1835), 2 Bing. N. C. 202; *Alliance Bank of Simla* v. *Cary* (1880), 5 C. P. D. 429.

obligations, either entered into or to be performed extraterritorially. In doing so we shall adhere to the classification of the subject indicated in § 57, *ante*, and accordingly commence with that branch of it which relates to the intrinsic validity and effects of contracts. Now the question of the validity of a contract (apart from its formalities, which will be considered presently) may arise either with reference to the contracting of the agreement, or with reference to its performance. Upon a question of the former kind the weight of English authority is in favour of deciding it in accordance with the law of the place where the contract is entered into.[1] This is the "broad rule," affirmed by the Court of Appeal in *Jacobs* v. *Crédit Lyonnais*,[2] as presumably governing the nature, the obligation, and the interpretation of a contract, unless the contrary appears to be the express intention of the parties. On the other hand, if the question is one which relates to the time, mode or conditions of performance, an English Court will unquestionably apply, subject of course to what has been said in § 58, the law of the place of performance.[3] Story adopts the same view,[4] and so does Chancellor Kent.[5] We find it also very emphatically affirmed in a decision of the Supreme Court of Commerce of the German Empire, of the 28th June, 1875,[6] where it was laid down that, in all that concerns payment or performance, the law of the place of payment or performance will rule. It is on a similar principle that questions of interest and currency

[1] *The Peninsular and Oriental Steam Navigation Co.* v. *Shand* (1865), 3 Moo. P. C. N. S. 290; *Branley* v. *South Eastern Rail. Co.* (1862), 12 C. B. N. S. 63; *S. C.*, 31 L. J. C. P. 286; and Foote, p. 369, 2nd ed. This is also the rule recognised by the great majority of continental Jurists: Fiore, I., § 146, pp. 174, 175.

[2] (1884), 12 Q. B. D. 599.

[3] *Branley* v. *South Eastern Rail. Co.* (1862), 12 C. B. N. S. at p. 71; *Santos* v. *Illidge*, 8 C. B. N. S. 867.

[4] *Conflict of Laws*, § 280.

[5] *Comment.* ii. 393.

[6] *Treschow* v. *Bockelman*, quoted at p. 571, note 5, of Gillespie's translation of Bar's *Priv. Inter. Law*. Cf. also Fiore, I., § 147, p. 175.

CHAP. V.

are determined. For, as regards the former, the obligation to pay interest is always an accessory of some other leading or principal obligation, and hence the question whether interest is due, and from what point of time and up to what point of time it is due, must be dependent on the same territorial law to which the leading obligation is itself subject.[1] Thus on default of payment by the acceptor of a bill of exchange, he is liable to pay interest at the rate fixed by the law of the place where the bill was payable,[2] and for the like reason the same principle prevails in regard to compound interest.[3] So also in regard to questions of currency, in cases of doubt the coinage recognized at the place of payment, or, if no place is fixed for payment, at the place where the contract was made, must be taken to be the proper medium of payment,[4] the acknowledged theory being that the creditor has a right to be put in the same position as if payment had been made at the place and time stipulated for.[5] "*Æstimatio rei debitae*," says Everhardus, "*consideratur secundum locum ubi destinata est solutio, non obstanta quod contractus alibi sit celebratus.*"[6] Accordingly, if a debt payable abroad is recovered in England, the judgment must be for so much money as, if remitted to the country where it ought to have been paid at the rate of exchange current at the time the judgment is recovered, will there produce the amount of the debt.[7] So in case of failure by the drawee to accept a bill of exchange, or of failure in payment by the acceptor of a bill

[1] Bar, § 264, p. 578, Gillespie's translation; Westlake, § 225, p. 264, 3rd ed. Cf. also *State Fire Insurance Co., In re*, 32 L. J. Ch. 300.

[2] *Cooper* v. *Waldegrave* (1840), 2 Beav. 282. This question is not specifically dealt with by sect. 72 of the Bills of Exchange Act, 1882. Cf. Westlake, § 234, pp. 271—273, 3rd ed.

[3] *Fergusson* v. *Fyffe* (1841), 8 C. & F. 121.

[4] Bar, § 259, p. 569, Gillespie's translation; 2 Burge, 860—861; Story, *Conflict of Laws*, § 271 *a*; and Fiore, I. § 182.

[5] *Cash* v. *Kennion* (1804 and 1805), 11 Ves. 314.

[6] *Consilia*, 78, No. 9.

[7] Westlake, § 226, p. 265, deducing rule from *Scott* v. *Bevan* (1831), 2 B. & Ad. 78, and *Bertram* v. *Duhamel* (1838), 2 Moo. P. C. 212. See as to bills of exchange sect. 72 (4) of the Act of 1882, *post*, § 61.

of exchange or the maker of a promissory note, the necessity and sufficiency of demand, protest or notice of dishonour, by the (last?) holder, in order to charge any other party to the bill or note, is determined by the law of the place where it was payable.[1]

Rights, duties, and liabilities of parties to bills of exchange drawn in one country and negotiated or payable in another, now regulated in England by statute law.

61. But the law affecting bills of exchange drawn in one country and negotiated, accepted, or payable in another is now, so far as English Courts are concerned, regulated by the Bills of Exchange Act of 1882 (45 & 46 Vict. c. 61), and requires special treatment. Section 72 of that Act determines the rights, duties, and liabilities of the parties to such bills as follows:—

"(1) The validity of a bill as regards requisites in form is determined by the law of the place of issue, and the validity as regards requisites in form of the supervening contracts, such as acceptance or indorsement or acceptance *supra protest*, is determined by the law of the place where such contract [*sic*] was made.

Provided that—

(a) Where a bill is issued out of the United Kingdom, it is not invalid by reason only that it is not stamped in accordance with the law of the place of issue:

(b) Where a bill, issued out of the United Kingdom, conforms, as regards requisites in form, to the law of the United Kingdom, it may, for the purpose of enforcing payment thereof, be treated as valid as between all persons who negotiate, hold, or become parties to it in the United Kingdom.

"(2) Subject to the provisions of this Act, the interpretation of the drawing, indorsement, acceptance, or acceptance *supra protest* of a bill, is determined by the law of the place where such contract is made.

[1] Westlake, § 231, p. 269, 3rd ed.; and cf. sect. 72 (3) of Bills of Exchange Act.

CHAP. V.

Provided that, where an inland bill is indorsed in a foreign country, the indorsement shall, as regards the payer, be interpreted according to the law of the United Kingdom.

"(3) The duties of the holder[1] with respect to presentment for acceptance or payment, and the necessity for, or sufficiency of, a protest or notice of dishonour, or otherwise, are determined by the law of the place where the act is done or the bill is dishonoured.

"(4) Where a bill is drawn out of, but payable in, the United Kingdom, and the sum payable is not expressed in the currency of the United Kingdom, the amount shall, in the absence of some express stipulation, be calculated according to the rate of exchange for sight drafts at the place of payment on the day the bill is payable.

"(5) Where a bill is drawn in one country and is payable in another, the due date thereof is determined according to the law of the place where it is payable."

Observations on the above provisions.

62. The rule embodied in sub-section 2, it will be observed, uses the word "interpretation" only, and it is not very clear what meaning was intended to be given by the British Legislature to it, whether, for instance, it was intended, as Westlake supposes,[2] to include "obligation"? But whatever may be the construction put upon the word, inasmuch as the

[1] Westlake thinks that this must be interpreted to mean the *last* holder, so as not to conflict with the doctrine laid down in *Horne* v. *Rouquette* (1878), 3 Q. B. D. 514. But this opinion is controverted by Gillespie in his learned Note AA on §§ 219—316 of his translation of Bar, at p. 694. Gillespie thinks the statute has adopted Bar's theory in favour of the law of the place where each obligation is undertaken, just as there was but one rule applicable to all holders by the law of Scotland, prior to the statute, in regard to all incidents of the original contract, among which are included the necessity of presentation of a protest, and of notice of dishonour, as well as the sufficiency of these when made. Page 694 of his translation of Bar. See *post*, p. 123, where the subject is further discussed.

[2] Westlake, § 229 3rd ed.

sub-section embodies the principle established by the previous case law, the nature and obligation of the contract of the drawer and indorser, and the extent of their liability, must be *primâ facie* determined by the law of the place where they contracted, in the absence, that is, of any clear indication that the parties intended to contract on the basis of any other law. This is the "broad rule" which, as we have seen, the Court of Appeal,[1] in *Jacobs* v. *Crédit Lyonnais*, said *presumably* governed the nature, the obligation, and the interpretation of ordinary contracts, unless the contrary appears to be the express intention of the parties. So also in regard to all matters relating to performance or non-performance by the acceptor, the law of the place of performance where the bill is accepted and payable, if both concur at one place, will govern. Where, however, the acceptor has accepted in one country a bill payable in another, the sound view appears to be that the intrinsic validity of the acceptance, that is to say, whether it is binding at all, is regulated by the law of the place where it was made, while the measure of his liability and the other incidents of payment would be determined by the law of the place where the bill is payable; in other words, by the law of the place of performance of his obligation.[2] In the above view, the liability of the drawer and acceptor, if complete by the law governing each of them respectively, would not be

1 (1884), 12 Q. B. D. 589, 599. Thus a marriage settlement was construed partly according to English law, and partly according to Scotch, in obedience to the plain intent of the settlement itself. *Chamberlain* v. *Napier* (1880), 15 Ch. D. 614.

2 Cf. Foote, *Private Inter. Juris.*, p. 435, 2nd ed., where the result of the authorities is given. Sect. 22 (1) of the English Bills of Exchange Act, 1882, says, generally, in regard to the question of capacity, that "Capacity to incur liability on a party is co-extensive with capacity to contract." The Indian *Negotiable Instruments Act* (XXVI. of 1881) declares (§ 134) that, in the absence of a contract to the contrary, the liability of the maker or drawer of a foreign promissory note, bill of exchange or cheque, is regulated *in all essential matters* by the law of the place where he made the instrument, and the respective liabilities of the acceptor and indorser by the law of the place where the instrument is made payable.

CHAP. V.

affected by the invalidity of an indorsement on the bill in a contest between them and the indorsee, or anyone who follows him.[1] The principles embodied in sub-sections (2) and (5) may be further curiously illustrated by a case[1] which arose out of a bill which became payable in France during the Franco-German War (1870—71). The bill had been drawn and indorsed in England, and was payable in France on the 5th October, 1870. But during the currency of the bill, and in consequence of the invasion of French territory by the German army, the Emperor Napoleon issued an edict extending the right of action on all negotiable instruments then current for one month, and deferring payment for that time (*moratorium*). After the change of government, similar laws were passed from time to time, with the ultimate effect of extending the day of payment of the bill in question to the 5th September, 1871, and on that day it was duly presented, dishonoured, and protested. Notice of dishonour and protest was then sent, in accordance with the law of France, to the English indorsee, who, having paid the sum due upon the bill, sued his indorsers for indemnity. It was contended for the defendants that they were discharged from liability by reason of failure to present the bill for payment at the time fixed in the bill, and to give notice of dishonour accordingly. But the contention was overruled, on the ground that everything had been rightly done by the law of the country where the bill was payable, which, as sub-section (5) of the English statute now enacts, is the law which determines the due date of a bill drawn in one country and payable in another.[2] The effect of the French enactments giving a period of grace (*moratorium*) has, however, given rise to considerable controversy on the Continent, where great conflict of opinion still exists as to whether the compulsory enlargement of the time by such enactments could affect any

[1] Bar, § 306, pp. 676, 677, Gillespie's translation.

[2] *Rouquette* v. *Overmann* (1875), L. R. 10 Q. B. 525.

one, save the indorsers who are subject to them. It is said, on the one hand, that the question is not as to the usual days of grace (which is, perhaps, all that sub-section 5 of the English statute contemplates), or periods of protestation, which are beyond doubt to be ruled by the law of the place of payment, and the reasons for refusing to recognize the extended period allowed by the French Government as prolonging the endurance of the liability of subsidiary obligants, drawees, or indorsees not subject to the law of France, are very forcibly put by the Supreme Commercial Court of the German Bund, of the 21st February, 1871. "The bill," says that judgment, "provides that it shall fall due at a specified time. The obligation is that payment shall be made at that very period. The guarantee undertaken by the other obligants is for a day certain—it binds them to see that payment is made upon the day fixed in the bill. Neither drawer nor indorser undertakes any obligation as to payment after this time. They are not responsible for possible changes in the position of the acceptor after the bill is due."[1] This reasoning is further supplemented by Bar in the following manner. Days of grace, he says, are merely intended to provide a convenient means of disposing of formal delays and impediments, and it is merely playing with words to say that they may just as well last for seven or eleven months as for two to ten days. And if the French measures be regarded as importing a prohibition of protest, the question is then reduced to this shape, viz.: Does the obligation on the bill continue to subsist, if protestation, which in other circumstances is necessary for its continued subsistence, is made impossible by a *vis major*, which is the character of the prohibition by a foreign Government? The sound answer to this question he thinks is, to regard a protest not so much an obligation incumbent on the creditor in the bill, but rather a condition of his right. If, then, accident or *vis major* makes

[1] Bar, § 310, pp. 682, 683, of Gillespie's translation.

CHAP. V.

it impossible for this condition to come into being, the loss falls, not upon the debtor, but upon the person whose right is qualified by this condition. Of course legislation may, by a fiction, hold that the condition has been satisfied, *i.e.*, that the protest was taken in due time, and in that case the holder has his right of recourse. He has this right, however, only as against an obligant in the bill by whose own law an obligant's obligation continues even where protests are hindered or forbidden by a *vis major;* he has no such rights as against obligants whose own law proceeds on the opposite footing.[1] On the other hand, in France, Italy, Sweden, the United States, and, so far as the point has yet arisen, in England also, the excuse of *vis major* is admitted in regard to omissions to protest even against subsidiary obligants. Gillespie is, however, of opinion that it is doubtful whether, in a case to which § 72 (2) of the English Bills of Exchange Act, 1882, was applicable, an English Court would now follow the decision in *Rouquette* v. *Overmann* above cited.[2] Foote, on the contrary, thinks[3] that case good law, and in strict accordance with the principle, established by the decision in *Allen* v. *Kemble*[4] and *Gibbs* v. *Frement*,[5] that the proper time for payment, and the proper time for notice of dishonour, was the time fixed by the law of the country where payment was to have been made.[6] In regard to the time within which protest must be made, and the observance

[1] Bar, § 310, p. 684, Gillespie's translation.

[2] *Ibid.* Note AA, at p. 695.

[3] *Private Int. Juris.*, p. 435, 2nd ed.

[4] (1848), 6 Moo. P. C. 314. But see the remarks of Cockburn, C. J., on *Allen* v. *Kemble* in his judgment in *Rouquette* v. *Overmann*, L. R. 10 Q. B. at p. 541. Westlake (§ 230, p. 269), does not agree with the reasoning of the judgment, though he supports the decision on the ground that the drawer and indorser were sued where they became parties to the bill, so that the law of that place was, in fact, the *lex fori*.

[5] (1853), 9 Exch. 25.

[6] The Indian *Negotiable Instruments Act* (XXVI. of 1881) lays down the same rules: *vide* section 135.

of the forms prescribed for the same, the decisions in Paris and Russia follow the old rule of the Scotch Courts prior to the passing of the Bills of Exchange Act, 1882, and apply the *lex solutionis*, or law of the place of payment, to such matters. Sub-section (3) of section 72 of the English statute, however, adopts the theory advocated by Bar,[1] that just as the law of the place at which each obligation on a bill is undertaken will regulate it (which is also the doctrine underlying the rule embodied in sub-section (2) in the case of a foreign bill), so also by strict logical necessity as against each holder the *lex loci actus* should regulate his conduct,[2] or, as the English statute states the rule, his duties in regard to presentment for acceptance or payment, and the necessity for, or sufficiency of, a protest on notice of dishonour, or otherwise, are to be regulated by the law of the place where the particular act is done or the bill is dishonoured. There seems to be no objection in principle why this statutory rule should have been intended only to apply, in the case of notice of dishonour, to the "last holder," and not to the case of an indorser who has been made duly liable and seeks recourse against a prior indorser or the drawer, as Mr. Westlake seems to think[3] must have been the real intention of the framers of the Act. Mr. Westlake's argument is, that the notice of dishonour which an indorser who has been made duly liable is bound to give *his* indorser, or to the drawer, if there be no intermediate party, depends on the law governing the contract made by the indorsement to him or by the drawing, *i.e.*, in general the law of the place where the bill or note was signed by the indorser or drawer.[4] But the obligation on a bill is undertaken not merely with reference to one particular individual and his assignees, but with reference to *any* lawful

[1] § 304, pp. 673—675, and p. 695; and § 306, p. 677, Gillespie's translation.

[2] Bar, § 306, p. 677; and § 312, p. 687, Gillespie's translation.

[3] § 232, p. 270, 3rd ed.

[4] § 233, p. 271, 3rd ed.

CHAP. V.

holder of the bill. The different obligants of the bill are in a manner tied up together, and each obligant who takes part in its circulation guarantees that payment shall be made at the place stipulated for in the bill. Inasmuch, therefore, as the object of protest is merely to show that payment has been demanded at the proper place from the principal obligant—that is the acceptor, or in certain circumstances the maker, of the bill—it follows that the law of the country in which the protest must be made—*i.e.*, the place of payment, must regulate the form, the place, and time of taking it, and, if so, there is surely no exaggeration of principle to hold that it must also regulate the sufficiency of the notice of the fact of the bill being dishonoured to the drawer, as well as to all the intervening indorsers, not only as regards the *last* holder, but *any* holder.[1] Upon this subject the previous theories were most divided. Some insisted on the application of the law of the domicil of the person who takes recourse, others on the law of the place of issue, others again on the law of each debtor on the bill, while Salpius draws a distinction between the necessity of notice of dishonour, which he thinks should be determined by the law of the person to whom the notice should be given, and the form of the notice, including the period of the notice, which, in his opinion, should be regulated by the law of the place from which the notice proceeds. In this conflict of opinion and practice, it cannot be said that the English Legislature offended against any generally recognized international practice by enacting that the sufficiency of notice of dishonour shall depend on the law of the place where the bill is dishonoured, without drawing any distinction between the last holder and any other holder of the bill.[2]

Proper law to be applied to *obligations quasi ex contractu.*

63. We have now considered the law regulating, in an international sense, the validity and effects of ordinary con-

[1] Cf. Story, § 306.

[2] The Indian Act, as we have seen, lays down the same rule in very general terms and without drawing any such distinction (§ 135).

tracts and of bills of exchange. But there are certain obligations which arise out of relations resembling those created by contract, which differ, however, from the latter in this respect, that whereas contractual obligations arise from agreements which are *intended* to produce an actionable obligation between the contracting parties, the primary object of the former is *not* the creation of an obligation. Hence they are said to arise *quasi ex contractu*, "as it were from contract." They are also said to arise *ex lege*, because, although the person obliged, *i.e.*, against whom the right *quasi ex contractu* is available, has not undertaken a special duty to the person entitled, *i.e.*, in whom that right resides, yet the law casts that duty upon him as if he had so undertaken it.[1] Examples of such obligations are the following:—

(a) The right of a person who is interested in the payment of money which another is bound by law to pay, or, as the English law expresses the rule, *who is compellable by law to pay it*, and who therefore pays it, to be reimbursed by the other.

(b) That of a person who lawfully does anything for another person, or delivers anything to him, *not intending* to do so gratuitously, and such other person *enjoys the benefit* thereof, to receive compensation from the latter in respect of, or to compel him to restore, the thing so done or delivered. In the Roman law a person who rendered a voluntary service of this kind was called a "*negotiorum gestor*."

(c) To return money paid by mistake or under coercion.

(d) The responsibility of a finder of goods to take such care of the goods as a man of ordinary prudence would, under similar circumstances, take of his own goods.

[1] See my *Jurisprudence*, 2nd ed., §§ 241, 242, pp. 281—287.

It will be observed that in these examples the obligation, as in the case of a delict or tort, arises from the act of one party, but inasmuch as that act is a lawful one, it more resembles an obligation arising from contract than from tort. Hence it is that some writers, like Laurent,[1] propose to treat such *quasi* contractual obligations after the analogy of real contracts, and would apply the personal law of the parties, if both belong to the same nationality, or the law of the place where the act is done if the parties are of different nationalities. English jurisprudence is very barren of authority on this subject. But the case of *De Greuchy* v. *Wills*[2] affords some slight indication of the rule which an English Court would apply. That was a case where a man domiciled in England was also married there after the passing of the Married Women's Property Act, 1870, and the question was whether he was liable, beyond the assets derived through his wife, for antenuptial debts contracted by the wife in Jersey. The solution of this question depended on whether the English statute or the law of Jersey was the proper law to be applied, by the former of which he would not be further liable, but by the latter he would. Since the husband's liability in any view could only be said to arise as an obligation *quasi ex contractu* on the marriage relation, there were two possible *criteria* for determining the proper law of such an obligation, depending either on the place of the celebration of marriage or the domicil of the marriage. In the case actually before the Court both *criteria* concurred, for the marriage took place in England, and the husband had his domicil there, accordingly the English law undoubtedly applied, and the husband was held not liable. But Lopes, J., was of opinion that if the marriage had taken place in Jersey the law of that place would have applied and the husband

[1] *Le Droit Internat.* Vol. VIII., § 2, pp. 6 *et seq.*
[2] (1879), 4 C. P. D. 362.

would have been further liable, and Grove, J., with more hesitation, was inclined to the same view. If this view should hereafter be adopted, the rule propounded by Laurent, that the place where the act occasioning the obligation occurred, if the parties belong to different nationalities, would supply the law of the obligation, would practically be upheld. Mr. Westlake, however, contends that the law of the place with which the act which occasions the obligation *quasi ex contractu* "has the most real connection," is the proper law.[1] According to this view in the above case, had the marriage even taken place in Jersey the decision ought still to have been the same, because the domicil of marriage, with which, as Mr. Westlake admits, the act occasioning the obligation on the part of the husband had the most real connection, was English, and consequently English law would still have applied to regulate the nature of the obligation. This view seems to receive some support from the decision of the same Court, that the question whether an insured person is accountable to the insurer who has paid him, for money received *aliunde* in respect of the loss, depends on the law governing the contract of insurance.[2]

Proper law governing formalities of contracts.

64. The law regulating the form and interpretation of contracts has next to be determined. In dealing with the former we at once meet with a striking instance of that real *communis consensus* amongst civilized States which justifies the possibility of formulating a system of private international law. For there is no rule of any one particular system of positive law which can be more definitely stated, or which has received more universal international recognition,[3] than that which is expressed in the maxim, *locus regit actum*. Accord-

[1] § 235, p. 273, 3rd ed.

[2] *Burnand* v. *Rodocanachi* (1880), 5 C. P. D. 424.

[3] See the provisions of the modern European codes summarized by Phillimore, Vol. IV., §§ 639—647. Cf. also Fiore, I., cap. VI., §§ 210 *et seq.*, p. 221.

CHAP. V.

ing to this rule, setting aside cases of a purely special character, and subject to what will be stated hereafter as to questions of evidence and proof (as matters affecting procedure, and not the solemnities of the contract)[1] being subject to the law of the *forum*, a legal transaction, *so far as its mere form is concerned*, will be held to be validly concluded if it conforms to the requirements of the law of the place where it takes place (the *lex loci celebrationis*).[2] How this rule came to obtain the almost universal recognition which is now conceded to it, is somewhat difficult to explain. It certainly cannot be defended, as Laurent attempts to do, on *à priori* grounds, and most other attempts to justify it on any first principles of law have proved to be equally unsatisfactory.[3] We must rest content, therefore, with the knowledge that whatever may have been the grounds which recommended this rule to general observance, it is now sanctioned by a *comitas gentium*, and is fully recognized in English jurisprudence, indeed to such an extent that it may be said to be subject (apart from matters affecting procedure) to only a single undoubted exception.[4] That exception refers, in the English, American, and Scotch systems, to the supremacy which the principle of the *lex situs* demands, as we have seen, in everything that refers to immoveables, and which is thus enunciated by Lord Mansfield:[5] "In every disposition or

[1] See the distinction drawn by Jervis, C. J., in *Leroux* v. *Brown* (1852), 12 C. B. 801.

[2] Burge, Vol. I., p. 29; Story, *Conflict of Laws*, §§ 260—262; Bar, § 4, pp. 5 and 6; and § 117, p. 262, Gillespie's translation; Westlake, § 207, p. 249, 3rd ed.

[3] Bar, § 117, pp. 262—264, Gillespie's translation.

[4] See, in addition to authorities quoted under § 55, *Benham* v. *Mornington*, 3 C. B. 133; *Warrenden* v. *Warrenden*, 9 Bligh, 110. As to bills of exchange, see § 61, *ante*.

[5] In *Robinson* v. *Bland* (1760), 2 Burr. 1079. See, also, *Waterhouse* v. *Stanfield* (1851), 9 Ha. 234; and (1852), 10 Ha. 254; *Hicks* v. *Powell* (1869), L. R. 4 Ch. App. 741; Bar, § 119, p. 267, Gillespie's translation; and Fiore, I., § 88, p. 112.

contract where the subject-matter refers locally to England, the law of England must govern, and must have been intended to govern. Thus, a conveyance or will of land, a mortgage, a contract concerning stocks, must all be sued on in England, and the *local nature of the thing requires them to be carried into execution according to the law here.*" But although a contract may be unimpeachable in point of form by the proper law, if it requires to be enforced in another country it may be necessary to have to resort to a different law, in order to determine the mode of proving it—whether, for instance, by parol or written evidence—to entitle the party to any remedy under it at the hands of the Court whose assistance is sought. "What evidence," said Lord Brougham in a leading case,[1] "the Courts of another country would receive and what reject, is a question into which I cannot at all see the necessity of the Courts of any one country entering. Those principles which regulate the admission of evidence are the rules by which the Courts of every country guide themselves in all their inquiries. The truth, with respect to men's actions, which form the subject-matter of their inquiry, is to be ascertained according to a definite course of proceeding, and certain rules have established that in pursuing this investigation some things shall be heard from witnesses—others not listened to; some instruments shall be inspected by the judge—others kept from his eye. This must evidently be the same course, and governed by the same rules, whatever be the subject-matter of investigation; nor can it make any difference whether the facts, concerning which the discussion arises, happened at home or abroad; whether they related to a foreigner domiciled abroad or a native living and dying at home. As well might it be contended that another mode of trial should be adopted as that

[1] *Yates* v. *Thomson* (1835), 3 Cl. & Fin. pp. 585—588.

CHAP. V.

another mode of evidence should be admitted in such cases." Accordingly, the English Courts act upon the principle that whatever relates to the enforcement of the remedy sought must be determined by the *lex fori* of that country where the action is brought. The distinction upon which the application of different laws is based in such matters is well put by Tindal, C. J., in *Huber* v. *Steiner*.[1] "The distinction," he says, employing the phraseology of Bartolus in his Commentaries on the Code,[2] "between that part of the law of the foreign country, where a personal contract is made, which *is* adopted, and that which is *not* adopted by our English Courts of law, is well known and established; viz., that so much of the law as affects the rights and merits of the contract, all that relates *ad litis decisionem*, is adopted from the foreign country; so much of the law as affects the remedy only, all that *ad litis ordinationem*, is taken from the *lex fori* of that country where the action is brought." In other words, the English Courts will leave the formalities or ceremonies required to establish the *vinculum obligationis* to be regulated by the law of the place where the contract is made, provided of course it does not relate to immoveables, and provided also there is nothing in the provisions of the foreign law contrary to the stringent policy of the English law.[3] If the contract does not fulfil the requirements of the foreign law as regards its solemnities, so as to be *available* as a contract, it is, according to the English view, "void all the world over."[4] Nor can it make any difference in principle whether the foreign forms are prescribed in the interests of the *fisc* (or revenue

[1] (1835), 2 Scott, 304; 2 Bing. N. C. 202.

[2] T. I. 1.

[3] Fiore practically argues in favour of the same principle, Vol. I. §§ 184—185, p. 201. See also Laurent, Vol. VIII. §§ 20—21, pp. 40—44.

[4] Per Lord Ellenborough in *Clegg* v. *Levy* (1812), 3 Camp. 167. Cf. also *Alves* v. *Hodgson* (1797), 7 T. R. 241; and *Bristow* v. *Secqueville* (1850), 5 Exch. 275; and *Richards* v. *Goold* (1827), 1 Molloy, 22.

laws), or in that of the parties. Accordingly, if neglect of the stamp laws, which are in force at the place in which the transaction is concluded, draws with it the penalty of nullity, the same effect must be attributed to that neglect in a foreign country also, and it is no good objection that the fiscal or revenue laws of one State have no force in another.[1] Such an objection influenced indeed the older decisions (ever since, as we have seen,[2] the time of Lord Hardwicke) in England[3] and, as some think, those of Scotland,[4] and is still found in Wharton.[5] The prevailing doctrine in England was that "a British Court cannot take notice of the revenue laws of a foreign State." But in *Bristow* v. *Secqueville*[6] it was admitted by Rolfe and Alderson, BB., that if for want of a stamp a contract made in a foreign country is void, it could not be enforced in England. In that case, however, the document (a receipt proving payment) was admitted in evidence, though without a stamp, which could not have been so used where it was given, for want of the stamp required in that country. But there was no question here of proving the contract itself, but only of proving that the case provided for by the contract had arisen through the fact of a certain payment having been made. The probativeness of the document for this collateral purpose was a question appertaining to the law of process, and as such was governed by the *lex fori*. The rules of procedure of the foreign Court may indeed have prevented the fact of payment being proved by such a document—that is to say, a Court there of taking judicial cognizance of it; but as

[1] Bar, § 126, p. 281, Gillespie's translation.

[2] *Vide* § 59, *ante*.

[3] *James* v. *Catherwood* (1823), 3 Dowl. & Ry. 190; *Holman* v. *Johnson* (1775), Cowp. 343; *Wynne* v. *Jackson* (1826), 2 Russ. 351.

[4] *Stewart* v. *Gelot* (1871), 9 Ct. of Sess. Repts., 3rd Series, 1057; Bell's *Prin.*, § 328. But cf. *Valery* v. *Scott* (1876), 3 Ct. of Sess. Repts., 4th Series, 965.

[5] Vol. I., p. 147.

[6] (1850), 5 Exch. 275.

CHAP. V.

the Courts of each country must be guided in matters of strict procedure by the law of their own State, and the English law did not render the receipt inadmissible, the English Court, in *Bristow* v. *Secqueville*, was clearly entitled to act upon all admissible evidence of a fact, and, once having had the fact properly brought before it, to draw the legal inferences from it, implied as well (it would seem) by the *lex loci actus* as by its own law. The case of *Leroux* v. *Brown*,[1] above cited, was one of a different kind, but may be supported on the same grounds. There an English Court gave effect to the 4th section of the Statute of Frauds, which provides that no action shall be brought upon certain contracts that are not evidenced by writing, although the contract was made abroad and would have been available there to found an action. The *ratio decidendi* is thus stated by Jervis, C. J.: "It is not denied that if s. 4 of the Statute of Frauds applies to the contract itself, or to the solemnities of the contract, it cannot be enforced here. I am of opinion that the section in question *applies not to the solemnities of the contract, but to the procedure*, and *therefore* that the contract cannot be sued upon here." It was thus a question which related to the enforcement of a remedy, and that remedy could only be obtained in accordance with the rules sanctioned by the law of that Court where the action was brought. In France, however, the maxim *locus regit actum* receives a more rigid observance, as may be illustrated by a case almost the converse of that of *Leroux* v. *Brown*. In *Benton* v. *Horeau*,[2] decided by the Court of Cassation, a contract had been concluded verbally in England between a Frenchman and an Englishman; the Englishman sued upon the contract in France, and it was contended that under the French law it was incompetent to

[1] (1852), 12 C. B. 801.

[2] 26th August, 1880, quoted in Mr. Gillespie's Note E. on §§ 117—128 of Bar, at pp. 286, 287, of his translation.

prove the debt arising on the contract otherwise than by writing, because it exceeded 150 francs. To this contention it was answered, that by the law of England, where the contract was made, writing was not necessary to constitute the obligation, and the rule to be applied was *locus regit actum*, this being a question as to the validity of the *vinculum obligationis*. The Court admitted parol proof of the debt, on the ground that the form of the contract and the proof of the execution must be governed by the law of the place of the execution. The intention of the parties was to bind themselves by the law of the place where they were at the time. So in Scotland, a contract verbally concluded in England and valid there, may be proved in Scotland and receive effect, although writing would have been required to constitute the contract in Scotland.[1] In both these last mentioned countries, therefore, the rule *locus regit actum* receives a more liberal extension than it does in England. But there is a further distinction between the English application of the rule *locus regit actum* and that followed (according to an overwhelming majority of precedents) on the Continent and, in a modified form, in Scotland. The English view,[2] as we have seen, is that the rule is imperative, subject only to the limitations already discussed. But according to the prevailing view on the Continent the rule in question merely imports a faculty, it does not involve any compulsion or restriction upon the parties.[3] Accordingly, mutual contracts may either be in conformity with the forms of the *lex loci contractus*, or with the forms which are recognized at the domicil of both the contracting parties. So in cases in which there are several joint obligants or subsidiary obligants in-

[1] *Dale* v. *Dumbarton Glass Co.* (1829), 7 Ct. of Sess. Repts., 1st Series, p. 369.

[2] Per Lord Ellenborough in *Clegg* v. *Levy* (1812), 3 Camp. 167.

[3] Bar, § 123, pp. 274—278, Gillespie's translation.

CHAP. V.

volved, the question is open to the same considerations for every one of them. But the Scotch Courts take a middle line. They admit the imperative nature of the rule, unless where the forms prescribed by the *lex loci solutionis* are adopted, and will therefore recognize a contract, and give effect to it, if the formalities of the law of the place of performance are, instead of those of the place of execution, observed in concluding the contract.[1] In regard to bills of exchange, the English statute (45 & 46 Vict. c. 61, s. 72 (1)), as already pointed out,[2] while adopting as a general rule the law of the place of issue as regulating the validity of a bill as regards requisites in form, recognizes two broad exceptions, namely, *first*, that where a bill is issued out of the United Kingdom it is not invalid by reason only that it is not stamped in accordance with the law of the place of issue; and *second*, that where a bill, issued out of the United Kingdom, conforms as regards requisites in form to the law of the United Kingdom, it may, *for the purpose of enforcing payment thereof*, be treated as valid as between all persons who negotiate, hold, or become parties to it *in the United Kingdom*.[3] With respect to wills of foreigners, so far as they affect personal property, an English Court will apply the *lex domicilii* of the testator in deciding all matters relating to formalities of execution. But in respect to wills executed since the 6th August, 1861, by British subjects, the question as to requisites of form is now regulated, in the United Kingdom, by the statute which has already been quoted (*i.e.*, 24 & 25 Vict. c. 114).[4] A distinction is drawn by that

[1] Per Lord President Inglis, in *Valery* v. *Scott* (1876), 3 Ct of Sess. Repts., 4th Series, p. 965.

[2] See § 60, *ante*.

[3] Section 136 of the *Indian Negotiable Instruments Act*, 1881, follows the same rule. See also as to stamping of bills drawn out of British India, and subsequently negotiated in India, § 5 of the *Indian Stamp Act*, 1879.

[4] And in India, in the case of wills executed on or after the 1st January, 1866, by persons other than Hindus, Muhammadans, or Buddhists, by

statute between wills made by British subjects out of or within the United Kingdom. In the case of the former (§ 1), a will of personal estate will be held to be well executed if made (1) according to the forms required either by the law of the place where the same was made; or (2) by the law of the place where such person was domiciled when the same was made; or (3) by the laws then in force in that part of Her Majesty's dominions where he had his domicil of origin. In the case of the latter, the forms prescribed by the third of the above alternatives must be observed.

International rule for the interpretation of contracts.

65. Passing now to the interpretation of contracts, we shall, with Savigny,[1] confine the subject to the solution of the doubts which may spring from the wording of them. We have seen[2] that in regard to bills of exchange it is not very clear in what sense the English Legislature used the term "interpretation;" and by some foreign writers[3] it is assumed to include the whole subject-matter of contracts. But confining "interpretation" to mean, in the limited sense recommended by Savigny, the construction of what the parties really meant by the language employed by them, it is, of course, manifest that the true intention of the parties must be the primary guide in this matter. If that intention is made sufficiently clear from their words, as expressed in the document, where their agreement is in writing, or from their acts or surrounding circumstances, the intention must above all considerations receive due effect wherever a Court has to adjudicate upon their rights or liabilities. Language, however, is not always skilfully used, and it thus very often happens that the words employed by the parties do not very clearly express their meaning, either because

Act X. of 1865. The excepted persons are governed in the matter of making wills by their own personal laws.

[1] *System*, Vol. VIII., § 374, pp. 243, 244, Guthrie's translation.

[2] *Vide* § 62, *ante*.

[3] Fiore, § 183, p. 200; Laurent, Vol. VII., §§ 479—482, pp. 582—590; Wharton, §§ 431—439.

CHAP. V.

they are capable of a double meaning, and the particular sense in which they have been employed is not indicated with sufficient distinctness, or because their collocation is defective, and they fail in consequence to convey any intelligent meaning. Or, again, particular words may have acquired a particular technical meaning. In all such cases a Court has to import rules of construction to aid it in the interpretation of the contract, and where the parties belong to different nationalities, or the contract is made in one country and is to be performed in another, the primary question will be—To what national law the Court is to look for such rules? Starting, therefore, with the principle that the intention of the parties is the fundamental guide to all rules of construction, it is supplemented in certain unexpressed or doubtful cases by *presumptions* or *primâ facie* rules, based, as was observed by the Court of Appeal in *Jacobs* v. *Crédit Lyonnais*,[1] "upon common sense, upon business convenience, and upon the comity of nations." One of these presumptions (subject of course to being displaced wherever the clear intention of the parties can be gathered from the contract itself) is, that the law of the country where the contract is made governs the interpretation of it. This is very explicitly laid down by Lord Esher, M. R., in a very recent case,[2] in accordance with previous authorities.[3] That was a case of a contract made in London, written in English, for carriage of goods on board a German ship. In the course of his judgment, the learned Master of the Rolls pointed out the general rule that, in the case of a foreign contract, the Court which has the duty of construing it must do so according to the canons of construction

[1] (1884), 12 Q. B. D. 599. Cf. also Story, *Conflict of Laws*, § 27.

[2] *The Industrie* (1894), 6 Reports, 31.

[3] For instance, in *King of Spain* v. *Machado*, 4 Russ. 225, 239; *Duncan* v. *Campbell* (1842), 12 Sim. 616; *Di Sora* v. *Phillips* (1863), 10 H. of L. 633; *Jacobs* v. *Crédit Lyonnais* (1884), 12 Q. B. D. 599.

in use in the country to which it belongs. And in dealing with the question of the intention of the parties, he observed, that the intention as to what law was to be applied to the construction was to be gathered not from *one* fact, but from *all* the facts relating to the contract. It thus appears that the rule favoured by the English Courts is that the *lex loci celebrationis* applies, unless the contrary is shown to have been the intention of the parties. If it appears that they have contracted with reference to a particular foreign law, that intention will be respected within the limits of the reference, and not generally.[1] So that where an English policy provided for general average "as per judicial foreign statement," it was held that the foreign law could not be invoked to decide what were and what were not "perils of the sea."[2]

Law governing construction of marriage contracts and wills.

66. In the case of marriage contracts and wills, however, there is a strong tendency to apply, in the former case, the law of the domicil of the husband at the celebration of marriage,[3] and, in the latter case, that of the testator at the date of the will, as the proper interpreter of all doubtful expressions and provisions. In the case of *Chamberlain* v. *Napier*,[4] the decision really turned upon the intention of the parties, and it was inferred from the trusts of the marriage contract that one set should be construed as being English and the other as being Scotch. For it is undoubtedly open to the spouses domiciled in one country to select the law of another as the law that shall construe their contract. And an inference to this effect may be drawn from the language of the contract, if it discloses an intention to live in a particular

[1] Cf. *Ex parte Dever, Re Suse and Smith*, 18 Q. B. D. 660.

[2] *Greer* v. *Poole* (1880), 5 Q. B. D. 272.

[3] Westlake, § 39, p. 71, 3rd ed.; Bar, § 188, p. 422, Gillespie's translation. And as regards the law of Scotland showing this tendency, cf. *Earl of Stair* v. *Head* (1844), 6 Ct. of Sess. Repts., 2nd Series, 905; and *Anstruther* v. *Adair* (1834), 2 M. & K. 513.

[4] (1880), 15 Ch. D. 614.

CHAP. V.

country, and to be ruled by its law.[1] Generally speaking, however, it is the law of the matrimonial domicil, as being the place in which the performance of the contract is contemplated, and that from which the personal law of one party at least is derived, to which the interpretation of a marriage settlement or contract will be referred.[2] Bar, indeed, argues in favour of dealing with marriage contracts like other obligatory contracts, and thus referring the interpretation of all doubtful expressions to the law of the place of the execution of the contract.[3] But the English rule appears to be settled as stated. As to wills of *personal* estate, there is a consensus of authorities that all questions affecting the proper construction of the documents must be decided in accordance with the testator's domicil (at the date of the will if there has been any subsequent change of domicil between that date and the date of the testator's decease), unless there is sufficient on the face of the will to show a different intention in the testator.[4] Thus in *Enohin* v. *Wylie*,[5] Lord Westbury says: "To the Court of the domicil belongs the interpretation and construction of the will of the testator." So in *Anstruther* v. *Chalmer*,[6] where a Scotch lady died domiciled in England, having made a will in the Scotch form whilst on a visit to Scotland, it was held that the law of England governed the construction of the will, with the consequence that the gift to a legatee who had died in the testator's lifetime lapsed, although this would not have occurred under the Scotch law,

1 *Earl of Stair* v. *Head*, 7 Ct. of Sess. Repts., 2nd Ser., 905.

2 Westlake, § 39, pp. 71, 72, 3rd ed.

3 Bar, § 188, p. 423, Gillespie's translation.

4 Westlake, § 123, p. 134, 3rd ed. Cf. Burge, Vol. II., pp. 857, 858; Story, *Conflict of Laws*, §§ 479 *et seq.*; Fiore, I., § 183, p. 200; Laurent, Vol. VII., § 483, p. 590.

5 (1862), 10 H. of L. 1. This case was not governed by Lord Kingsdown's Act.

6 (1826), 2 Sim. 1.

in the technical language of which the will was written. And in accordance with this rule, the currency in which a legacy is given must in general be interpreted to be that of the testator's domicil.[1] But by the law of Scotland (as it was by that of England prior to Lord Kingsdown's Act[2]) it is still said the law of the *last* domicil will regulate the construction of testamentary instruments in regard to moveables, unless the frame of the deed, the circumstances of its execution, and the history of the testator, point to another law as intended by the testator to be taken as the canon of construction.[3] In questions as to real estate, the same law recognizes the supremacy of the *lex rei sitæ* in matters of construction of wills as in all other matters affecting such property. It will be presumed to supply the test for the interpretation of ordinary non-technical language, or of words which have a technical meaning in the law language of the *situs*. If such words have a double technical meaning, according as the law of the *situs* or the law of the place of execution of the document or of the testator's domicil is applied, the presumption will always be in favour of the *lex situs* in case of doubt as to which meaning was intended by the testator. If, however, foreign words are used, they must be so translated as the intention of the testator shall receive due effect.[4] As regards the English doctrine for the construction of wills relating to

[1] *Saunders* v. *Drake* (1742), 2 Atk. 465; *Pierson* v. *Garnet* (1786), 2 Bro. C. C. 38.

[2] 24 & 25 Vict. c. 114. The general language of sect. 3 would seem to render it applicable to the testaments of aliens, although the title of the Act, if it could be referred to for the purpose of interpretation of the enacting part, would limit its operation to wills of personal estate made by "*British subjects.*"

[3] Cf. Gillespie's Note OO. on Bar, § 377, p. 830. Mr. Gillespie does not notice the effect of Lord Kingsdown's Act. The *Indian Succession Act* has no express rule on this point, but in regard to succession to *moveable* property it recognises the law of the country in which the testator had his domicil *at the time of his death* (sect. 5).

[4] *Ibid.*, p. 830.

CHAP. V. immoveables, any stringent rule of interpretation existing by the *lex situs* of the immoveables concerned will no doubt be recognized as preventing the will from affecting the immoveables, except in accordance with it. But otherwise, and in order to give due effect to the real intention of the testator, an English Court will look to all the circumstances, including the domicil of the testator.[1] Foote, indeed, goes further, and states that "the construction of wills is in *all* cases a matter for the law of the domicil alone, even when the destination of immoveables situate in some country other than that of the domicil is affected by it."[2] He quotes in support of this statement the decision in the Scotch appeal of *Trotter* v. *Trotter*,[3] in which Lord Lyndhurst no doubt said: "A will must be interpreted according to the law of the country where it was made, and where the party making the will has his domicil." But Lord Lyndhurst was here merely stating a general rule, and his language must be considered with reference to the class of case he was dealing with, which was where the heir-at-law is put to an election between immoveables, as to which a devise was inoperative by the *lex situs*, and money given him by the will: the question being one of the construction and operation of a will as affecting the disposition of the *moveable* estate, the law of the place where the will was made and where the testator had his domicil was, in accordance with the rule already given, naturally applied. There is certainly nothing in the decision which can be said to ignore the qualification of the supremacy of the *lex situs*, where that law contains a stringent rule for the construction of wills affecting immoveables governed by it, and an English Court accustomed to recognize this supremacy in regard to English

[1] Westlake, § 170, p. 193, 3rd ed. Cf. also Wharton, §§ 592 and 597.

[2] *Private Inter. Jurisprudence*, 2nd ed., p. 199. And cf. Phillimore, Vol. IV., §§ 866 and 867.

[3] (1829), 4 Bligh, N. S. 502; *S. C.*, 3 Wils. & Sh. 407.

land[1] is least of all likely to do so. And we come to this conclusion with less hesitation seeing that, in the later case of *Yates* v. *Thomson*,[2] Lord Brougham distinctly affirmed the qualification. "Accordingly," he says, "where the question is what a person intended by an instrument relating to the conveyance of a real estate situated in a foreign country, *and where the lex loci rei sitæ must govern*, we decide upon his meaning by *that* law, and *not* by the law of his country where the deed was executed, because we consider him to have had that foreign law in his contemplation."

Interpretation affected by commercial and agricultural customs.

67. The interpretation of a contract may also be affected by the existence of commercial or agricultural customs. It will be presumed, until the contrary is proved, that the parties have contracted with reference to them. Thus a lease of English land made abroad will be construed in England with reference to the agricultural customs of the country where the land is requisite—another instance of the supremacy of the *lex situs*—for such customs are deemed to be part of the Common Law of the land, and are enforced as such, except when excluded by proof that the parties intended otherwise. So in regard to commercial customs, the rule to be followed is explained by Lord Kingsdown[3] in these terms: "When evidence of the usage of a particular place is admitted to add to or in any manner affect the construction of a written contract, it is admitted only on the ground that the parties who made the contract are both cognizant of the usage, and must be presumed to have made their agreement with reference to it. But no such presumption can arise when one of the parties is ignorant of it."

[1] Cf. Lord Mansfield's decision in *Robinson* v. *Bland* (1760), 2 Burr. 1079, cited *ante*, § 64, p. 128, n. 5.

[2] (1835), 3 Cl. & Fin. 585, 588.

[3] In *Kirchner* v. *Venus* (1859), 12 Moo. P. C. 361, 399.

CHAP. V.

Proper law governing questions arising out of agency.

68. The subject of agency presents but little scope for specific treatment in an international sense, and positive authority on questions connected with it is very meagre. It may be considered, however, in its relation (1) to the principal, and (2) to third parties, and with reference to the authority of the agent, ratification by the principal of unauthorized acts of the agent, and the revocation of the agent's authority. As between the principal and his agent, the *form* of the contract of agency and the extent and character of the authority conferred by it, where this is not sufficiently indicated by the terms of the instrument itself, will, no doubt, generally speaking, be determined by the law of the country where the contract was made.[1] This rule, however, or rather the last branch of it, presupposes that the parties to such a contract have met together in a certain place, and have made a contract there in the presence of each other, intending, presumably, to submit themselves to the law of that place. But this may not always happen. Suppose, for instance, a merchant in England orders his correspondent in Paris to buy goods for him there, which the correspondent executes. In such a case, the approved opinion is that the contract between the principal (*mandans*) and the agent (*mandatarius*) is created in the place of residence of the agent.[2] In the absence of anything to indicate a contrary intention, the fact that a person is authorized to act as an agent in a *foreign* country, where he is resident, and where he receives his authority, is thus taken to show that the relation between principal and agent would be governed by the law of that country, where it is deemed to be created by the person accepting the duties

[1] *Great Northern Rail. Co.* v. *Laing* (1848), 10 Ct. of Sess. Repts., 2nd Series, 1408; *Kerslake* v. *Clark* (1820), More's Notes to Stair, Vol. VI., quoted by Gillespie in his translation of Bar, Note S. to §§ 267—269, p. 592, 2nd ed.

[2] Story, § 286; Phillimore, Vol. IV., § 702.

of agency. In dealings with third parties the law of England, Scotland, and America acts upon the principle *qui facit per alium, facit per se*, in determining what law shall regulate the rights and obligations of the principal against, and to third parties arising out of contracts effected through, an agent. The contract in such a case will be treated as if it had been concluded by the principal in person. "If I send an agent," said Lord Chancellor Lyndhurst, in a Scotch appeal,[1] "to reside in Scotland, and he, in my name, enters into a contract in Scotland, the contract is to be considered mine where it is actually made. It is not an English contract because I actually reside in England. If my agent executes it in Scotland, it is the same as if I were myself on the spot, and executed it in Scotland." The same view has very recently been taken as to the Scotch law, even in cases of undisclosed principals, by Lord Kyllachy, who propounds the general rule to be, "that whether the principal is disclosed or undisclosed, contracts made by an agent on behalf of his principal are the contracts of his principal, who may sue and be sued upon them, and to whom, in the case of sale, the property passes by delivery to the agent." Accordingly, the nature and extent of an agent's authority are to be measured, against third parties, by the law of the place where he is acting as agent.[3] But the English law will certainly require

[1] *Albion Insurance Co.* v. *Mills* (1828), 3 Wils. & S. 218, 233; 1 Dow. & Cl. 342. Cf. Story, *Conflict of Laws*, § 285; Fiore, I., § 130, p. 164, adopting the opinion of Casageris, *Disc.* 179, n. 2; Esperson, *Il principio di nazionalità*, p. 138; Masse, *Droit Commercial*, I., p. 482. Cf. Laurent, VII., §§ 454—455, who seems to admit the general principle stated in the text, but finds a difficulty in its application when the foreign agent happens also to be the vendor of the goods ordered by the principal. Casageris and the Italian jurists reply that as the agent fully represents the absent principal, the vendor and purchaser must both be deemed to be present at the place where the agent resides, and thus the law of the latter place is the law which would always govern.

[2] *Delaurier* v. *Wyllie* (1889), 17 Ct. of Sess. Repts., 4th Series, at p. 191.

[3] *Maspons y Hermano* v. *Mildred* (1882), 9 Q. B. D. 530, affirmed (on

the question of an undisclosed principal's right to sue, if the contract is made by a foreign agent of a foreign principal with an Englishman to be performed in England, to be determined by the law of the contract between the agent and the third party—that is to say, the English law, and not by the law of the mandate or agency. And the rule that an undisclosed principal is liable on the contracts which are made on his behalf by his agent, is not applicable to the case of a foreign constituent contracting by an English commission merchant in England. "The great inconvenience that would result," said Blackburn, J., in *Armstrong* v. *Stokes*,[1] "if there were privity of contract established between the foreign constituents of a commission merchant and the home suppliers of the goods has led to a course of business, in consequence of which it has been long settled that a foreign constituent does not give the commission merchant authority to pledge his credit to those from whom the commissioner buys them by his order and on his account." So also the Indian Contract Act (sect. 230 (1)) provides that where a contract is made by an agent for the sale or purchase of goods for a merchant resident abroad, it shall be presumed to be enforceable by or against the agent personally. In connection, moreover, with contracts by agents in England with reference to goods situated in England, the provisions of the Factors Act, 1889 (52 & 53 Vict. c. 45), are to be kept in mind. By that Act a mercantile agent has power to give a good title to *bonâ fide* third parties by sale, pledge, or other disposition of the goods of which he is in possession by consent of the true owner, and the Indian law is to the same effect.[2] Accord-

different grounds) sub nom. *Mildred* v. *Maspons* (1883), 9 App. Cas. 874, Cf. Phillimore, Vol. IV., § 705.

[1] (1872), L. R., 7 Q. B. 598, 605; *Hutton* v. *Bullock* (1873), L. R. 8 Q. B. 331; 9 *ibid.* 572.

[2] *Vide* sect. 178 of the Indian Contract Act; and cf. sect. 108 *ibid.* as to

ingly, as these laws permit real rights to be constituted by contracts made between the agent and third parties, without considering the nature of the agent's authority under his mandate, the principal will be held bound by such contracts without regard to the law which determines the character of the agency in other respects. This is the result, as Bar[1] points out, of the universal validity of the *lex rei sitæ* in the law of things. In the case of maritime contracts made in a foreign port, the law of the flag which the ship carries being the law which would presumably govern contracts made by the owner himself if he were present in person and contracting, will also govern such contracts made on behalf of the owner by the shipmaster. This is very clearly enunciated by Blackburn, J., in *Lloyd* v. *Guibert*,[2] where he is reported to have said: "We think that the power of the master to bind his owners personally is but a branch of the general law of agency. And it seems clear that if a principal gives a mandate to an agent containing a condition that all contracts which the agent makes on behalf of his principal shall be subject to a defeasance, those who contract through that agent, *with notice of that mandate containing such a limit on his authority*, cannot hold the principal bound absolutely. And, we think, as far as regards the implied authority of the master of the ship to bind his owners personally, the flag of the ship is notice to all the world that the master's authority is that conferred by the law of that flag—*that his mandate is contained in the law of that country*, with which those who deal with him must make themselves acquainted at their peril." In regard to the effect of ratification by the principal of unauthorized acts of his agent, inasmuch as a subsequent

sales. Cf. *Brocklesby* v. *Temperance Permanent Building Society*, (1893) 3 Ch. 130.

[1] § 269, p. 590, Gillespie's translation.

[2] (1865), L. R. 1 Q. B. 115.

CHAP. V.

affirmation or recognition of an act which was originally voidable gives validity to it from its inception (*omnis ratihabitio retrotrahitur et mandato priori æquiparatur*), so the contract, when ratified, would seem to be rightly governed, as between the principal and the third party, by the law of the place of contract, and not by that of the place of ratification.[1] Hertius, however, would draw a distinction between a ratification which has for its object to supply additional proof or weight to the contract (*ad conciliandum contractui majorem fidem*), and a ratification which gives validity to the contract (*ut contractus sit validus*). In the former case, in his opinion, the law of the place of the contract would prevail, but in the latter that of the place of ratification. This opinion Phillimore[2] thinks is not unreasonable. But the rule as previously stated appears to be based on a sounder principle, and is approved by Story, while that suggested by Hertius makes the decision unnecessarily complicated. There is as little unanimity amongst juristical writers in regard to the proper law governing a revocation of the agent's authority. Upon principle, the question as to its effect upon transactions concluded by the agent in ignorance of it would seem to necessarily depend, as between the principal and third parties who have dealt with the agent in the *bonâ fide* belief that his authority continued—as, for instance, in ignorance of the principal's death—upon the same law which regulates the transaction of business by an agent for a foreign principal: in other words, its effect is to be decided according to the law of the State where the agent is acting as

[1] Story, *Conflict of Laws*, § 286, n.; Fiore, I., § 131, p. 165. But Laurent combats this view and maintains that as the ratification alone gives validity to a contract which an agent has entered into without authority, it is the law of the country where the ratification takes place which ought to govern. Vol. VII., §§ 457, 458, pp. 546 *et seq.*

[2] Phillimore, Vol. IV., § 703.

such.[1] Story, indeed, inclines to the application of the law of the State where the principal resides;[2] but his opinion in this matter appears to be based on analogies which are at least questionable, and is itself unsound and unjust. The Italian jurist Fiore[3] goes, perhaps, to the opposite extreme in holding that, *even as between the principal and agent*, the death of the former would not necessarily put an end to the relation created by the agency, if that relation would still continue to subsist in regard to transactions completed by the agent in ignorance of the fact of his principal's death, by the law of the place in which the agency was to have operation. We have already seen that no theory of testing contracts of agency, as between the immediate parties, exclusively by the law of the place where they are to have effect, can be absolutely set up. The place where the contract was made will generally, in the absence of any contrary intention, rule the relation between the parties to it; but circumstances may occur where the completion of the contract must be referred to the place where the agent resides, in which case the law of that place will be presumed to govern the relation. Fiore's view does not fit in with either of these rules, and is open to a serious objection raised by Bar,[4] founded on the practice, which is said not to be uncommon, of the operation of powers of attorney not being confined to any particular place, but which are intended to have effect wherever the person holding the power thought fit to use it. If Fiore's theory were followed in the case supposed, the relation of principal and agent would have to be ruled by an infinite variety of local laws, which would be very embarrassing in determining the rights and liabilities of those parties *inter se*. But the

[1] Phillimore, Vol. IV., § 705; Fiore, I., §§ 129, 130, pp. 163, 164.

[2] *Conflict of Laws*, § 286d.

[3] Sect. 335.

[4] *Private Inter. Law*, § 269, p. 591, Gillespie's translation.

CHAP. V.

German jurist is not content with merely exposing the fallacy of his Italian contemporary's doctrine on this subject. He next dissents from Phillimore's criticism on Story. "If a man," he says, "contracts as the agent of a foreigner on the ground of a power of attorney given him in a foreign country, the third party contracting with him cannot reasonably be held excused, if he makes no enquiry at all as to the foreign law by which that power of attorney is ruled. The principle of protecting a third party who contracts in good faith must have some limitation, if it is not to be turned into a source of legal uncertainty. As, then, in the case we have put (that of a transaction concluded by an agent, in ignorance of the mandant's (principal's) death, in his name in favour of a *bonâ fide* third party), the third party is much better able to protect himself than the person who gave the power of attorney—supposing that this power of attorney is, as the solution given by Phillimore suggests, to subject him to a law of which he knows nothing—then, in the interest of legal security, we must decide in favour of the person who gave the power of attorney"[1]—that is to say, by the law of *his* domicil, according to which (in the case supposed) the death of the principal would *ipso facto* cause a revocation of the agent's authority. But this reasoning is scarcely convincing. It may, of course, be conceded that it is the duty of a third party to make himself acquainted with the nature and limits of the power conferred upon an agent by his absent principal. Where the instrument conferring the power speaks plainly on the point, it is no doubt conclusive in determining whether the agent's acts are within the scope of his authority. But where that instrument or power of attorney is not explicit, there would seem to be not only nothing unreasonable in measuring the nature and extent of the agent's authority, so

[1] § 269, p. 591, Gillespie's translation.

far as third parties may be affected by it, by the law of the place where the agent is found acting as such, but it is by that law that every one who deals with the agent there must presumably be held to have had clearly in view, and to have regulated his inquiries. This, at all events, is the theory which the English Courts,[1] as well as those of France[2] and Louisiana,[3] act upon.

Proper law applicable to torts committed abroad.

69. We have now completed our inquiry as to the proper law by which the validity, the form, and the interpretation of obligations, whether expressly arising out of contract or out of relations resembling those created by contract, and which are usually described as *quasi ex contractu*, must be regulated in view of Private International Law. But there are obligations of still another kind, which do not rest upon any intention to create a legal duty of this nature, or which cannot be said to arise out of any relation resembling one created by contract. Obligations of the kind here referred to are those which are commonly spoken of as arising *ex delicto* or *quasi ex delicto*, and are also included in the general denomination of torts. The law to be applied internationally for the determination of claims arising out of such obligations depends upon the adoption of one of two prevailing theories, namely, that which maintains the exclusive authority of the *lex loci delicti commissi*, and that which insists upon a concurrence of the *lex fori* and *lex loci delicti commissi* in order that an act or omission may be deemed tortious. The former is the theory adopted by Continental nations[4] (although Germany, under the influence of Savigny[5] and Wächter,

[1] See *Maspons y Hermano* v. *Mildred* (1882), 9 Q. B. D. 539, above cited.

[2] *Code Civil*, Art. 2008.

[3] *Code Civil of Louisiana*, § 300.

[4] *Vide Nouveau Traité de Droit Inter. Privé*, by C. Brocher, p. 315.

[5] *System*, Vol. VIII., § 374, p. 254, Guthrie's translation,

will recognize nothing but the *lex fori*), and is thus supported by one of its latest and ablest exponents. "We must," writes Bar,[1] "recognize everywhere claims of damages which have validly arisen according to the law of the place where the act was done. It is only by holding fast to this principle that we shall achieve a real equality of natives and foreigners in relations of private law in all civilised States, and it is only in this way that a man who lives in this or that territory can know on what guarantees for his legal rights he may rely, since foreigners cannot withdraw themselves from their obligations to pay damages by betaking themselves to their own country." Nevertheless in dealing with the question of liability for damage done by beasts, or by other persons, such as children, servants, &c., the same author does not appear to adhere consistently to his main doctrine; on the contrary, he there seems to reach finally much the same conclusion as the advocates of the rival theory would under similar circumstances. "The liability," he says, in such a case, on the one hand, "can never be broader or go further than the law of the place where the damage takes place permits. But just as little can it go beyond what is sanctioned by the law of the nationality or domicil of the person against whom the claim is made. . . . If the *lex fori* should be such as to make the judge who is dealing with the case think that it would be altogether unreasonable to fix liability on the defender, he could not well find him liable even according to the *lex loci actus*."[2] Brocher, also, while maintaining the exclusive authority of the *lex loci delicti commissi*, is constrained to yield to the judge of the *forum* the right of taking into account considerations of "public order." So that from

[1] *Private Inter. Law*, § 286, p. 636, Gillespie's translation.
[2] *Ibid.* § 287, pp. 639, 640, Gillespie's translation.

different standpoints it seems to be admitted that the *lex loci delicti commissi* cannot claim an absolutely exclusive authority. A broad exception in favour of the stringent policies of the law of the *forum* must be allowed. And we have here, at least, a qualified recognition by writers of different schools of juristic thought of the principle of coercitive law, which, rightly understood in the sense accepted by the author himself in an earlier part of his book,[1] requires that the legal system and Courts of a State cannot lend themselves to the direct realisation of legal relations or claims which would be rejected by their law as absolutely untenable. This principle is substantially the basis of the other theory we have mentioned, according to which claims arising out of *delicts* or *quasi delicts* are only sanctioned so far as they can be maintained both by the *lex fori* and the *lex loci actus*. In dealing with such claims the territorial law of each State may not unreasonably assume a coercitive character. In the interests of public order it has the right to regulate men's conduct within its own boundaries, but a rule of conduct proper within those boundaries may not be suitable in the territories of another State. The comity of nations may, it is true, demand that respect should so far be paid by the Courts in State A. to the laws of State B. that the sovereign power of the latter of regulating men's conduct within its boundaries should not be invaded, which would be the case if conduct which did not give rise to a right to damages by the law of the place where the tortious act is committed should be permitted to have this effect, if the action were brought in consequence of it in another country. If this concession to the laws of a foreign country were not allowed, a native who thought that, while abroad, he was wronged by a foreigner, might subsequently assert a claim to damages in conformity

[1] Bar's *Private International Law*, § 36, p. 96, Gillespie's translation.

CHAP. V.

with his own law in his own courts, which would be nothing short of an attempt to make a foreigner, in his own country, conform to another law in regulating his conduct of which he could not be expected to know anything. To sanction such a claim would be palpable injustice. But inasmuch as the domestic tribunals of the State where an action is brought cannot (on the other hand) be required to lend themselves to the realisation of claims which would be rejected by their laws as absolutely untenable, it equally follows that no act which is not an actionable wrong by the *lex fori* should be treated by the *forum* where the action is raised as actionable, merely because it is so by the law of the place where the act was done. Hence the theory now thoroughly established in the jurisprudence of England and the United States, and apparently recognized also by the Scotch Courts, that the *lex fori* and the *lex loci delicti commissi* must concur, in order that an act or omission may be deemed tortious.[1] Formerly, indeed, and for three centuries, the doctrine prevailed that, in respect to wrongs to immoveable property in a foreign country, no action could be brought in an English Court, mainly on the ground that it was absolutely necessary that the locality of the alleged grievance should be within English jurisdiction, where the action in question could be tried according to English law.[2] But since the abolition of the formal distinction between local and transitory actions, effected by the passing of the Judicature Acts,[3] it is doubtful whether the above doctrine, questioned even by Lord Mans-

[1] Per Brett, J., in *Chartered Bank of India* v. *Netherlands India Steam Navigation Co.* (1883), 10 Q. B. D. at pp. 536, 537. Cf. Westlake, §§ 196, 197, pp. 237, 238, 3rd ed.; Foote, pp. 476—481; Phillimore, Vol. IV., Gillespie's Note N. on §§ 286, 287, of Bar, p. 640.

[2] *Skinner* v. *East India Co.* (1665), cited in Cowp. 168; *Doulson* v. *Matthews* (1792), 4 T. R. 503.

[3] 38 & 39 Vict. c. 77; Order XXXVI. r. 1.

field so far back as 1775,[1] would now be maintained in the Supreme Court, there being in it no local venue. In the case of *The M. Moxham*, which was an action brought by an English company who owned a pier in Spain against an English shipowner for damage done to the pier by the defendant's vessel coming into collision with it, and in which the parties had agreed that the dispute thence arising should be tried in England, Lord Justice James observed that, but for such agreement, "Very great difficulties, indeed, might have arisen as to the jurisdiction of this Court to entertain any action or proceedings whatever with respect to injury done to foreign soil."[2] But as regards personal injuries, and wrongs to personal property, the rule is now perfectly settled in England, that no action can be maintained in an English court for such injuries or wrongs, committed within the jurisdiction of a foreign country, unless the act is wrongful by the law of the country where it is committed and also wrongful by the law of England. This was so said by Mellish, J., in the case of *The M. Moxham* already cited, and by Willes, J., in *Phillips* v. *Eyre*.[3] An act, however, may be wrongful in the sense of the public law in the foreign country where it was committed, but yet no civil action may be permitted to be brought with respect to it by the law of that country; or, again, it may be that a civil action is only permitted under conditions, for instance, of first proceeding against the wrongdoer under the criminal law. In the former case, it appears that no action would be permitted in respect of such a wrong in an English court, on the broad ground that the foreign law, by refusing a civil action to the person injured, and only permitting criminal proceedings against the wrongdoer, practically views the act *not* as a

[1] In *Mostyn* v. *Fabrigas*, Cowp. 180.
[2] (1876), 1 P. D. 109.
[3] (1870), L. R. 6 Q. B. 1, 28.

CHAP. V.

wrong to the *individual* but to the *State;* and the case therefore falls within the first part of the general rule formulated by Mellish, J., that the act to be actionable in England must, as a first condition, be wrongful—*i.e.*, in the sense of perpetrating a private wrong—by the law of the country where it is committed. The prosecution of the wrongdoer criminally would only be with the object of the vindication of the law affecting public order, and of deterring others from commission of the like act. This wrong, accordingly, in the case supposed, is not one which, in the country where it was committed, would create a civil obligation to the injured person, and we have already seen, in regard to civil obligations generally, that it is the law of the place where the act which gives rise to the obligation is done that defines its character.[1] The exact point, however, has not been definitely settled in England, and the *obiter* opinions expressed upon it in the case of *Scott* v. *Seymour*[2] were very divergent. But upon principle the sounder view appears to be, that the act must amount to an actionable wrong by the law of the country where it is done, to entitle the injured person to maintain an action for damages upon it in an English court. And this is the view which has very recently been adopted in Scotland.[3] Where, however, the foreign law only postpones the civil remedy till after the criminal law has been vindicated, the matter stands on a different footing. Here the actionable nature of the wrongful act being admitted by the law of the place where it is done, the question of the right mode of pursuing the civil remedy is one that affects procedure, and is

[1] See sect. 63 *ante*, and opinion of Laurent there discussed: and cf. sect. 60. "The civil liability arising out of a wrong," said Willes, J., in *Phillips* v. *Eyre*, "derives its birth from the law of the place, and its character is determined by that law;" (1870), L. R. 6 Q. B. 29.

[2] (1862), 1 H. & C. 219.

[3] *Rosses* v. *Thakur Sahib of Gondul* (1891), 19 Ct. of Sess. Repts., 4th Series, p. 31.

consequently governed by the *lex fori*.[1] Another important question may, however, arise when the act complained of is done in a country over which no municipal law extends, or at least none (as in the case of a country belonging to a savage race) to which the subjects of civilised States can be made subject. In such a case, what law is to govern? Inasmuch as there is no *lex loci delicti commissi* which can be applied, the only recourse obviously is either (1) to the law of the *forum* where the action is brought, or (2) to the personal law of the injured person, or (3) to that of the defendant. The first of these alternatives is the view which is accepted by a leading authority in England[2] and in the United States,[3] but it is rejected by Bar[4] as a dangerous mode of avoiding a difficulty, and replaced by that of the personal law of the person against whom the claim is made. It only remains to add that in the case of torts committed by means of the collision of one ship with another upon the high seas, the extent of liability of the delinquent ship in an English court is now regulated by the Merchant Shipping Act, 1894 (57 & 58 Vict. c. 60), which enacts that:—

The owners of a ship, British or foreign, shall not, where all or any of the following occurrences take place without their actual fault or privity, that is to say,

> Where any loss of life or personal injury is caused to any person carried in any other vessel by reason of the improper navigation of the ship:
>
> Where any loss or damage is caused to any other ship or boat, or to any goods, merchandise or other

[1] Westlake, § 199, p. 239, 3rd ed.; Foote, pp. 482—486.
[2] Foote, p. 481. But cf. Westlake, § 202, p. 242, 3rd ed.
[3] Story, *Conflict of Laws*, § 423.
[4] *Private Inter. Law*, § 287, p. 639, Gillespie's translation.

things whatsoever on board any other vessel by reason of the improper navigation of the ship;

be answerable in damages in respect of loss of life or personal injury, either alone or together with loss or damage to vessels, goods, merchandise, or other things, to an aggregate amount exceeding 15*l*. for each ton of their ship's tonnage; nor in respect of loss or damage to vessels, goods, merchandise, or other things, whether there be in addition loss of life or personal injury or not, to an aggregate amount exceeding 8*l*. for each ton of their ship's tonnage (sect. 503).

Under the previous statute (53 Geo. III. c. 159, § 1), the limitation of liability not being in express terms extended to foreigners, it was held that the statute was only applicable to cases where *both* the litigants were British, and that consequently the English law could not be invoked either for or against either plaintiff or defendant in an English Court where a foreign ship was concerned.[1] The statute, in fact, was treated[2] as a contract that, whereas by the natural law the owner of the ship or property that has been injured would be entitled to damages to the full extent of the loss that he has sustained, all those persons upon whom the Legislature can impose such a contract, shall forego that which the natural law—the Common Law as we should call it in England—would give them, and shall be entitled only to the amount of the value of the ship by which the injury had been inflicted, and of the freight due, or to grow due, in respect of such ship during the voyage—this being the limit fixed by the former Act. How far such a theory of a contract could be successfully maintained according to juristic principles, or how far the British Legislature could impose such a contract upon foreigners, are questions which would

[1] *Cope* v. *Doherty* (1858), 4 K. & J. 367; affirmed (1858), 2 D. J. 614; *The Wild Ranger* (1862), 1 Lush. 553.

[2] Per Wood, V.-C. (afterwards Lord Hatherley), in *Cope* v. *Doherty*.

now only possess an academic interest. The later statute has distinctly extended the limitation of liability to the owners of foreign ships, and no British Court could do otherwise than obey the command of the Legislature to which the law it administers is subject. The question was indeed raised in *The Amalia*,[1] very shortly after the statute of 1862 was passed, that this statute had only limited the *liability* of foreign owners of ships, and had not affected the *rights* of foreign owners against British owners. But the Privy Council held that the statute applied whenever the rights or liabilities of foreign owners came in question in an English Court, so far as to limit their right to recover and their liability to pay damages by one and the same rules. Accordingly, it is no longer open to foreign owners to plead the law of their flag as exempting them from liability when sued as defendants in a British Court for damage by collision at sea. Thus, in the case of *The Leon*,[2] Spanish owners were held to be subject to liability in England for damage caused on the high seas wholly by the negligence of the master or mariners, notwithstanding that by the law of Spain they were freed from liability in such a case. But although the measure of the remedy which a British Court may award to or against a foreign owner of a ship may be governed by the English statute, there are other questions relating to sailing and navigation in respect to which the regulations prescribed by the British Merchant Shipping Acts cannot be held to bind foreign owners outside the limits of British territorial jurisdiction. These are regulations of a purely municipal character, which cannot be imposed upon or claimed to be enforced by foreigners against British owners in the case of collisions on the open seas, inasmuch as they have no real connection with the measure of remedy which a British

[1] (1863), 1 Moo. P. C. N. S. 471.
[2] (1881), 6 P. D. 148.

CHAP. V. Court can award, and the British Legislature cannot claim, and is not to be assumed as attempting to exercise, a power of regulating the conduct of foreign vessels on the high seas. Accordingly, the rule of the road to be followed when two ships are in danger of collision at sea, is that which is *common* to their flags, or if at the time no rule is common to their flags, then by the rule which was once common to all maritime nations of Europe, and which is presumed to continue to exist in the absence of any other common rule applicable to both ships.[1] The principle to be applied in such a case is that the law of the place where an action originated is to govern, while the forms of remedies and the order of judicial proceedings are to be referred to the *lex fori*.[2] Thus, in *The Zollverein*,[3] it was contended on behalf of the owners of a Russian brig, in defence to an action brought against them by the owners of a British vessel, that the British vessel had violated the rule of the road laid down in § 296 of the Merchant Shipping Act, 1854, and was thus responsible for the collision that had occurred. But Dr. Lushington held that the English statute was inapplicable in determining the merits of a collision between a foreign and a British vessel. "I am of opinion," he said, "that, in its true meaning, § 296 is wholly applicable to the merits of the case; it determines how vessels shall conduct themselves at the time of collision on the high seas; *the Legislature of this country has no power to bind foreign vessels in such a condition*. It is true that § 298 relates to remedy, but the application of the section is entirely founded on, and emanates from, § 296. Then comes the question whether, in a trial of the merits of a collision, a foreigner may urge in his defence that the British vessel,

[1] Westlake, § 205, p. 246, 3rd ed.
[2] Story, *Conflict of Laws*, § 558.
[3] (1856), Swab. 96.

though free by the law maritime,[1] has violated his own municipal law, and so, being plaintiff, cannot recover? Reverse the position: suppose the foreigner plaintiff, and to have done his duty by the law maritime. I am clear that he must recover for the damage done; if so, it is contrary to equity to say that the British shipowner, *in eâdem conditione*, shall not recover against the foreigner. What right can the foreigner have to put forward British statute law, to which he is not amenable, so far as the merits are concerned?" In this case the collision occurred in the open seas, outside therefore the limit of the territorial waters of England. But in *The Saxonia*,[2] the collision took place in the Solent, between the Isle of Wight and the mainland of Hampshire, and consequently within the three mile limit from the coast, which the law of nations concedes as falling within the territorial jurisdiction of the State to which the coast belongs.[3] But it was nevertheless held that the British statu-

[1] The law here spoken of is that which the English Court of Admiralty is accustomed to apply to certain transactions happening out of British dominions, to which the ordinary statute law of the realm does not, in the absence of an expressed intention to that effect, apply. In this sense it was no doubt correctly described, "to avoid periphrasis," as "the law of England," by the Court of Appeal, in *Lloyd* v. *Guibert* (1865), L. R. 1 Q. B. 125. But it is not a law peculiar to England; it is founded upon, and has no doubt originated from, the principles and practice followed by all, or at least a majority of, maritime nations, the product, as it were, of approved maritime usage, and not peculiar to one nation, or anomalous in itself.

[2] *The Eclipse and The Saxonia* (1862), 15 Moo. P. C. 262; 1 Lush. 410.

[3] Cf. the English Territorial Waters Act, 1878 (41 & 42 Vict. c. 73), which defines territorial waters of Her Majesty's dominions as "any part of the open sea within one marine league of the coast, measured from low-water mark." At the meeting of the Institute of International Law at Paris for 1894, one of the chief questions dealt with was as to the proper limits of jurisdiction in territorial waters. The resolutions finally arrived at declared, *inter alia*, that territorial waters should extend to *six marine miles* (reckoning sixty miles to each degree of latitude) from low-water mark, or in the case of bays and straits, where their width does not exceed the width of twelve marine miles at the mouth, subject, however, to any continuous usage by which any greater extent may have been established (*Revue de Droit International*, Brussels, Vol. XXVI., No. 3).

CHAP. V.

tory rule did not apply to foreign vessels, even within the limit. In the case of *The Repeater* v. *The Braga* or *Kragerœ*,[1] the Court of Admiralty of Ireland, it is true, applied the British statutory rule as between a British and a Norwegian ship, but that was in consequence of a convention between the King of Norway and the Queen of England. There is one other question connected with collisions at sea which may be briefly considered here, namely, how far the compulsory employment of a pilot will exempt the owners of a ship, in an English Court, from liability for damage caused in foreign territorial waters by the pilot's fault, whatever be the flags and the laws of them? For the right solution of this question we must resort to those general principles which are recognized as sound in other departments of private international law, and which, in the absence of any statutory rule or international approved usage to the contrary, must be held to govern in questions of maritime liability also. Now by English statute law (57 & 58 Vict. c. 60, s. 633, "The Merchant Shipping Act of 1894") no owner nor master of any ship is to be "answerable to any person whatever for any loss or damage" occasioned by the fault or incapacity of a qualified pilot within the district where the employment of such a pilot is compulsory. And it has been previously stated to be an established rule of English jurisprudence, that no act done extra-territorially can be treated as a wrong in England which is not such in the defendant, both by the principles of English law and by the law of the place where the act is done. In applying the English statute an English Court holds that the mere compulsory employment of a pilot will not exempt the owners of a ship from a claim for damages, *unless, as in England, the pilot supersedes the master in the control of the ship*. Accordingly, inasmuch as the *lex fori*

[1] (1865), 14 L. T. N. S. 258.

and the *lex loci delicti commissi* must both concur to found an action, in an English court, on a tort committed abroad, it was held by the Judicial Committee of the Privy Council that a suit, founded upon a liability by the law of Belgium, could not be maintained for damages in England, arising from a collision which was due to the act of the pilot, whom the shipowner was compelled by the law of Belgium to employ, and in whose selection he had no voice, on the ground that the pilot could not be regarded as the shipowner's agent, and the shipowner was not, therefore, responsible for the consequences of his act.[1] Where, however, the master does not, by compulsory pilotage, lose the control of the ship in accordance with the rules regulating the employment of pilots prevailing in the territorial waters where the pilot is engaged, the shipowner is not exempt from liability in an English court, although it may be on different grounds to those which the law of the place where the collision occurred would recognize. Thus, where a collision occurred between two English ships on entering the port of Havre, where compulsory pilotage prevails by French law, but by the same law the pilot does not supersede the master in the control of the conduct of the ship, it was held, in England, that a plea of non-liability founded on compulsory pilotage could not be sustained, although it appeared that, as a matter of fact, the master had given up the charge of the vessel to the pilot.[2] The prevailing view

[1] *The Halley* (1868), L. R. 2 P. C. 193. Cf. Abbot *on Shipping*, 12th ed., p. 580.

[2] *Augusta* v. *Chilian* (1887), 5 L. T. 326. Cf. also *The Guy Mannering* (1882), 7 P. D. 132, where the *locus* of the collision was the Suez Canal, the rules of which as to compulsory pilotage are similar to those in force in France; and *The Agnes Otto* (1887), 12 P. D. 56, where the *locus* of the collision was the Danube, and by rule 92 of the International Rules for the Navigation of the Danube, the responsibility of the pilot is confined to pointing out the navigable channels and the peculiarities of the navigation

CHAP. V.

on the Continent, however, is in favour of the exclusive application of the *lex loci actus* to damages resulting from collisions between ships in any harbour, or in waters subject to any definite sovereign power;[1] and this is in accordance with the ordinary rule followed there as to *delicts*.[2] In the case of collisions in English territorial waters the statutory rule is, that in any cases arising in any British court of justice concerning matters happening within British jurisdiction, foreign ships shall, so far as regards such regulations, be treated as if they were British ships.[3] The Court of the German Empire has, in like manner, applied the law of Germany to all collisions occurring in German waters.[4]

of the river, and the captain who abandons the direction of the vessel to the pilot does so on his own responsibility.

[1] Bar, § 327, p. 717, Gillespie's translation.

[2] *Vide* p. 149, *ante*.

[3] Sect. 418, Merchant Shipping Act, 1894 (57 & 58 Vict. c. 60).

[4] Bar, § 327, p. 718, n. 58, Gillespie's translation.

CHAPTER VI.

IMMATERIAL RIGHTS, AND HEREIN OF COPYRIGHT, TRADE-MARKS, AND PATENTS.

CHAP. VI.

Classes of immaterial rights proposed to be considered.

70. In this chapter, those immaterial rights (*jura incorporalia*) will be considered which have received a special consideration in the jurisprudence of most civilized nations under the three general heads of Copyright, Patents, and Trade-marks. From an international aspect these special classes of rights have considerable importance, and various conventions, resting on the principle of reciprocity, exist between different States in respect to them, while in each State they are usually regulated, as in England, by domestic legislation. But a *jus cogens* regulating rights of this description is a product of modern commercial and intellectual activity, and finds no place, for instance, in the jurisprudence of the Roman Empire, which in other branches of the law has furnished Europe with principles and rules for universal guidance, and of imperishable value. Other immaterial rights, such as rights of action and rights of succession, which, as the jurist Casaregis says,[1] are neither moveable nor immoveable, but constitute a class by themselves, have already been considered under the head of Property, although, correctly speaking, they are only the means of obtaining property. These rights, however, are more directly associated with the individual,

[1] "Quæ bona neque dicuntur *mobilia* neque *immobila*, sed *tertiam* speciem componant et dicuntur *incorporalia*," quoted by Story, *Conflict of Laws*, § 399, n. 1.

although immaterial in their nature, than the particular rights included within the same general classification which have been reserved for separate treatment in this chapter. The former must necessarily diminish if their enjoyment is not exclusive and individual, while the latter, arising out of intellectual effort, are capable of common enjoyment without necessarily impairing that of the individual.

Rules of international copyright are founded on reciprocity.

71. Thus, to take the instance of Copyright, which we shall first consider, and which consists in the author's right of prohibition against the public of re-printing and re-publishing his original work, the whole object is not to exclude a common enjoyment of the intellectual product over which it extends its protective ægis, but to so control that enjoyment that the author himself shall be secured a special share of it, as a reward for his intellectual labour, and as an encouragement to other able and gifted men to work for the common good. This was the underlying object[1] of the earliest statute law in England on the subject—that of 8 Anne, c. 19—prior to which the right of an author was of a very uncertain character. And the right only restricts the common enjoyment in a particular way and for a definite period; it commences by publication, and controls re-publication under certain conditions. In the case of an unpublished manuscript, the possibility of future publication has of course to be kept in mind, and if the law did not protect the author in regard to such productions also, he might be deprived of

[1] Cf. *Jeffreys* v. *Boosey* (1854), 24 L. J. Exch. 81; *S. C.*, 4 House of Lords' Rep. 815. And so with respect to the 25 & 26 Vict. c. 68, which first gave copyright in paintings, drawings, and photographs, the object of the statute has been said by Lopes, L.J., to be "to protect property, to protect the artistic faculty in painting, drawing, and photographing, and to prevent any interference by reproduction thereof with either the artist's reputation or the commercial value of the work." *Hanfstaengl* v. *Empire Palace*, (1894) 3 Ch. at p. 131. This decision has since been affirmed by the House of Lords.

all benefit from his intellectual product at the very moment, perhaps, when he was completing lucrative arrangements for its publication. Again, it is right that the option of publication in the first instance, during the author's lifetime, should be left to the author himself. Were this not so the reputation of the author might be seriously affected by the publication of writings which were either never intended by him to be published, or upon which he had not devoted that final revision which the manuscript would no doubt have received at his hands if the publication had been made with his consent. In the interests of the general public, also, it is desirable that the responsibility for publication should primarily rest with, or at least be materially shared by, the author, who under the sense of a personal responsibility would be more likely to produce honest, useful work, which would enhance his reputation, than work of an indifferent character or carelessly executed, which would be certain to seriously injure, if not entirely to wreck, any reputation he may already have acquired, or the chances of any success in the future. But the distinction between the right of an author in *published* writings and that of his rights in *unpublished* products of his brain, may be well illustrated by reference to the view which the common law of England took of this question. After publication the author's exclusive rights are lost at common law.[1] But *before* publication the common law gives him an exclusive right in his work, and this right has been carried to the extent of being applied to letters written and transmitted to the person for whose perusal they were intended. No person, whether the addressee or anyone else, can publish such letters without the writer's consent in his lifetime,[2] or

[1] Per Lord St. Leonards: a view in which Lord Brougham concurred in *Jeffreys* v. *Boosey*.

[2] *Oliver* v. *Oliver* (1878), 11 C. B. N. S. 139. And see as to the law of Scotland, which puts the right on the ground of just and expedient interference for the protection of reputation, Bell's *Principles*, § 1356.

CHAP. VI.

that of his heir after his death; and an injunction can be obtained to prevent a threatened invasion of this right, as it was by the late Earl of Lytton with reference to the unpublished letters of his father.[1] And this common law right is one that is as freely open to, and exerciseable by, a foreigner as by a British subject, to both of whom British courts are open, without distinction, for the vindication of their rights in this, as well as in any other, description of property. But it is especially with reference to his published writings that an author more frequently needs the protection of courts of justice, and it is the increasing facilities which exist for re-publishing literary and artistic work in the author's own, as well as in neighbouring, countries which early induced the Legislature to come to his aid, so far as it was possible to do so within the sphere of its legitimate activity, and which finally led to that important agreement in 1885 between independent States which is known as the Convention of Berne, and which has given to Copyright a truly international character. That Convention was drawn upon the lines sketched by the great German jurist to whose unrivalled work on Private International Law all writers on that subject resort, as to a fountain of universal knowledge and information. Prior to that Convention efforts were no doubt made to arrive at some general international concord on the subject of Copyright, and the German Confederation was foremost in proposing that the right should be as much respected throughout the different States which composed the Confederation as through the different provinces of a single State.

In 1837 the German Diet introduced a Convention upon the subject between the different members of the Confederation, to which Austria and Prussia gave in their

[1] (1885), 54 L. J. Ch. 293.

adherence on behalf of those portions of their territories which did not fall within the jurisdiction of the Confederation. In the same year Prussia, ever active in promoting the recognition of Copyright, passed a law of reciprocity in this matter with all foreign States, and England followed in 1838 by legislating in the same direction (1 & 2 Vict. c. 59), while two years later (in 1840) Austria and Italy entered into a Convention, to which the other States of Italy, and one of the Cantons of Switzerland, gave their adherence. Later on England entered into agreements with Prussia, Hanover, France, Belgium, and Austria-Hungary, whereby the authors and artists of the contracting countries were declared entitled to enjoy the same rights as those which the legislation of each State had granted to its own subjects, with respect to works of literature and art published or edited after a certain date—for instance, after the 17th January, 1852, in France, and the 28th January, 1852, in England. Translations were included within these Conventions, as well as unprinted dramatic works, and articles in newspapers and periodicals which were not of a political character. But it was necessary, to entitle the author to the privilege of Copyright, for him to notify on the title-page that he reserved the right of translation; and with respect to other works of literature and art, that the author should have duly registered the same within three months of their first publication, at certain stated public offices—for instance, in France, at the office of the Minister of the Interior, and in England at Stationers' Hall, with or without the deposit of a copy or of a print, according to the nature of the work and the law of the State. It was not until the passing of the statute 1 & 2 Vict. c. 59, that foreigners, however, were conceded Copyright in England with reference to works first published by them abroad: for neither the common law nor the statute of 8 Anne, c. 19, or of 54 Geo. III. c. 136,

CHAP. VI.

covered such cases.[1] The statute of 1838 was subsequently repealed by 7 & 8 Vict. c. 12; but it is unnecessary to do more than to refer in passing to the latter statute, or to the subsequent ones of 15 & 16 Vict. c. 12, and 38 & 39 Vict. c. 12, as the subject of international Copyright is now mainly regulated, as pointed out in an earlier chapter,[2] by an Act passed in 1886 (49 & 50 Vict. c. 33), the object of which was to give effect to the Convention of Berne[3] of the preceding year. The Act is accordingly strictly one of reciprocity, and § 4 (2) provides that Her Majesty, before making an Order in Council giving effect to the main provisions of the Convention of Berne, shall be satisfied that the foreign country with reference to which the Order is to be made has made such provisions for the protection of the authors of works first produced in the United Kingdom as she shall think expedient. Assuming, therefore, that an Order in Council has been duly made, the foreign author will, in England, be governed by the following rules:—

(a) He shall not have any greater right or longer term of copyright in any work than that enjoyed in the foreign country in which such work was first produced (§ 2, sub-sect. (3));

(b) A literary or artistic work, in which category a photograph is declared to fall,[4] first produced simul-

[1] Cf. *Chappell* v. *Purday* (1845), 14 M. & W. 303; *Jeffreys* v. *Boosey* (1854), 24 L. J. Exch. 81; *S. C.*, 4 House of Lds. Rep. 815; *Boucicault* v. *Delafield* (1864), 33 L. J. Ch. 38; *S. C.*, 9 Jur. 1282; *Cassell* v. *Stiff* (1856), 2 Kay & Johns. Rep. 279; and *Wood* v. *Chart* (1870), L. R. 10 Eq. 193.

[2] *Vide* § 52, *ante*.

[3] This Convention was mutually ratified at Berne on the 5th of September, 1887, on behalf of the Governments of the German Empire, Belgium, Spain, France, England, Italy, Switzerland, Hayti, and Tunis. Cf. "*Morocco Bound*" *Syndicate, Limited* v. *Harris*, (1895) 1 Ch. 534, as to remedy of English author to restrain threatened infringement in a foreign country.

[4] By sect. 11 of the Act of 1886. Cf. *Schauer* v. *I. C. & J. Field*, (1893) 1 Ch. 35. But the representation of pictures by *tableaux vivants*, formed by grouping, in the same way as the figures in the pictures, living persons in the same dress and the same attitudes, is not an infringement of the copy-

taneously in two or more countries of the Copyright Union, shall be deemed, for the purposes of copyright, to have been first produced in that one of those countries in which the term of copyright is shortest (§ 3, sub-sect. (1));

(c) He will be entitled to the same right of preventing the production and importation of any translation in and into the United Kingdom of a book or of a dramatic piece first produced in a foreign country as he would have of preventing the production and importation of the original work; provided that this production shall cease if no translation is produced under the author's licence within ten years after the book, or each number of it, is published (§ 5, sub-sects. (1) and (2));

(d) He will be entitled to the same protection in respect to a lawfully produced translation as in the case of an original work (§ 5, sub-sect. (3));

(e) Any article of political discussion which has been published in any newspaper or periodical in a foreign country may, if its source is acknowledged, be republished or translated in any newspaper or periodical in England. Other articles so published may be republished or translated, unless the author has signified his intention of retaining his copyright and right of translation in some conspicuous part of the newspaper or periodical. If he has done so, his article will receive the same protection as books receive, without the necessity of observing the same formalities (§ 7 of Act 15 & 16 Vict. c. 12, the provisions of which are saved by the Act of 1886);

right. *Hanfstaengl* v. *Empire Palace*, (1894) 2 Ch. 1. See also *Hanfstaengl* v. *Newnes*, (1894) 3 Ch. 109, where it was held that the sketches in the *Daily Graphic* were not copies of plaintiff's pictures, within the meaning of sect. 1 of the Fine Arts Copyright Act, 1862.

CHAP. VI.

(f) Any interests arising from or in connection with any work lawfully produced in the United Kingdom, subsisting or valuable at the date of any Order in Council, shall not be diminished by the terms of the Act of 1886 (§ 6). Thus the rights of a bandmaster who had bought for five shillings the right to perform a French polka before the date of the Order applying the convention to French subjects, were held to be excluded from the operation of the statute of 1886.[1] The same restriction to the otherwise retrospective character of Orders in Council under the Berne Convention is to be found in the Protocol to the Franco-German treaty of 1883, which contains the provision that dramatic and musico-dramatic works, which have been publicly performed in the original or in a translation before that treaty shall have come into force, shall only enjoy protection in the terms in which that was conceded by the treaties concluded previously with the individual States of Germany. But, subject to such legislative restrictions, the effect of conventions of the kind here discussed, both in England and elsewhere, would appear to be, that the protection secured by the treaty will apply to works antecedently published.[2]

How far a foreign author possesses copyright in England outside the provisions of the International Copyright Act of 1886.

72. The question will still remain, By what law are foreign authors to be governed who belong to a nation which has refused, like Russia and the United States of America, to join the Berne Convention, with respect to works first published by them (1) in a foreign country and (2) in England? So far as British Courts are concerned, the answer to the first

[1] *Moul* v. *Grœnings*, (1891) 2 Q. B. 443.

[2] Bar, § 347, pp. 750, 751, Gillespie's translation.

of these questions is simple enough; but the answer to the second is involved in some conflict of opinion. We have already seen that by the common law a work as soon as it is published loses its distinctively individual character of private property, and the author's exclusive rights are thenceforth lost. A foreigner, therefore, with respect to a work previously published in a foreign country, would derive no advantage by appealing to the common law in a British court. Nor, on the other hand, would the statute law prior to 1886, and so far as it is still existent, help him to obtain any redress in such a case. For as appears from the summary of that legislation given in Serjeant Stephen's *Commentaries*,[1] it uniformly proceeds on that principle of reciprocity which, in common with most other nations, England has consistently followed, and which is still maintained in the legislation of 1886; and where there was no such reciprocity between the nation to which the foreign author belonged and England as the statute law contemplates, the foreign author would be excluded by its express terms from appealing to it. But the matter would stand in a different light where the foreigner published a work for the first time in England. By the judgment in the case of *Jeffreys* v. *Boosey* already cited, a foreigner who by residence in England owes a temporary allegiance to the Crown, and who first publishes a work there, is an "author" within the meaning of 8 Anne, c. 19, no matter where his work was composed, or whether he came to England solely with a view to its publication. But if at the time of publication the foreign author is not in England, he is not deemed a person whom the statute meant to protect. In the subsequent case of *Routledge* v. *Low*, which also went up to the House of Lords, it was finally held that an alien friend who, during the time of his temporary residence in a

[1] Vol. II., pp. 41, 42, ed. of 1858.

British colony, publishes, in the United Kingdom, a book of which he is the author, is, under 5 & 6 Vict. c. 45, entitled to the benefit of English copyright.[1] Lord Cairns and Lord Westbury were of opinion, however, that the presence of the foreign author within British territory, at the time of publication, which the judgment in *Jeffreys* v. *Boosey* had fourteen years before declared to be necessary, was immaterial. In this conflict of opinion in the highest tribunal the question as to the necessity of the author's presence on British soil at the time of a first publication in England cannot be said to be settled.

American legislation on the subject of copyright.

73. As English authors mostly suffer from piratical publications of their works in the United States, it may be convenient to mention the most recent legislation in that country on the subject of copyright. As stated in the preceding paragraphs, the United States did not join the Berne Convention. But in March, 1891, an Act of Congress was passed whereby it is enacted that all authors shall have the sole right of publishing, copying, and dramatising their works on complying with certain conditions, the main one being that two copies of the book, or in the case of statuary, painting, &c., a photograph of the original, must be deposited with the Librarian of Congress. *These copies must have been printed or the photograph reproduced from types set up or negatives made within the limits of the United States.* A copyright so obtained lasts for the author's lifetime, and for a period of fourteen years after his death for the benefit of his widow and children. While it subsists it will be illegal to import into the United States any copies not made from type so set up, or negatives so made. In the case of books English translations of which alone have been copyrighted, this prohibition applies

[1] (1868), L. R. 3 H. of L., p. 100; *S. C.*, 37 L. J. Ch. 454.

only to those translations, and not to the originals. This Act is also based on the principle of reciprocity, for sect. 13 provides that the Act shall only apply to a citizen or subject of a foreign State or nation when such foreign State or nation permits to American citizens the benefit of copyright on substantially the same basis as its own citizens, or when that foreign State or nation is a party to an international agreement which provides for reciprocity in the granting of copyright, to which agreement (as in the case, for instance, of the Berne Convention) it is open to the United States to become a party. And as in England it is left to an Order of the Queen in Council to apply the provisions of the English Act upon Her Majesty being satisfied that the requisite conditions of reciprocity have been fulfilled by the foreign country with reference to which the Order is to be made, so in the United States the existence of the conditions prescribed by sect. 13 are to be determined by a proclamation of the President. It will be observed from the above provisions that the copyright of a foreign author is practically restricted to copies of his book actually printed in the dominions of the United States.

International aspect of, and rules governing, patent rights.

74. Upon general principle an inventor is as much entitled to protection as the author of a literary or artistic work. An invention is as much the product of one man's brain as a book or engraving is that of another's, and the author of the former is in point of equity as largely entitled to benefit from his skill and intelligence as that of the latter is from his. The outside public, too, is as greatly interested in encouraging the one class of intellectual achievements as the other. And the right which is, therefore, conceded to the inventor is analogous to that of the author of a literary or artistic work, distinguished by the same prohibitive character as the latter, and having the same object of securing him a fair share of reward for his skill while extending the use and

CHAP. VI.

enjoyment of the invention for the benefit of the public at large. But it is said that there is this distinction between the two cases: that an invention is not capable of being marked by the same impress of individuality as that of a literary composition. Two persons may indeed, without any previous consultation, simultaneously write a book on the same subject, and the general ideas permeating their respective works may even be the same. But in the execution, in the collocation of the materials, and in the style of each production, there must be something to mark the individuality of the particular author, unless indeed the one is a mere plagiaristic imitation of the other. It is perfectly conceivable, however, that the discovery of the same invention may have occurred to two minds quite independently of each other. To entitle a person, therefore, to any right of prohibition against the public in use of what is claimed as an invention there must be some distinctive element of novelty about it. This right is called a Patent Right, and as it is founded on a grant from the sovereign authority in a particular State, its ambit obviously does not extend beyond the territorial limits of that authority.[1] So jealously indeed was this principle formerly maintained of regarding patents as mere creatures of the municipal law of the State which grants them, that it was judicially decided in France to be lawful for a Frenchman to make or counterfeit the subject of a patent granted by a foreign State. Grants securing patent rights have no doubt been extensively made in various countries for centuries past. Grotius[2] mentions two granted by the States-General in connection with an invention in sawmills, bearing date

[1] The grant of letters patent by a foreign country is an act of State within 14 & 15 Vict. c. 99, s. 7, and is therefore provable by a copy of the letters patent, purporting to be sealed with the seal of such foreign State, without proof of the seal or signature, or judicial character of the person signing the same. *Re Betts' Patent* (1862), 1 Moor. P. C. N. S. 49.

[2] See *Opinions of Grotius*, by D. P. De Bruyn, p. 115.

respectively the 16th August, 1630, and 16th March, 1632. But all such grants were strictly territorial, and received no international recognition. It was not until 1883 that a more liberal policy found favour, and that independent States came to see that the true interests of progress demanded a recognition at their hands of the application of the principle of *comitas gentium* to this subject also. Experience has more than justified the notion that the practice of granting patents was helpful to the march of industry; and it was generally acknowledged that the time had come when rights of this kind should be placed on an international footing. Accordingly, on the 20th March, 1883, a general Convention for the protection of industrial property was concluded at Paris by Belgium, Brazil, Spain, France, Guatemala, Italy, the Netherlands, Portugal, St. Salvador, and Switzerland, with a power reserved to other nations of joining it, under which England subsequently became a party on the 17th March, 1884. To give effect to this Convention the British Parliament enacted 46 & 47 Vict. c. 57,[1] which, following the lines of the Convention, deals not only with patents, but also with the protection of industrial designs and trade-marks. Henceforth, therefore, patent rights secured by a foreigner under the Convention will be respected in England if application is made, in accordance with the formalities prescribed by the statute, within seven months after applying for a patent abroad, and the date of the patent is to be deemed to be that of the date of the application abroad, with the reservation that the patentee shall not be entitled to damages in a British court for infringements happening prior to the date of the actual

[1] This Act was subsequently amended by 48 & 49 Vict. c. 63. The United States of America acceded to the Convention on the 30th July, 1887; and by Order in Council, of 12th July, 1887, sect. 103 of the Trade Marks Act, 1883, was, so far as regards trade-marks, applied to the United States.

acceptance in England of his complete specification. Any person, moreover, who has applied for protection of an invention in any State with which the Queen has made arrangements for mutual protection will be entitled to a patent under the Act in priority to other applicants, and his invention is not to be deemed invalidated by any publication or use of the same within the United Kingdom between the date of his application abroad and that of the date of the actual acceptance of his complete specification under the Act. The 43rd section of the Act introduces an important limitation to the right of a patentee to prohibit the use by a foreign vessel in British waters of an invention covered by an existing British patent, as declared in *Caldwell* v. *Van Vlissengen.*[1] It is now provided by that section that a foreign vessel of any such State as gives British vessels within its waters reciprocal protection for inventions similarly used there, shall not be prohibited by the existence of a British patent from using an invention for the purposes of her own navigation within British waters, nor shall the use of a foreign invention on board of such a vessel within these limits be prevented by such a patent, unless the invention in question is used for the manufacture of something which is intended to be sold in the United Kingdom or exported from it. But the Act is not intended to have operation in British possessions having an independent Legislature, although by sect. 104 it is made lawful for the Queen in Council to apply the provisions of sect. 103 (by which arrangements are authorized to be made with any foreign State for the mutual protection of inventions) if Her Majesty is satisfied that the Legislature of the possession concerned has made satisfactory provision for the protection of inventions. This further point has to be noticed in regard to the British

[1] (1851), 9 Hare, 415; *S. C.*, 21 L. J. Ch. 97.

legislation of 1883, that, whereas the statutory law in most Continental nations (the Italian, French, Austrian, Belgian, and Prussian) has some provision making the duration of a patent for a foreign invention conditional on the subsistence of any patent right previously taken out in the foreign country, the English statute has, apparently designedly, omitted to adopt any limitation of the kind.

Remedies for infringement of industrial designs and trade-marks under (1) the common law and (2) the statute law.

75. Industrial designs and trade-marks are also, as we have seen, dealt with by the Convention of Paris and by the English statute. The design, when registered as required by the Act, is protected for a period of five years; but if a registered design is used in a foreign country and is not used in this country within six months of its registration under the Act, the copyright in such design shall cease to exist. Foreign inventors of designs in States with which the Queen has made arrangements for mutual protection, may apply for registration within four months[1] after application in the foreign State for protection, and the other provisions of § 103 and those of § 104 of the Act apply to designs as well as to patents. The effect of registering a design, however, is only to prevent the application of that design to goods in this country, and the sale of goods in this country to which such a design shall have been applied. It cannot, therefore, operate to restrain even a British subject from using the registered design beyond the territorial limits to which the Act applies.[2] To have extended by express language the prohibition to acts of subjects of this country when abroad could not have been justified in principle, and would only have prejudiced such of them as had manufacturing establish-

[1] Cf. *In re Californian Fig Syrup Co.* (1888), 40 Ch. D. 620, where the application not having been made within the time required was rejected.

[2] *Potter & Co.* v. *Braco de Prata Printing Co., Ltd.* (1891), 18 Ct. of Sess. Rep., 4th Ser., p. 511.

CHAP. VI. ments abroad in their competition with foreigners, by subjecting them to a prohibition which could have no effect against foreigners.[1] The Act, however, does not use such language, and the Scotch Court, in holding that it was not to be extended by implication to the case of British subjects using the registered design abroad, acted in accordance with sound principle. In regard to trade-marks and trade-names, the right to use them does not rest upon statute law, although they are now, in an international sense, regulated by the same Act as deals with patents and designs. Fair and honest competition is undoubtedly beneficial for trade, and is open to everyone. But, as was said by the learned Chief Justice (Sir J. H. De Villers) of the Supreme Court of South Africa, in a case[2] decided in that court in January, 1888, "no one has the right to take an undue and improper advantage by means of falsehoods, the effect of which is to benefit himself at the expense of another." It has accordingly long been held that when once a manufacturer has used a certain symbol in his trade to indicate where, by whom, and at what manufactory the article to which it is affixed was made, his right in its application becomes exclusive, and will be protected by law.[3] So in the case of a fancy name. The principle is, as stated by the Master of the Rolls in *Reddaway* v. *Banham*,[4] that, if a man in any particular market has acquired the right to the use of a fancy name for his goods, although he has no patent and no question of a trade-mark arises, another person cannot make use of that fancy name. And it would seem that the owner of a natural source of an article which nature manufactures is in the same

[1] Cf. Bar, § 356, p. 773, Gillespie's translation.

[2] *Combrinck & Co.* v. *De Kock*, 5 Juta, 405, quoted in *Opinions of Grotius*, by D. P. De Bruyn, p. 123.

[3] *Leather Cloth Co., Ltd.*, v. *American Leather Cloth Co., Ltd.*, 11 Jur. N. S. 513.

[4] (1895) 1 Q. B. at page 291.

position as a manufacturer by the hands of his workpeople.[1] If a man, therefore, in order to deceive the public, avails himself without leave given of the same name, or of the same trade-name or symbol, as another to describe his goods, he is open to an action of damages at the instance of the person who has already used such name or symbol, and acquired a *quasi*-right of property therein, as the first producer of the particular goods identified with a particular name, on the ground of unfair competition, or what the French law calls *concurrence déloyale*.[2] But a man may call the goods he is selling by the name by which anyone wanting to buy or sell the goods would in ordinary course call them in any market in which he wanted to buy or sell them, although in so doing he calls them by the name by which the person who complains has called his goods in a market, until in that market the name alone is taken to mean his goods alone.[3] This exclusive right in symbols or names which constitute trade-marks or trade-names is not peculiar to the common law of England. It is a right equally known to the laws of the United States,[4] of France, and other nations. "The right," said Sir Robert Phillimore, delivering the judgment of the Privy Council, "to the exclusive use of a name in connection with a trade or business is familiar to our law, and any person using that name, after a relative right of this description has been acquired by another, is considered to have been guilty of a fraud, or at

[1] Per Fry, L. J., in *Re The Apollinaris Company's Trade-Marks*, (1891) 2 Ch. 186, at page 226.

[2] See Art. MCCCLXXXII., *Code Civil.*

[3] Per Lord Esher, M. R., in *Reddaway* v. *Banham*, (1895) 1 Q. B. at page 292. See also as to "fancy words" not being open to registration if merely descriptive, deceptive, or geographical, the very recent case of *In re* DENSHAM'S TRADE-MARK (the *Mazawattee* tea trade-mark), Weekly Notes, 2nd Feb. 1895, page 19.

[4] *Marsh* v. *Billings*, 7 Cush. (U.S.) 322.

least of an invasion of another's right, and renders himself liable to an action, or to be restrained from the use of the name by an injunction."[1] So also, in another case,[2] Lord Chancellor Cranworth described the right in the following terms: "Where the manufacturer has been in the habit of stamping his goods which he has manufactured with a particular stamp, mark, or brand, so that thereby people purchasing goods of that description know them to be his manufacture, no other manufacturer has the right to adopt the same mark. By doing so he would be substantially representing the goods to be of the manufacture of the manufacturer who had previously adopted the stamp or mark in question, and so would or might be depriving him of the profits he might have made by the sale of the goods which, *ex hypothesi*, the purchaser intended to buy. The law considers this to be a wrong towards the person whose mark is thus assumed." The same doctrine was affirmed in the well-known case of the *Singer Manufacturing Co.* v. *Wilson*,[3] where it was laid down that when the first producer of an article has identified it with a particular name, whether his own or another, such name becomes a trade-mark, and cannot be adopted or employed by another person. The character of the right is, therefore, like that secured by a patent, prohibitive, and is based on the fundamental principle that to take an undue and improper advantage by means of deception and falsehood is not compatible with honest trade and fair competition, which it should alone be the object of every civilized country to protect and encourage. The law accordingly will prevent a person, by resorting to means of the above description, from attracting custom to himself which would otherwise flow to

[1] *De Boulay* v. *De Boulay* (1869), L. R. 2 P. C. 441.
[2] *Seixo* v. *Provezende* (1866), L. R. 1 Ch. App. 196.
[3] (1877), 3 App. Cas. 376; *S. C.*, 47 L. J. Ch. 481.

another.[1] This doctrine is well illustrated by two cases, one of which was decided by the American Courts, and the other (already cited *supra*) by the Supreme Court of South Africa. In the former case, a coach proprietor, running carriages between a railway station and a town, was held to have no right falsely to hold himself out as being in the employment of a particular hotel-keeper, by fixing to his carriages the name of the hotel, and as this was done to the detriment of the plaintiff, who alone was lawfully entitled to the privilege in question, it was a fraud on the plaintiff and a violation of his right, for which an action would lie without proof of actual or specific damage.[2] In the South African case[3] the question raised was whether a person who, by falsely and fraudulently representing himself to be the agent of a particular tradesman (in that case a firm of butchers of Cape Town), induces a third party to sell to him articles which have been offered for sale to such tradesman (who is known to be an extensive purchaser of such articles), is liable to an action at the suit of such tradesman? The question was answered in the affirmative, and the learned Chief Justice (Sir J. H. de Villers) in delivering judgment drew an ingenious analogy in support of this view from the case of a vendor of goods fraudulently selling goods bearing a false trade-mark. "The liability of the seller," he observed, "is based upon the ground that it is a fraud on his part to attract to himself that course of trade or custom which, but for the false representation, would have flowed in the ordinary course to the tradesman or manufacturer who has established a reputation as a vendor of certain articles. But the reputation of being a liberal purchaser of cattle may be as valuable to a

[1] Cf. *Collins Co.* v. *Brown*, and *Same* v. *Cohen* (1857), 3 Kay & Johns. 423; *Collins Co.* v. *Reeves* (1859), 28 L. J. Ch. 56.

[2] *Marsh* v. *Billings*, 7 Cush. (U.S.) Rep. 322.

[3] *Combrinck & Co.* v. *De Kock* (1888), 5 Juta, 405.

butcher as that of being a vendor of particular articles to a tradesman, and the damage done to a butcher requiring cattle for slaughter by the fraudulent representation of another that he is a purchaser on behalf of such butcher, may be as great as the damage done to a manufacturer by the infringements of his trade-name." The *ratio decidendi* in both cases proceeds upon the principle above adverted to, that no one has the right to take an undue and improper advantage by means of falsehoods, the effect of which is to benefit himself at the expense of another. And as most civilized nations now admit foreigners to an equality with natives in regard to civil rights, an alien friend, and even an alien enemy,[1] is as competent to institute, by the common law of England, a suit for an injunction restraining the defendant from an infringement of his rights of trade-mark in foreign goods and for damages for loss of profits as a native subject with respect to a similar infringement in the case of English goods. Thus where an alien friend manufactured, in his own country, goods which he distinguished by a peculiar trade-mark, and such goods had obtained considerable reputation both in his own country and in various other foreign countries, though it was not shown that any goods of this manufacture had ever been introduced or imported into England, it was held that he was intitled to an injunction against the defendant, who was in the habit of manufacturing in and selling in England goods similar in appearance, and with an exact copy of the plaintiff's peculiar trade-mark.[2] So in another important case a similar injunction was granted to an American trading company, incorporated by the law of the State of Connecticut in the United States of America, restraining a Birmingham manufacturer from continuing the fraudulent use of the trade-

[1] See Phillimore, Vol. IV., § 580c.

[2] *Collins Co.* v. *Brown; Same* v. *Cohen* (1857), 3 Kay & Johns. Reps. 423. Cf. also *Collins Co.* v. *Reeves* (1859), 28 L. J. Ch. 56.

marks of the company, and for an account of the profits made by him from such use.[1] And the Transvaal High Court granted an injunction to the English firm of Rose and Co., the well-known manufacturers of lime juice cordial, against a trader of Johannesburg in the South African Republic, who made lime juice and sold it in bottles of Rose and Co., and in others of similar shape, which latter were labelled with an almost exact imitation of plaintiff's label. It was contended for the defendant that no Roman-Dutch authorities treated of the subject, that it was therefore not a common law right in South Africa, and that, in the absence of special legislation Rose and Co.'s trade-mark could not be recognised in the Transvaal. But the High Court (in August, 1891) held that such a right did exist, that Miller's representation was likely to mislead the public, and under these circumstances granted the injunction prayed for.[2] In all these cases the Court has acted on the principle affirmed in *Collins Co.* v. *Cohen* that "every subject of every country . . . has a right to apply . . . to have a fraudulent injury to his property arrested." It would seem, however, that if the foreign mark came into conflict with an existing mark used in England, the former by the common law had to give way to the latter, and the question whether one mark is sufficiently distinguishable from another or not was left for decision by the Judge according to the law of the *forum* and not by that of the law of the country to which the mark belongs.[3] But this and the preceding question of a foreigner's right to sue for damages arising out of an infringement of his trade-mark are now somewhat differently regulated by statute law. By sect. 77 of the Act of 1883 (46 &

[1] Phillimore, Vol. IV., § 580D.

[2] *Rose & Co.* v. *Miller*, quoted in *Opinions of Grotius*, by D. P. De Bruyn, p. 123.

[3] *In re Farina* (1879), 27 W. R. 456.

CHAP. VI.

47 Vict. c. 57) "a person shall not be entitled to institute any proceedings to prevent or to recover damages for the infringement of a trade-mark, unless, in the case of a trade-mark capable of being registered under this Act," it has been so registered. This section would seem to apply (1) to all trade-marks belonging to countries with which Her Majesty has made arrangements under sect. 103, and (2) to all trade-marks belonging to other foreign countries which have the characteristics required for registration in England, since, under sect. 62, any person, without distinction of country, may apply for registration. For the future, therefore, to entitle a foreigner to sue in a British Court to prevent or to recover damages for the infringement of a trade-mark, he must have (1) registered his trade-mark in England, or (2) he must have duly applied to register his mark in one of the favoured countries, or (3) if he has not done so his mark must be one that is *not* capable of being registered under the English Act. Again, in regard to trade-marks registered in the country of origin, if such country is included in an Order of Council made by Her Majesty under the provisions of sect. 103 of the Act, the old view requiring that the capability of the trade-mark for registration should be determined by the law of the *forum*, is now superseded by a proviso attached to sub-sect. 3 of sect. 103, which enacts that "in the case of trade-marks, any trade-mark, the registration of which has been duly applied for in the country of origin, may be registered under this Act." In such cases the qualification prescribed by the foreign law is substituted for that required by the English Act. On the other hand, the character and extent of the remedy must be determined by the *lex fori*, where that law does not expressly enact otherwise; and it is immaterial that the foreigner's trade-mark enjoys a less complete protection in his own country.[1] In conclusion

[1] Bar, § 358 (4), p. 781, Gillespie's translation.

it is to be noted that an injunction will be granted against foreign manufacturers and their agents to prevent them from sending to England or to India, or to any country with which the person complaining has an established trade, goods bearing an imitation of a British trade-mark, fraudulently adopted by the foreign manufacturer.[1]

The assignment of immaterial rights is subject to the same general principles as regulate the transfer of other rights.

76. The assignment of immaterial rights, such as those of copyright, or of a trade-name or a trade-mark, is subject to the same general principles of private international law which have already been discussed in regard to the transference of other rights of property and the assumption of obligations.[2] As an accessory of property, a trade-name or a trade-mark may be sold and transferred upon the sale and transfer of a man's business, or of the manufactory of the goods at which the trade-mark has been used to be fixed, and may thereafter be lawfully used by the purchaser.[3] A purchaser may also, as the proprietor of the trade-mark, apply to have the same registered under the Act if it has not already been registered.[4] But it is to be observed that if the goods derive their increased value from the personal skill or ability of the adopter of the trade-mark, he cannot give other persons the right to affix his name or mark upon their goods, for the effect thereof would give them a right to practise fraud upon the public.[5] Grotius also draws a distinction between a patent granted in respect of a certain person and of an invention, and restricts the right of transfer to a patent of the latter description.[6]

[1] *Siegert* v. *Findlater* (1878), L. R. 7 Ch. D. 801.

[2] Bar, § 340, p. 741, Gillespie's translation; *Ibid.* § 353, p. 768; § 356, p. 773.

[3] Per Lord Cranworth, in *Leather Cloth Co., Ltd.* v. *American Leather Cloth Co., Ltd.*, 11 Jur. (N. S.) 513.

[4] 46 & 47 Vict. c. 57, s. 62 (1).

[5] Per Lord Kingsdown, in *Leather Cloth Co., Ltd.* v. *American Leather Cloth Co., Ltd.*, 11 Jur. (N. S.) 513.

[6] *Opinions*, No. 11 (1), p. 115, De Bruyn's ed.

CHAP. VI.

Invasions of the rights of trade-mark are punishable by the criminal law in some countries.

77. Invasions of the right of trade-mark are also in some countries, as in England, made amenable to the criminal law. Thus, by sect. 2 of the Merchandise Marks Act, 1887 (50 & 51 Vict. c. 28), every person who forges a trade-mark, or sells, or has in his possession for sale, or for trade or manufacture, any goods marked with a forged trade-mark, or with a mark so closely resembling a trade-mark as to be calculated to deceive, shall be guilty of an offence against the Act, and shall be liable to the forfeiture of the "chattel, article, instrument, or thing, by means of, or in relation to, which the offence has been committed." And by sect. 16 (based on Art. X. of the Paris Convention) all goods liable to forfeiture under sect. 2 may be seized at the Custom House, and the same power of seizure may be exercised with respect to goods which are truly of foreign manufacture, but bearing a name or trade-mark which is the name or the trade-mark of a manufacturer, dealer, or trader in the United Kingdom, unless such name or trade-mark is accompanied by a definite indication of the country in which the goods are made. Inasmuch, however, as criminal laws are by their nature strictly territorial, and cannot affect the laws and rights of citizens of another country,[1] the provisions of sect. 2 of the English Act would be confined, in their operation against foreigners, to acts done in the territories to which the Act applies. But a person in one country may abet the commission of an offence in another, and, accordingly, to meet such a contingency, sect. 11 provides that any person who, *being within the United Kingdom*, procures, &c., or is accessory to the commission, *without the United Kingdom*, of any act which, if committed in the United Kingdom, would be a misdemeanour under the Act, shall be guilty of that misdemeanour as a principal. This Act, accordingly, completes the measures which British municipal

[1] Per Grove, J., in *Ogden* v. *Folliott* (1790), 3 T. R. at p. 735.

legislation has introduced for the protection of trade-marks, and it must be admitted that it has gone as far in this direction as could be possibly justified. Indeed, it is questionable whether the policy underlying sect. 11 is a sound one, even within the restricted limits of its provisions. It is certainly open to abuse by the large power it concedes to officers of Her Majesty's Customs to act upon their suspicions, and in its ultimate consequences it may damage importation even to a larger extent than a protective duty would do.[1] But these are questions of policy with which Courts of justice have no concern. For them the voice of the Legislature is enough, and their duty lies in administering the law of their State as they actually find it, not as some of them, perhaps, might wish to see it.

[1] Cf. the criticisms of Bar on such legislation, § 361, p. 788, Gillespie's translation.

CHAPTER VII.

PROCEDURE, AND HEREIN OF FOREIGN JUDGMENTS AND *LIS ALIBI PENDENS.*

CHAP. VII.

Nature of the inquiry indicated.

78. The subject which has been reserved for the concluding chapter of this treatise is that which refers to the law of process, or the procedure regulating actions in a court of justice. In no country can justice be effectively administered unless the conduct of its courts is regulated by certain specific rules. But as these rules are fixed mainly with reference to the local requirements, customs, and habits of the people and the constitution of the courts exercising judicial functions within the territorial area to which they are intended to apply, it is only natural that considerable diversity should be found to prevail between the rules of procedure followed in one country and those sanctioned by the laws of another. It may thus often happen that the success of a litigant party may depend upon the determination of the question whether the law of process of the State where an obligation was entered into, or that of the State where its enforcement is sought, is to govern the mode of trial. Suppose, for instance, the existence of the obligation which the plaintiff seeks to enforce is denied by the defendant. Here, before the plaintiff can obtain any relief at the hands of the court in which the action is pending, he must *prove* the existence of the obligation to the satisfaction of that Court. But the *lex fori* may require *written* evidence as the only admissible *proof* of the particular obligation, whereas the law of procedure of the place where the contract out of which the obligation has

arisen was entered into may, in the like case, be satisfied with oral evidence. Now, the plaintiff may not be in a position to produce evidence of a character to satisfy the former rule, but he may have abundant and trustworthy evidence to satisfy the latter. By which law then is he to be governed? Again, the rules of prescription or limitation of one country may be widely different from those of another, and the plaintiff's suit, if brought in the courts of State A. may be barred by the territorial law, whereas it would not be so barred if the *lex loci contractûs*, or the *lex domicilii*, that is, the law of State B., were to apply. Here also the same question would arise, and the success of one party or the other would depend on the answer to it. It is plain, therefore, that in an international view, there is no question which possesses greater practical importance than that which we shall now proceed to consider, namely, By what law a Court of justice is to be guided in the trial and disposal of a suit?

Difficulty of compressing the subject within the four corners of any general or universal rule.

79. At the very threshold of this inquiry we are confronted with a rule which at first sight seems to solve the whole question we have set ourselves to consider. *De his quæ pertinent ad litis ordinationem, et inspicitur locus judicii*, is the general rule which Bartolus propounds, and in accordance with this fundamental canon it is commonly said that matters which relate to the order of procedure, including therein not only the modes of proceeding in an action but the forms of remedies, are governed by the *lex fori*,[1] while those touching the essentials of a right of action (*quæ spectant decisoria causæ et litis decisionem*) by the law regulating the obligation itself. A formulary of this kind is only calculated, however, to conceal the real difficulties which lie beneath the surface of so wide a generalization. It is not very easy, for instance, to

[1] Per Baron Parke in *General Steam Navigation Co.* v. *Guillon* (1843), 11 M. & W. 894.

CHAP. VII. say offhand what matters are intended to be included among the *ordinatoria litis*, which are determinable by the *lex fori*, and what among the *decisoria litis*, governed *lege loci contractûs* or *lege domicilii*. For, as soon as we begin to define the matters which relate simply to the formalities of procedure, and to distinguish them from those which touch the essentials of a right of action, we realize the difficulty which still lies in the path of those who have to apply the general rule, that procedure is governed by the law of the forum, in a practical sense. A process at law is composed of several elements, and some of these not only deal with the jural relation itself, which is made the subject of a judicial contest in its aspect as the subject of an action, but they operate still further by controlling the efficacity of that relation, as the substantive foundation of a right, and even annihilating its very existence as such. It is difficult, for instance, to understand on the one hand that a substantive jural relation is submitted to the operation of the law of the Court which is charged with the process, only in so far as the provisions of that law on the matter of procedure are concerned, but that it is not submitted to any rules that may be found in that law dealing with the relation apart from its aspect as the subject of an action,[1] when, on the other hand, by the operation of the

[1] Bar, § 388, p. 845, Gillespie's translation. So Rocco says, it is a firm and settled principle of international jurisprudence, that rights duly acquired in one State should not be subject to defeasance in another State (cap. xi.). And Fiore argues, following Savigny (VIII., § 374), that since the juridical value of an obligation consists in the rights which the creditor acquires to compel the debtor to perform it, so the existence and nature of the action ought to be strictly regarded as connected with the *vinculum juris*, and not made to depend except upon the same law which regulates the obligation. It is inconsistent, he says, to hold that the substance and validity of the obligation ought to depend upon one law, and the admissibility of an action or of a peremptory exception upon another law. It is only exceptions founded on the law of procedure that ought to be properly governed by the law of the place where the action is brought (I., § 153, p. 79). But here, again, arises the difficulty noticed in the text: What are *these* exceptions, and

law of the Court regulating the limitation of actions, the relation itself may be practically extinguished; or, again, by reason of a law of the Court imposing a condition precedent to the recognition of the relation as the subject of an action, namely, that it should be evidenced by writing, the validity of the relation as such, although unimpeachable by the law properly applicable to it, may be called into question and pronounced non-existent. It is for this reason that some jurists, like Rocco,[1] contend that a foreign tribunal which has to enforce the contract, ought not to reject a species of evidence which the law of the place of the contract would have admitted. It is impossible, therefore, to be satisfied with the bare statement of a general rule, that procedure is governed by the *lex fori*, without some further amplification indicating the various elements which are to be deemed included in the term "procedure." Fœlix,[2] for instance—supported, as Phillimore says,[3] "by the highest French judicial authorities"—contends that the question as to the admissibility of oral evidence to sustain or impeach an obligation, is one that does not properly relate to the *forme de procéder*. But the contrary view is clearly that of the English Courts. Again, there is doubt whether the question in whose name an action is to be brought is one that affects title or merely the form of the remedy.[4] In the former view the law which created it would govern, while in the latter the *lex fori* would be the proper law to apply. We have already

by what hard and fast rule are they to be defined? Among the former class Fiore would include the *exceptio non numeratæ pecuniæ;* the *exceptio excursionis*, and the *exceptio doli* (I., § 154, p. 180).

[1] *Loc. cit.*

[2] § 233.

[3] Vol. IV., § 917.

[4] Cf. Story, *Conflict of Laws*, § 565; *Trimbey* v. *Vignier* (1834), 1 Bing. N. C. 151; *Bradlaugh* v. *De Rin* (1868), L. R. 3 C. P. 538, and L. R. 5 C. P. 473; and *Alivon* v. *Furnival* (1834), 1 C. M. & R. 277.

seen[1] how this question arose before the Judicature Acts in regard to the assignment of a *chose in action*, and to state the proposition in the way Mr. Westlake does, that the *lex fori* determines in what name an action must be brought, *so far as that question can be separated from the question of the title sued on*,[2] is to leave the real difficulty unsolved. The *crux* of the whole question lies precisely in the qualification which Mr. Westlake tacks on to the rule, for it is by no means easy to distinguish between the name in which the action must be brought, from the title on which it depends. Take, for instance, a case[3] which has actually occurred, where two out of three syndics of a French bankrupt sued, in accordance with French law, in England, *on a chose in action* of the bankrupt, without joining the third. By the English law it was contended they could not do so. In this conflict, the question whether the two plaintiffs could sue in their own names alone was one which could not be decided without reference to their *title* to do so. Baron Parke, in answering the question in the affirmative, did so expressly with reference to the French law, according to which syndics of a bankrupt act as mandatories, or agents, for the creditors, the whole, or any two, or one of them having the power to sue for and recover the debts in their own names. "This is a peculiar right of action," said the learned Baron, "*created by the law of that country*, and we think it may be, by the comity of nations, enforced in this, as much as the right of foreign assignees or curators, or foreign corporations, appointed or created in a different way from that which the law of this country requires." So in the case of an assignment of a bill of exchange, the question whether the assignee can sue in his own name depends on the validity of the title created by the

[1] *Ante*, § 53, p. 91.

[2] § 342, p. 361, 3rd ed.

[3] *Alivon* v. *Furnival* (1834), 1 C. M. & R. 277.

assignment in his favour, and this question is certainly not one that the Court in which the action is brought can claim to decide according to its own law if the assignment occurred at a place where a different law prevailed. And so in the case of a plaintiff in an action generally, the question of his *locus standi* as such is so intimately involved in the question of his title to demand relief against the defendant, that it is almost indistinguishable from the latter. On the other hand, as regards liability to be sued, we have to bear in mind, at the outset, that no person can be made liable by the *lex fori* who would not be so liable by the law which governs the nature and character of the act, or of the contract in respect of which the action is brought. As the Roman law expressed the principle, *Debitor intelligitur is a quo invito exigi pecunia potest:* he is deemed a debtor who can be compelled to pay.[1] And this compulsion must depend on the law which regulates the obligation. Thus, where a defendant, an acting director and shareholder of a French company, was sued for injury done to the plaintiff's ship on the high seas, by a vessel of which he (the defendant) was alleged to be the owner, and the defence was substantially a denial that the defendant was personally or individually liable at all by the French law, Baron Parke said: "*If the defendant was not liable for the acts of the master by that law which is to govern the case, he has a good defence to the action.* For the defendant, it is contended that the plea means to aver that by the law of France he was not liable for those acts, but that a body established by the French law, and analogous to an English corporation, were the proprietors of the vessel, and alone liable for the acts of the master. . . . *If such be the true construction of the plea, we are all strongly inclined to think that there is a good defence to the action.*"[2] But the mere non-joinder of the other

Chap. VII.

[1] *Dig.* 50, 16, 108.

[2] *General Steam Navigation Co.* v. *Guillou* (1843), 11 M. & W. 895; *S.C.*, 13 L. J. Exch. 168

CHAP. VII.

members of an *unincorporated* firm, *if the defendant is jointly liable with them*, will be immaterial if the law of the Court permits the action to be brought in this form.[1] So that while the *lex fori* will regulate the *mode* in which an *existing* liability should be *judicially constituted*,[2] the question whether the defendant *is liable at all* must be decided according to the law governing the act or contract which gives rise to the action. Of course, this question is independent of the power of every State to place certain persons under special disabilities. Thus, alien enemies in British India can only sue with the permission of the Governor-General in Council;[3] and a foreign State is only allowed to do so when (a) it has been recognized by Her Majesty or the Governor-General in Council, and (b) the object of the suit is to enforce the private rights of the head or of the subjects of the foreign State.[4] Here the question is not in *what name* the action is to be brought, but whether the plaintiff is a person who is *capable* of invoking the remedial jurisdiction of the Court, a question which must be decided with reference to the law of the Court. These examples will suffice to show that it is not enough to say that in the law of procedure the *lex fori* shall exclusively rule. For many laws are only apparently rules of procedure, but, in reality, are rules of substantive law, or, at least, are so mainly.[5]

Law of evidence is the *lex fori* which governs the Courts.

80. It is preferable, therefore, under these circumstances, to avoid the dilemma of enunciating, or attempting to enunciate, in this matter a rule for general application, which, in practice, would only be found to be approximately correct, and to need explanations and definitions which it

[1] *Bullock* v. *Caird* (1875), L. R. 10 Q. B. 276.

[2] Per Lord Campbell, in *Bank of Australasia* v. *Nias* (1851), 16 Q. B. 734.

[3] Sect. 430, Act XIV. of 1882.

[4] Sect. 431 *ibid.* Cf. as to English law, *Hullett* v. *King of Spain* (1828), 1 D. & Cl. 169; and *Emperor of Austria* v. *Day* (1862), 30 L. J. Ch. 690.

[5] Bar, § 390, p. 850, Gillespie's translation.

would again be difficult to formulate without the admission of exceptions. It must suffice if certain matters are specified as clearly determinable by the law of the *forum*—at least, according to the doctrine of the English Courts — leaving other questions that may arise in practice to be settled by analogy, as far as it may be possible to do so, or with reference to the fundamental principles of the particular jurisprudence which has to deal with them. Thus, no one will doubt the reasonableness of the proposition that no Court ought to be governed in conducting its inquiries into a *matter of fact* by the law of evidence of any other country except its own.[1] "What evidence," said Lord Brougham, in a judgment which has already been quoted above,[2] "the Courts of another country would receive, and what reject, is a question into which I cannot at all see the necessity of the Courts of any one country entering. Those principles which regulate the admission of evidence are the rules by which the Courts of every country guide themselves in all their enquiries."[3] And in a later case, the same learned judge expressed himself as follows: "The law of evidence is the *lex fori* which governs the Courts. Whether a witness is competent or not; whether a certain matter requires to be proved by writing or not; whether certain evidence proves a certain fact or not—that is to be determined by the law of the country where the question arises, and where the remedy is sought to be enforced, and where the Court sits to enforce it."[4] So also the question whether a payment is to be presumed or not must be determined by the law of the country in which the remedy is sought. In like manner, whether a parol agreement is to be given up, or can be enforced, must be tried by the law of the

[1] Cf. *Robertson* v. *Burdekin* (1843), 1 Ross' Comm. Ca. 818.

[2] *Ante*, § 64, p. 129.

[3] *Yates* v. *Thomson* (1835), 3 Cl. & Fin. 544.

[4] *Bain* v. *Whitehaven and Furness Junction Railway* (1850), 3 H. of L. 1.

country where the law is set in motion to enforce the agreement, and so must all questions of the admissibility of evidence.[1]

The *lex fori* regulates the time within which an action can be brought, or an appeal filed.

81. Again, since all statutes of limitation are statutes of repose,[2] on the same principle that Lord Brougham ruled that presumptions as to payment must be determined by the *lex fori*, the question whether a particular claim is time-barred or not must be equally determined by that law. It must obviously be left to each State to determine within what period its Courts shall be open to give relief in personal actions, either by way of original suit or by appeal to a higher Court, in case of an adverse decision by an inferior Court,[3] and statutory provisions of this kind must, therefore, be regarded as part of the stringent policy of the State, which must override all contrary provisions of the law of any other State. "A certain period," said Lord Hatherley, in *Pardo* v. *Bingham*,[4] "is fixed by the statute, which binds everybody who comes to sue before this *forum*." The wisdom of the Legislature in one country may fix a longer or a shorter period for the enforcement of personal claims than may be deemed expedient in another. Thus, in India, there is no distinction between specialty and simple contract debts, while in England a longer period of limitation is allowed for the former than for the latter. Accordingly, where a suit was brought in England on a *sealed* bond executed in India, the action was held to be maintainable with reference to the limitation applicable to such instruments in England, although the debt had become time-barred by the law of India.[5] So, on the other hand, in an old Indian case which was decided at a time when proceedings in the old Supreme Court of

[1] Per Lord Brougham in *Don* v. *Lippmann* (1837), 5 Cl. & Fin. 15.

[2] Burgundus also holds that prescription is akin to payment (IV. 28).

[3] *Tulloch* v. *Hartley* (1841), 1 Y. & C. Chan. 114; *Lopez* v. *Burslem* (1843), 4 Moore, P. C. 300.

[4] (1869), L. R. 4 Ch. 735.

[5] *Alliance Bank of Simla* v. *Carey* (1880), L. R. 5 C. P. D. 429.

Calcutta were governed by the English Statute of Limitations, it was held by the Privy Council that in applying the English statute in a case in which the parties were Gentoos and the action was founded on contract, the Supreme Court did not violate the provisions of its charter requiring that the Gentoo laws of contract should be observed between Gentoos.[1] In both cases the law of the *forum* was held to determine the question of limitation, quite irrespective of the law of the place of contract or the nationality of the parties. And so thoroughly established is this principle in English jurisprudence, that even where a foreign judgment has pronounced a claim to be barred by its local law, this fact offers no bar to a similar action being maintained in England if the law there allows a longer period, and such period is still unexpired.[2] How far such a doctrine could be maintained in a British court in India, in a case similar to the one just mentioned, may be open to some doubt with reference to the special provisions of sect. 13 of the Code of Civil Procedure of 1882, which enacts that the final determination by *any* Court of competent jurisdiction of *any* issue arising in a case shall not be open to contest in any subsequent suit between the same parties or their representatives in interest. A foreign court properly seised of the suit would certainly fall (as the High Court of Bombay has held)[3] within the category of "*any* competent court," and having finally determined an issue as to whether the claim was "time-barred," it might be open to contention that the decision on *that* issue was operative under the section extra-territorially, and within British India, as *res judicata*. But the more correct view would probably be that the question of the *foreign* limitation was alone *res judicata*, and that the British Court would have to determine for itself whether

[1] *Ruckmaboye* v. *Mottichand* (1853), 5 Moore, Ind. App. 234.

[2] *Harris* v. *Quine* (1869), L. R. 4 Q. B. 653; *S. C.*, 38 L. J. Q. B. 331.

[3] *Babalhat* v. *Narharbhat*, I. L. R. 13 Bomb. 224.

CHAP. VII. the suit was nevertheless within limitation according to the law of British India. It must be also added that the Continental view as to the application of the *lex fori* in questions of prescription or limitation of actions is generally opposed to the English doctrine above stated. On the other hand, the greatest discord prevails amongst foreign writers as to the true theory to be applied if that of the *lex fori* is rejected. Thus, according to the French writer Fœlix,[1] the theory which is the best established, and adopted also by the Douay and Paris Courts (and by the German Imperial Court at Leipsic),[2] is that which holds that the *lex loci contractûs*, or the law of the place where the contract was made, should rule. But this theory is severely handled by Bar,[3] and is as unsound as that advocated by Pothier,[4] that the law of the creditor's domicil should rule. Fiore[5] thinks that the more reasonable doctrine is to hold that in personal obligations the law which governs the obligation ought to prevail in regulating the prescription of an action to enforce it, and this is the ruling theory in German science and practice.[6] It would seem, therefore, according as the place of execution or the place of performance of the obligation is held to regulate it, so is the one place or the other assumed as regulative of prescription. In connection, however, with the general rule recognised by the English Courts, it is necessary to sound a note of warning not to push the rule beyond its legitimate limits. The policy of the English statutes of limitation must, for example, be kept in mind. That policy is not to *actively* aid suitors in personal actions to *recover*

[1] Vol. I., § 100, p. 241. But cf. *Journal de Marseille*, 1866, 1, 36; 1867, 1, 116, as to the doctrine adopted by the Marseilles Court, which adopts the law of the place of performance of the obligation.

[2] In the case of *Hervey* v. *Engelbert*, 5th March, 1877.

[3] § 279, p. 618, Gillespie's translation.

[4] *De la Prescription*, No. 251. See also Fiore, Vol. I., § 159, p. 182.

[5] Vol. I., § 165, p. 186, following Savigny, Vol. VIII. p. 271.

[6] Bar, § 279, p. 615, Gillespie's translation.

stale claims after a certain period. But the *remedy* alone is refused after that period has expired. The statute does not profess to *extinguish* the *right* out of which the claim springs, and it may be possible for it to receive recognition in various ways, though it cannot form the basis of a suit. Accordingly it has been held that the right may subsist as to preserve a lien on the goods of the debtor,[1] and as to supply the necessary condition for a new promise to pay the barred debt.[2] So also a creditor in an administration suit was allowed to retain, without bringing into hotchpot, the proceeds of a foreign attachment on foreign assets for another debt, being a debt barred by the English statute but not by the foreign law.[3]

But a foreign law of limitation may receive effect if it extinguishes the *right* of action and not merely the remedy.

82. The distinction just adverted to between the mere loss of a remedy and the extinguishment of the *right* itself serves also to explain why in some cases an English Court will give effect to a foreign law of limitation and not in others. We have seen, for instance, in the case of the *Alliance Bank of Simla* v. *Carey* (quoted *supra*), that a claim barred by the Indian law was allowed to be enforced in an English court. But the Indian, like the English, law only barred the remedy and did not extinguish the right, and hence, as there was still a subsisting right, the action to enforce it was rightly governed by the law of the *forum* where it was brought. In a case, however, where the *right* itself is extinguished by the foreign law (*e.g.*, by the Prussian Land Recht),[4] and not merely the *remedy* to enforce it *by suit*, the

[1] *Spears* v. *Hartley* (1800), 3 Esp. 81, 82; *Higgins* v. *Scott* (1831), 2 B. & Ad. 413. So the Roman law said, *remanet propter pignus naturalis obligatio*: Dig. XXXVI. 1, 59, and Windscheid, Vol. I., § 225, pp. 721, 722.

[2] Sect. 25 of the Indian Contract Act.

[3] *In re Bowes, Strathmore* v. *Vane* (1889), W. N. p. 53.

[4] *Das Allgemeine Land-Recht*, I. 6, § 64: "If a person omits to bring his action of damages for wrong suffered, except in the case of a contract, within three years after the notice of the claim, and the persons responsible to him are within his knowledge, *he loses his right*."

question assumes a very different form. The better opinion would seem to be that there is here no obligation remaining upon which an action can be founded anywhere, either *in foro contractûs* or *in foro domicilii*, and consequently the plaintiff is barred *in limine*, and cannot appeal to the law of the *forum*, which can only properly help him to realise an *existing* right, and has no scope for its own operation when by the law governing the contract the right itself has ceased to exist, for, in such a case, there is nothing left to be enforced, and the law of process is not brought into play.[1] In such a case, on principle, the rule of the older Jurists would be best applicable—that this kind of extinctive prescription *pertinet ad decisionem litis, non ad ordinationem causæ.* But actual judicial authority in England and the United States has not hitherto gone beyond recognising the effect of a foreign law of limitation, even in the case here contemplated, except under an important condition. To constitute a bar to an action in an English court,[2] or in a court of the United States,[3] it must appear that the statutes of limitation of the State whose law governs the obligation generally, have absolutely extinguished the right, *and that the parties have been resident during the whole time that this law allowed for the action to be brought within its territorial jurisdiction.* The proposition in this form was ap-

[1] Cf. *Ellis* v. *McHenry* (1871), L. R. 6 C. P. 228, where the question as to what amounts to a discharge of a foreign cause of action is elaborately discussed. "There is no doubt," said Bovill, C. J., "that a debt or liability arising in any country may be discharged by the laws of that country, and that such a discharge, *if it extinguishes the debt or liability, and does not merely interfere with the remedies or course of procedure to enforce it*, will be an effectual answer to the claim, not only in the courts of that country, but in every other country. This is the law of England, and is a principle of private international law adopted in other countries."

[2] Cf. Burge, Vol. III., pp. 883, 884.

[3] Story's *Conflict of Laws*, § 582; Wharton, § 538; *Townsend* v. *Jemison*, 18 Cur. Rep. 201, 202; *S. C.* 9 How. 419; *Shelby* v. *Guy*, 11 Wheaton, 361; *Brent* v. *Chapman*, 5 Cranch's Reps. 358.

proved of by the Court of Common Pleas in *Huber* v. *Steiner*,[1] and in *Don* v. *Lippmann*.[2] Lord Brougham alluded to it in the following terms: "There is no occasion," he said, "with a view to the decision in this case, to question the doctrine laid down by Dr. Story in his able work on the Conflict of Laws, and approved of by the Court of Common Pleas in *Huber* v. *Steiner*, that if the *lex loci contractûs* makes the obligation wholly void after a certain time, and if the parties have resided within the jurisdiction during the whole of that period, it may be taken as the guide of the Court where the action is brought." The condition requiring the continued residence of the parties within the jurisdiction of the State in which the *forum contractûs* lies during the *whole* period that time is running by that law, may be supported on the principle that *bona fides* requires that a creditor who has thus by want of diligence actually *lost* his right by the law which governed the obligation, and which must be looked on as impliedly incorporated with it, should not be entitled to derive any advantage *in the prosecution of his suit* by a simple change of domicile on the part of his debtor *subsequent to the extinction of his right*. On the other hand, if before that period has expired the debtor has left the jurisdiction, taking his property with him, and has acquired a domicil elsewhere, it seems reasonable enough to hold—although Bar thinks otherwise [3]—that the creditor should be able to appeal to the law of the actual *forum* for the prosecution of a still subsisting right which he can no longer enforce, in consequence of the change of domicil, *in foro contractûs*. By the change of domicil the debtor has put an end to the jurisdiction of that *forum* for purposes of the law of process. But as the right of action against him still subsists, the period within which it must be enforced can only be governed, in accordance with the general

[1] (1835), 2 Bing. N. C. 202.
[2] (1837), 5 Cl. & Fin. 1.
[3] Bar, § 281, note 23, p. 621, Gillespie's translation.

CHAP. VII. rule which here is not displaced by the operation of any other law the recognition of which *bona fides* requires, by the law which ordinarily regulates the mode of realising a remedy, that is to say, by the law of the Court where the action is brought. This view has, however, been subjected to some hostile criticism, which will presently be noticed. Meantime this seems the proper place to refer to a somewhat novel rule which Bar laid down in the first edition of his work on Private International Law as the proper one to meet such a case, where, as supposed, a debtor changes his domicil while the period of limitation has not yet run out. In such a case he thought "there would require to be a proportional calculation of the different periods." So that if, for example, the period of limitation had run half its course according to the law of the earlier domicil, it should be held to be half run by the law of the subsequent domicil.[1] But this was a mere arbitrary device to meet a difficulty which had no sound basis of reason to recommend it, while the practical difficulties of applying such a doctrine added a further and fatal objection to its adoption, which induced the author himself to abandon it in his second edition in favour of the theory recommended by another German jurist (Grawein), according to which the debtor may appeal to the law of prescription of his former domicil, or to that of his subsequent domicil, whichever is more to his advantage.[2] The simplicity of this rule is certainly in its favour, but the other rule also, which, as we have seen, has the high authority of Story and Lord Brougham to recommend it, is equally simple of application, and it is not easy to discover how it can be said to be illogical, as Bar thinks it is.[3] But it must be added that two such eminent authorities as Dr. Phillimore and the learned editor of the English "Leading Cases," are not prepared to accept

[1] § 281, p. 621, Gillespie's translation.

[2] *Verjahrung und gesetzliche Befristung*, Part I., p. 202, Leipzig, 1880.

[3] § 281, note 23, p. 621, Gillespie's translation.

the English and American doctrine without a certain modification. Phillimore, for instance, thinks that "perhaps upon a fuller and further consideration it may be found that the residence of the parties *subsequent to the making of the contract*, cannot really affect the true question, namely, whether an *extinctive prescription*, at least, incident to the law of the place of the fulfilment of the obligation be not a matter which concerns the nature and essence of the obligation itself, whether it was not a condition provisionally contemplated by the parties at the time when the obligation was incurred." [1] And the editor of the "Leading Cases" criticises the doctrine as follows: "Supposing," he says, "the law of a foreign country to be that a contract is, after a certain time, to be deemed absolutely extinguished, it seems not quite reasonable to say that the removal of the parties out of the jurisdiction while that time is running, should authorize the Courts of this country to consider it *in esse* after the period prefixed. The authorities establish that the law of the country where the contract is made must govern it, and must be looked on as impliedly incorporated with it. Now, if the contract had contained a *proviso* that it should be absolutely void, if not enforced within a certain time, no doubt the English Courts would hold it void after the expiration of that time. But what difference can it make that such proviso is implied from the law of the country where the contract was made, instead of being expressed in terms? Is it not in both cases equally part of the contract? If, indeed, the rule of the foreign law be, that the contract shall, after the lapse of a certain time, become void, provided that the parties to it continue to reside all that time in the same country, the arrival of the period prefixed, or its avoidance, will depend on the contingency of their abstaining from absenting themselves, and, if they leave the country, never will arrive at all; and this is,

[1] *Private Inter. Law*, Vol. IV., § 804.

CHAP. VII.

perhaps, what Judge Story intends by the words, 'that the parties are resident within the jurisdiction all that period, *so that it has actually operated upon the case.*' For if the law be so framed as to *operate upon the case* without such residence, the qualification appears to be inapplicable."[1] Ordinarily, however, laws respecting the limitation of actions do *not* operate extraterritorially, and hence it is that the English Statute of Limitations is no bar to a party, whether he be a subject of the realm or a foreigner, who was not in England at the time the cause of action occurred, and who continues resident abroad.[2] It results from this principle that the debtor, by removing himself out of the jurisdiction of such a law before he has obtained a complete discharge under it, can no longer appeal to it, and thereby give it an extraterritorial effect when he has placed himself under a new jurisdiction the law of which still permits an action to be brought upon an obligation from which, up to the time of his entering that jurisdiction, he had not been validly discharged. And as to what is said about a contract containing a *proviso*, that it should be absolutely void if not enforced within a certain time, it is no doubt open to parties to stipulate in certain contracts—as, for instance, in a contract of guarantee—that liability shall not extend under them beyond a certain period. But it is, at least, open to grave doubt whether parties can, by contractual stipulations of the kind alluded to, create a law of limitation for themselves, applicable to *breaches* under the contract, different from that enacted by the general law of the land, which otherwise would bind them as well as all other persons living under its protection. And besides there is no real analogy between

[1] *Vide* note to *Mostyn* v. *Fabrigas* (1775), in Vol. I., p. 678, 9th edition.

[2] 21 Jac. I. c. 16, s. 7. Cf. also sect. 13 of Act XV. of 1877 (The Indian Limitation Act); and see *Atul Kisto Bose* v. *Lyon & Co.*, I. L. R. 14 Cal. 457; and *Maharaja Sir Partab Singh* v. *Provincial Bank of India*, No. 72, Panj. Record for 1891.

the discharge of an obligation as provided by the parties in terms of their contract, and the extinction of the same by the direct interposition of the law. At all events, the weight of English and American authority is at present on the side of adhering to the qualification as to residence of the parties in the case of *extinctive* laws of limitation incident to the place of the contract or its fulfilment. In the case of suits relating to immoveables the English,[1] like the Indian,[2] statute extinguishes the right after the prescribed period, and no other law, except the *lex sitûs*, would be applicable to such suits.[3] Consistently, moreover, with the doctrine applied by them in regard to the *absolute extinction* of obligations by a foreign prescription, the English Courts recognize a complete discharge obtained under a bankruptcy of the debtor in the special *forum* of the obligation—*locus contractûs* or *solutionis*, or *locus delicti commissi*—as having a similar effect in England.[4]

Execution or means of compulsion available to enforce an obligation governed by *lex fori.*

83. Again, it is generally recognised that the method of execution of foreign decrees or judgments, or the means of compulsion available for their enforcement, must depend on the law of the place of execution.[5] Nor will the exclusive application of this law be affected by any regulation which the judgment may contain, or which the law of the State where the judgment was pronounced may prescribe. Thus the circumstance that imprisonment was not allowed in civil actions by the *lex loci contractûs* will not prevent resort being had to this remedial process if permitted by the law of the *forum* where execution is proceeding. The same principle applies in regard to the enforcement of contracts generally

[1] 3 & 4 Will. IV. c. 27.

[2] Sect. 28, Act XV. of 1877 (The Indian Limitation Act).

[3] Westlake, § 171, p. 194, and § 343, p. 362, 3rd ed.

[4] Ibid., § 240, p. 281, 3rd ed.

[5] Bar, § 451, p. 968, Gillespie's translation; Foote, p. 516, 2nd ed.; Westlake, § 345, p. 362, 3rd ed.

CHAP. VII. in another country. In the absence of an express stipulation, the parties must be held to bind themselves generally, and to contemplate the possibility of enforcing it in another country. The breach of a contract cannot reasonably be supposed to be what the parties ordinarily contemplate, and, indeed, as Lord Brougham forcibly said in the leading case of *Don* v. *Lippmann*[1] (cited *supra*), "Nothing could be more contrary to good faith. It is supposing that when men bind themselves to do a certain thing they are contemplating not doing it, and considering how the law will help them in the non-performance of a duty." They must, therefore, be presumed to intend to take the law as they find it when they come to enforce their contract. "The distinction," continued Lord Brougham, in the same case, "which exists as to the principle of applying the remedy, exists with even greater force as to the practice of the courts when the remedy is to be enforced. No one can say that, because the contract has been made abroad, the form of action known in the foreign court must be pursued in the courts where the contract is to be enforced, or the other preliminary proceedings of those courts must be adopted, or that the rules of pleading, or the curial practice of the foreign country, must necessarily be followed. . . . No one will contend in terms that foreign rules of evidence should guide us in such cases; and yet it is not so easy to avoid that principle in practice if you once admit that, though the remedy is to be enforced in one country, it is to be enforced according to the laws which govern another country." But the case with which Lord Brougham was then concerned contained, as he was careful to point out, no express stipulations as to the nature of the remedy to be enforced under the contract. This is a matter which is no doubt subject to the control of the parties, who may certainly agree amongst themselves that the contract

[1] 5 Cl. & Fin. at pp. 13, 14.

shall be enforced against the property, and not against the person of the party making default—in other words, that there shall be no personal liability for the breach or non-fulfilment of the undertaking. The case of *Melan* v. *Fitz-James*[1] was, in the opinion of the majority of the Court, one of this kind. There the contract was made in France, and the defendant being held to bail in England the question arose, whether the nature of the contract was such that it created a personal obligation, or only bound the defendant's property? The Court of Common Pleas (Heath, J., dissenting) held that the latter was the right construction to put upon the contract with reference to the French law, and thereupon the bail-bond was ordered to be delivered up and cancelled on the defendant entering a common appearance. "If it appears," said Eyre, C.J., "that this contract creates no personal obligation, and that it could not be sued as such by the laws of France, there seems to be fair ground on which the Court may interpose, to prevent a proceeding so oppressive as a personal arrest in a foreign country at the commencement of a suit, in a case which, as far as we can judge at present, authorises no proceeding against the person in the country in which the transaction passed. If there could be none in France, in my opinion there can be none here. I cannot conceive that what is no personal obligation in the country in which it arises can ever be raised into a personal obligation by the laws of another. *If it be a personal obligation there, it must be enforced here in the mode pointed out by the law of this country; but what the nature of the obligation is must be determined by the law of the country where it was entered into, and then this country will apply its own law to enforce it.*"[2] Whether the particular facts of the case justified this decision has

[1] (1797), 1 B. & P. 141.

[2] Cf. also *Talleyrand* v. *Boulanger* (1797), 3 Vesey, 447; and *Flack* v. *Holm* (1820), 1 J. & W. 405, 417, 418.

been seriously doubted;[1] but on the assumption that the contract *really* created no personal liability, and, when properly construed by the *lex contractûs*, was only a mere hypothecation of property, the question was one which, in the language of Tindal, C.J.,[2] may be said to have related *ad litis decisionem*—that is, to the rights and merits of the contract, and not *ad litis ordinationem*, or to matters affecting the remedy only.

Proper law governing right of set-off.

84. The question whether the admissibility of a plea of set off is to be determined by the *lex fori* as relating to procedure, or by the *lex loci contractûs* as being a part of the original obligation, is not altogether free from conflicting authority.[3] But on principle it would seem that this is a proper case for the application of the *lex fori*, for the plea is intimately connected with the mode of trial of the suit and the nature of the relief which the plaintiff is entitled to ask at the hands of the Court which is seised with the action, and this is the prevailing opinion on both sides of the Atlantic.[4] In like manner the competency of a plea of compensation, as it is termed on the Continent, must be determined by the Court in accordance with its own law, in so far as it may fall to be repelled upon formal grounds of process, as, for instance, that both claims must be liquid. It clearly depends on the *lex fori* to regulate under what circumstances a plea of this kind can be legitimately raised. Thus by the Prussian law[5] no compensation can be pleaded against alimentary obligations; while in the older Roman law the right of *compensa-*

[1] By Lord Ellenborough in *Imlay* v. *Ellefsen* (1802), 2 East, 455. See also *De la Vega* v. *Vianna* (1830), 1 B. & Ad. 284.

[2] In *Huber* v. *Steiner* (1835), 2 Scott, 304; 2 Bing. N. C. 202, cited *supra*, § 62.

[3] Cf. *Macfarlane* v. *Norris* (1862), 2 B. & S. 783, with *Allen* v. *Kemble* (1848), 6 Moore, P. C. 314, and *Rouquette* v. *Overmann* (1875), L. R. 10 Q. B. 541, explaining latter decision.

[4] Story, *Conflict of Laws*, § 575, 7th ed.; Westlake, § 346, p. 362, 3rd ed.; Foote, p. 515, 2nd ed.

[5] *Alleg. Land-Recht*, I. 16, §§ 366, 367.

tio was only admissible in the *bonæ fidei judicia*, and then only if the claims made available had arisen *ex eadem causâ*, that is, from the same obligatory relation.[1] According to the Indian law,[2] a counterclaim can only be set off if it is for an ascertained sum of money, and the parties with respect to it fill the same character as they fill in the plaintiff's suit. It would seem, however, that the right to plead set off or compensation may be controlled by contract, *e. g.*, by express stipulation, just in the same way as the enforcement of personal liability may be similarly controlled, although sanctioned by the *lex fori*.[3]

Lex fori governs all priorities in an administration suit, except in regard to foreign assets.

85. Another matter which is undeniably regulated by the *lex fori* is that relating to priorities in an administration suit. Indeed, if the rule were not so, a hopeless deadlock would arise where there was a conflict between the laws applicable to rival debts: for, as Mr. Westlake observes,[4] if two debts were contracted under different laws, and each by the law under which it was contracted would be prior to the other, how shall their order be determined if not by the law of the *forum* where they meet? But it seems that if *foreign* assets are being judicially administered in England, the Court will apply them as the foreign representative should have done—that is, will assign to the creditors as against any particular assets that order of priority which is prescribed by the law under the authority of which those assets were reduced into possession.[5] Strictly speaking, the jurisdiction of the Court in matters of administration is merely territorial, but if by

[1] See my *Jurisprudence*, p. 226, 2nd ed.

[2] Sect. 111 of Act XIV. of 1882. But cf. I. L. R. XI. Cal. 557; XVI. *ibid.* 711; and VII. Allah. 284.

[3] Cf. Bar, § 277, p. 612, Gillespie's translation.

[4] *Private Inter. Law*, § 110, p. 119, 3rd ed.; and cf. Story, *Conflict of Laws*, §§ 524, 525.

[5] Westlake, § 111, p. 120, 3rd ed.

CHAP. VII.

reason of the submission of the foreign administrator the Court is called upon to exercise a wider jurisdiction, it will respect the title to priority already acquired by any particular creditor by the law under which the administrator obtained possession of the asset in question.

Law applicable to auxiliary proceedings taken in aid of a suit extraterritorially.

86. In the preceding paragraphs of this chapter we have dealt with matters of procedure which arise within the jurisdiction of the Court which is seised with the action. But a process at law consists of several steps, and some of these steps may have to be taken extraterritorially. It may be necessary, for instance, to cite a person or to examine a witness who is resident in another State, or to cause some inspection to be made in a different country, or to make a requisition upon another Court to give assistance. In such and the like isolated steps of procedure, the question will at times need decision by what law they are to be regulated: whether by the law of the place where they are carried out, or by that of the Court in which the action itself is pending? The answer to this question depends on whether the particular step is required to be taken through some foreign magisterial or judicial agency, or by means of a commission issued to a private person. Whenever the former course is taken, the foreign Court, judge or functionary, in so far as the conduct of the auxiliary process is concerned, must follow the procedure of his own law, for it is to that law that he owes implicit obedience. Thus, the form of oath to be administered to witnesses examined abroad, and the drawing up or manner of recording their evidence, must be in accordance with the rules prevailing at the place where the particular judicial act takes place. Accordingly, what is recognized as correct and formal in that country, should be so recognized everywhere.[1] In practice, however, a foreign Court pays due

[1] *Savage* v. *Hutchinson* (1853), 3 C. L. & Eq. Repts., p. 368; Phillimore,

regard to any reasonable suggestions made to it by a duly constituted tribunal of a friendly State, in so far as the same may not be expressly forbidden by, or contrary to, the stringent policy of its own law.[1] Formerly, the practice in England and the United States was to employ private agency to carry out such commissions; and, of course, it is always competent to the Court issuing such a commission to prescribe the procedure by which the private commissioner is to be guided.[2] But the inconvenience of resorting to such agency lay in the want of power of a commissioner so appointed to compel the persons whose evidence was required to attend before him, or to produce documents whose inspection was desired. The statutes 1 Will. IV. c. 22 and 3 & 4 Vict. c. 105 accordingly empowered English Courts to address requisitions to foreign Courts for assistance, and since then the former practice has fallen into disuse, more especially as in some States laws exist which positively prohibit the administration of an oath, or the exercise of any judicial function by any persons other than those authorised by such laws to administer or exercise the same. Thus proceedings were actually taken in Germany in the year 1886 for offending against a law of this kind, against an English barrister who had been appointed to take evidence there on commission by the High Court of Justice in England. By a later statute[3] the English Parliament authorised its own Superior Courts to comply with the requisition of a foreign Court in aid of any civil or com-

Vol. IV., §§ 913, 914; Wharton, § 752; Bar, § 392, p. 855, Gillespie's translation.

[1] Cf. *Hitchins* v. *Hitchins* (1866), L. R. 1 P. & M. 153.

[2] Taylor *on Evidence*, § 513.

[3] 19 & 20 Vict. c. 113, passed on the 29th July, 1856. By sect. 391c of Act XIV. of 1882 (the Indian Code of Civil Procedure) commissions issued by the Courts of any foreign country for the time being in alliance with Her Majesty, are to be executed in the manner provided for by Ch. XXV. of the Act.

mercial suit pending before it by ordering the examination upon oath, before any person or persons named in the order, of any witnesses within the jurisdiction of such Courts whose testimony the foreign Court might desire to obtain. A certificate of the Ambassador, Minister, or other diplomatic agent, or, in case there be no such agent, of the Consul-General or Consul of the foreign Power in whose Court the civil or commercial matter may be pending, setting forth that such Court has jurisdiction in the matter, and is desirous of obtaining the testimony of a certain witness or witnesses, is declared by the Act sufficient evidence in support of any application made under it. But in the absence of such a certificate, other evidence to the same effect may be admitted. Persons examined on oath under the Act are to be deemed guilty of perjury if they wilfully and corruptly give any false evidence, but every person so examined has the right to refuse to answer questions tending to criminate himself, or other questions which a witness in any cause pending in the Court by which the order for examination is made would be entitled to refuse to answer; and no person shall be compelled to produce, under any such order, any writing or other document that he would not be compelled to produce at a trial of such a cause.

But probative value of evidence taken in foreign country must be determined by Court trying the action.

87. Although where evidence is thus taken by a Court in one country in aid and at the request of a Court in another country, the form of oath, the manner of recording the evidence, and the protection accorded against incriminatory questions, are matters which are regulated *secundum legem actûs*, that is, by the law of the country where the evidence is actually taken, the probative value of the evidence when taken must be determined by the Court in which the action is pending according to its own law.[1] The German *Civil-*

[1] Cf. observations by Cockburn, C.J., in *Dessilla* v. *Fels*, 40 L. T. Rep. 423.

Process Ordnung, however, goes somewhat further, and enacts (§ 334) that "if evidence taken by a foreign official conforms to the law recognized in the Court where the suit depends, no objection can be taken to it by reason of its defects according to the foreign law." This, says Bar,[1] would make it incumbent on a German judge to treat as valid an oath which was taken abroad in the form prescribed by the German *Civil-Process Ordnung*, and was absolutely null by the foreign law, imposing not an iota of criminal responsibility on the party who emitted it. The criticism seems sound, but there is reason to believe that an English Court would follow the rule laid down in the German statute.[2] In regard, however, to the citation of parties outside the territorial jurisdiction of the Court issuing the same, all questions as to sufficiency of time allowed for appearance, or as to the form and contents of the citation, must be determined by the law of the Court issuing the same. The reason for this is based on the power of that law to regulate and dispose of the suit which is properly within its cognizance, and the obligation of the parties to submit to it in regard to all matters relating to the mode of trial.[3]

Practice of English Courts in regard to service of writs out of jurisdiction.

88. The existing rules followed by the English Courts in reference to the service of writs or notices of writs out of jurisdiction are as follows:—

"Order. XI. r. 1.—Service out of the jurisdiction of a writ of summons may be allowed by the Court or a judge whenever—

"(a) The whole subject-matter of the action is land situate within the jurisdiction (with or without rents or profits); or

[1] § 394, note 23, p. 861, Gillespie's translation.

[2] Taylor *on Evidence*, § 512; and *Dessilla* v. *Fels*, cited *supra*.

[3] Bar, § 391, pp. 852—54, Gillespie's translation.

CHAP. VII.

"(b) Any act, deed, will, contract, obligation, or liability affecting land or hereditaments situate within the jurisdiction, is sought to be construed, rectified, set aside, or enforced in the action;[1] or

"(c) Any relief is sought against any person domiciled or ordinarily resident within the jurisdiction; or

"(d) The action is for the administration of the personal estate of any deceased person who, at the time of his death, was domiciled within the jurisdiction; or for the execution (as to property situate within the jurisdiction) of the trusts of any written instrument, of which the person to be served is a trustee, which ought to be executed according to the law of England; or

"(e) The action is founded on any breach or alleged breach within the jurisdiction of any contract, wherever made, which, according to the terms thereof, ought to be performed within the jurisdiction, unless the defendant is domiciled or ordinarily resident in Scotland or Ireland;[2] or

"(f) Any injunction is sought as to anything to be done within the jurisdiction, or any nuisance within the jurisdiction is sought to be prevented or removed, whether damages are or are not also sought in respect thereof;[3] or

[1] An action to recover compensation for tenant right according to the custom of the country has been held to fall under this provision, *Kaye* v. *Sutherland* (1887), 20 Q. B. D. 147. But not an action for slander of title to land, *Casey* v. *Arnott* (1876), 2 C. P. D. 24.

[2] When a judge is in doubt whether there has been a breach of contract within the jurisdiction, the proper course is to make an order for service out of jurisdiction, at the same time imposing on the plaintiff the condition of recovering at the trial only the amount as to which it shall appear that service out of the jurisdiction was proper, *Thomas* v. *Hamilton* (1886), 17 Q. B. D. 592. The question whether the contract ought to be performed within jurisdiction may be *inferred* from the nature of the contract, *Robey* v. *Snaefell Mining Co.* (1887), 20 Q. B. 152.

[3] But the condition of granting service would no doubt be, that there was

"(g) Any person out of the jurisdiction is a necessary or proper party to an action properly brought against some other person duly served within the jurisdiction."[1]

Except in so far as the above statutory rules permit a Court to do so, service out of the jurisdiction being an interference with the ordinary course of law, is not allowable.[2] By the Indian Code of Civil Procedure, a summons may be served on a defendant outside of British India through the post, if there be postal communication between such place and the place where the Court is situate.[3] But in England Rule 6 of the Order above quoted prescribes that when the defendant is neither a British subject nor in British dominions, *notice of the writ and not the writ itself* is to be served upon him. Whence it follows that to justify the service out of jurisdiction of a *writ* the defendant must be a British subject; while in the case of a foreigner it can only be served if he is *within* the British dominions, and a *notice* of the writ must be substituted if he be outside those dominions. Any service effected on a foreigner in violation of this rule is not a mere error of procedure or irregularity, but an absolute nullity, affecting all the subsequent proceedings.[4] And such notices are to be given in the manner in which writs of summons are served (r. 7 of the same

a reasonable prospect of any such injunction being capable of being enforced in England. Cf. *Tozier* v. *Hawkins* (1885), 15 Q. B. D. 650.

[1] It is necessary that the party within jurisdiction should be served before an order for service out of jurisdiction can be made. *Yorkshire Tannery Co.* v. *Eglington Chemical Co.* (1884), 54 L. J. Ch. D. 81.

[2] *Re Busfield* (1886), 32 Ch. D. 123; *Re Maughan* (1874), 22 W. R. 748; *Re Brandon* (1886), 34 W. R. 352; *Re Anglo-African Steamship Co.* (1886), 32 Ch. D. 348.

[3] Sects. 89—92, Act. XIV. of 1882.

[4] *Fowler* v. *Barstow* (1881), 20 Ch. D. 246; *Great Australian Co.* v. *Martin* (1877), 5 Ch. D. 17; *Padley* v. *Camphausen* (1878), 10 Ch. D. 550; *Westman* v. *Aktiebolaget Ekmans Mekaniska Snickarefabrik* (1876), 1 Ex. D. 237.

Order)—that is to say, wherever practicable, in the manner in which personal service is made; but if it appear to the Court or a judge that the plaintiff is from any cause unable to effect prompt personal service, the Court or judge may make such order for substituted or other service, or for the substitution for service of notice by advertisement or otherwise, as may seem just.[1]

Mode of proving foreign law.

89. We have seen how frequently a Court in one country has to decide matters arising in a suit pending before it in accordance with the law of another country. But as a judge "has not organs to know and to deal with the text of the foreign law,"[2] he must look for extraneous aid to other sources of information which may be available to him. The onus, however, is on the party who relies on a foreign law to prove that it is different from the law of the land where the suit is pending.[3] In *Dalrymple* v. *Dalrymple*,[4] Lord Stowell, having to decide, in accordance with the law of Scotland, summarised the sources of information that were open to him as follow. "The authorities," he said, "to which I shall have occasion to refer are of three classes: first, the opinions of learned professors given in the present or similar cases; secondly, the opinions of eminent writers as delivered in books of great legal credit and weight; and thirdly, the certified adjudication of the tribunals of Scotland upon these subjects. I need only say that the last class stands highest in point of authority. Where private opinions, whether in books or writing, incline on one side and public decisions on the other, it will be the undoubted duty of the

[1] Order IX. (2) of 1883.

[2] Per Lord Brougham in *The Sussex Peerage Case* (1844), 11 Cl. & Fin. at p. 115.

[3] *Brown* v. *Gracey* (1821), Dow. & Ry. N. P. 41, note. Cf. Bar, § 37, pp. 98—101, Gillespie's translation; and sect. 137 of the Indian Negotiable Instruments Act, 1881.

[4] (1811), 2 Hagg. Consist. at p. 81.

Court which has to weigh them, *stare decisis*." The general practice, however, is to examine a person who is an expert, or one who is *peritus virtute officii* in the knowledge of the foreign law in each case, because it is possible that the law may have changed since it was last expounded.[1] The expert need not be a judge or a lawyer, but any person who is engaged in the performance of important and responsible duties in connection with which he is bound to make himself acquainted with the branch of law which is in question.[2]

Thus, a Persian Ambassador has been allowed to give evidence of Persian law, on his stating that members of the Persian diplomatic service were expected to be versed in law, and that there were no professional lawyers in Persia.[3] And in a more recent case the certificate of the Russian Ambassador was accepted as proof of the Russian law relating to the wills of the Russian Imperial family.[4] It is not, of course, to be supposed that the Court which has to form an opinion may not, with propriety, take upon itself to construe the words of a foreign law, and determine their application to the case in question, especially if there should be a variance or want of clearness in the testimony.[5] Thus, in *Bremer* v. *Freeman*, the Judicial Committee of the Privy Council held itself at liberty to form an opinion on the articles cited from the Code Napoleon;[6] and in the case of

[1] Taylor *on Evidence*, § 1042.

[2] Per Lord Langdale in *The Sussex Peerage Case*, cited *supra*, at p. 134. Cf. sect. 45 of the Indian Evidence Act. As to what questions may be asked of experts under the Indian Act, see I. L. R. 9 Cal. 455. In India the Court, in addition to examining experts, may refer to books, printed or published under the authority of the Government of the country, and containing a statement of the law. Sect. 38, Act. I. of 1872.

[3] *In the Goods of Dost Ali Khan* (1880), 6 P. D. 6.

[4] *Re Prince P. G. Oldenburg* (1884), 9 P. D. 234.

[5] Per Lord Langdale in *Nelson* v. *Bridport* (1846), 8 Beav. 537. Cf. also, *Concha* v. *Murrietta* (1889), 40 Ch. D. 543.

[6] (1857), 10 Moore, P. C. 306.

CHAP. VII. *Lindo* v. *Belisario*, in which the evidence as to foreign law was not clear and positive, Lord Stowell thought that he should not transgress his duty if he looked beyond the evidence, but not farther than the evidence fairly led.[1] Properly speaking, the evidence of witnesses skilled in the foreign law should not be confined to merely setting forth the contents of the written law, but to expound its effect and the state of law resulting from it. "The mere contents indeed," as Lord Denman observed in *The Baron de Bode's Case*,[2] "might often mislead persons not familiar with the particular system of law: the witness is called upon to state what law does result from the instrument." And although, by virtue of two statutes passed in the years 1859 and 1861 respectively, British Courts are empowered to ascertain what is the law of any foreign Court—English and Scotch Courts being considered as foreign to one another—by a direct requisition to such foreign Court, and this is now the more usual practice, it is still competent to examine witnesses as legal experts,[3] or to refer the question by a judicial remit to a foreign legal authority, such as a professor of law.[4] The former statute (22 & 23 Vict. c. 63) applies to cases where any Court *within* the British dominions requires information as to the law prevailing in any other part of the British dominions applicable to the facts of any given case. The other statute (24 & 25 Vict. c. 11) applies to cases where any Superior Court within the British dominions desires to ascertain the law of any foreign State with which Her Majesty shall have entered into a convention permitting a requisition for the purpose. The provisions in both statutes are substantially to the effect that, where it

[1] (1795), 1 Hagg. Consist. 216.

[2] (1844), 8 Q. B. Rep. 250.

[3] *Parnell* v. *Walter* (1889), 16 Ct. of Sess. Rep., 4th Ser., 917.

[4] *Goetz* v. *Aders* (1874), 2 Ct. of Sess. Rep., 4th Ser., 150.

shall be the opinion of any Court as above described that it is necessary or expedient for the proper disposal of any action to ascertain what is the law applicable to the facts of the case as administered abroad, or in any part of Her Majesty's dominions other than that where the Court is situate, the Court may direct a case to be prepared and laid before one of the Supreme Courts in the foreign country or in the other part of the British dominions whose law is to be ascertained, in order that such Court may give an opinion upon it. There is this distinction, however, in the treatment of the reply in the two cases: in the case of an opinion obtained from any other Court in the British dominions, the Court making the remit is bound to apply the opinion in the same manner as if it had been pronounced by such Court itself upon a case reserved. (22 & 23 Vict. c. 63, s. 3.) But Her Majesty in Council or the House of Lords may adopt or reject such opinion of any Court whose judgments are respectively reviewable by them, as the same shall appear to them to be well-founded or not in law. (Sect. 4.) On the other hand, in the case of a foreign Court, the Court making the remit may either re-remit the case for further consideration, or may make a fresh remit to any other Superior Court of the same country before proceeding to apply it. (24 Vict. c. 11, s. 2.)

Foreign judgments, how treated internationally.

90. Another method by which Courts in one country afford auxiliary help to those of another is by giving effect to the final judgments pronounced by the latter. This practice, with many local variations which a later jurisprudence has introduced, has an ancient history, which, like many other institutions of modern law, has to go back to Roman times to be properly understood. With the establishment of universal sovereignty, Roman tribunals, or tribunals exercising jurisdiction upon Roman principles, were formed in

CHAP. VII.

remote parts of the world. And in order to cement that notion of a central authority which Rome claimed as the acknowledged mistress of other nations, it soon became a settled theory that judges should universally respect the ultimate decisions of each other. Indeed, even when the reality of Roman political supremacy had dwindled into the shadow of a Holy Roman Empire, in which the majesty of territorial sovereignty was represented by a more or less effete Emperor with ambitious but unrecognised claims, and the spiritual by a Pope whose authority transcended every terrestrial basis, the universal influence which the principles of Roman law had formerly attained still survived in the daily practice of judicial tribunals. So that secular Courts, as well as the judicatories of the Church, felt bound to support each other, seeing that the law they each administered was substantially identical, based alike on Roman law. But as independent States gradually consolidated their power, the notion of strictly territorial sovereignty gained increasing development, and with it the authority of judicial tribunals was more closely restricted to their own territorial jurisdiction. It is not easy, however, to uproot a practice which has had the sanction of centuries in support of it, and thus Courts continued to put in execution the judgments of foreign Courts *ob reciprocum utilitatem et ex comitate*, subject, of course, to the necessary proviso that such Courts had jurisdiction to decide the subject-matter, and that the interests of their own State were not impaired by their doing so. Such, then, is the common genesis of the three prevailing theories which are known at the present day to the jurisprudence of modern Europe, and under some one form of which recognition is still accorded to foreign judgments. There is, in the first place, what may be called the Continental theory, according to which the foreign judgment is practically adopted and executed by the domestic Court as its own, conceding to it what the French call "*l'exécution parée*," with the modifications thereof requiring either (1) the formal requisition of the foreign Court (*commission rogatoire*), or (2) the existence of reciprocal treaties to this effect. This theory was regarded as thoroughly established in proceedings *in rem* in England so far back as 1667 in the old Court of Admiralty, and is still the basis of the practice of the Admiralty Division of the High Court. It was accepted in the former year by Sir Leoline Jenkins as "a *ruled* case that one judge must not refuse, upon letters of request, to execute the sentence of another foreign judge when the person or goods sentenced are within his jurisdiction, and, if he do, his superior must compel him to it, else it is sufficient ground for reprisals against the territory."[1] The practice was said to be due to the fact that "all the Courts of Admiralty in Europe are governed by the civil law, and are to be assistant one to another, though the matter were not originally determinable in our Court of Admiralty."[2] And so recently as 1879 Sir Robert Phillimore declared his duty, as a judge of the Admiralty Division of the High Court, to be "to act as auxiliary" to a Portuguese Court which had passed the original judgment, "and to complete the execution of justice which, owing to the departure of the ship, was necessarily left unfinished by that Court." "In other words," continued the learned judge, "it is my duty to place the English Court in the position of the Portuguese Court after its sentence has been given against the defendants."[3] This decision was, it is true, subsequently reversed on appeal, but only because it appeared that the Portuguese Court was not a court having admiralty jurisdiction, or jurisdiction equi-

[1] Wynn's *Life of Jenkins*, Vol. II., p. 762.

[2] Per Finch, afterwards Lord Nottingham, in arguing *Jurado* v. *Gregory* (1670), 1 Ventris, 32.

[3] *City of Mecca* (1879), 5 P. D. 28, at p. 33.

CHAP. VII. valent thereto, in proceedings on a maritime lien.[1] The same theory is partially recognised also by the Indian Code of Civil Procedure,[2] which authorises the Governor-General in Council to notify, from time to time, the native States, the decrees of whose Courts shall be recognised by British Indian Courts as enjoying this privilege; and all decrees of such Courts shall thereafter be enforced in British India as if they had been passed by a British Indian Court. *Secondly*, there is the theory more generally adopted by the English Courts—which is also as a general rule (subject to the special exemptions from it resulting from a notification by the Governor-General in Council of the kind already mentioned) followed by British Indian Courts—which regards the foreign judgment as giving rise to an obligation on which an action can be maintained. It is thus enunciated by Baron Parke, whose *dictum* has been approved of and followed in later cases: "Where a Court of competent jurisdiction has adjudicated a certain sum to be due from one person to another, a legal obligation arises to pay that sum on which an action of debt to enforce the judgment may be maintained." It is in this way that the judgments of foreign and colonial Courts are supported and enforced.[3] It is said, by Blackburn, J.,[4] to rest upon "what is loosely called international comity," a comity *usu exigente et humanis necessitatibus* which regards all obligations once created by an appropriate law as worthy of recognition in the tribunals of all other

[1] (1881), 6 P. D. 106.

[2] Sect. 229B, Act XIV. of 1882, as amended by sect. 39 (1) of Act VII. of 1888. This privilege has been at present extended to the following Courts:— 1. Courts of Kuch Bihar. 2. Courts of Mysore.

[3] In *Williams* v. *Jones* (1845), 13 M. & W. 633; *Russell* v. *Smyth* (1842), 9 M. & W. 810; *Godard* v. *Gray* (1870), L. R. 6 Q B. 139; *Schibsby* v. *Westenholz* (1870), *ibid.* 161; *Grant* v. *Easton* (1883), 13 Q. B. D. 302; *Hawksford* v. *Giffard* (1886), 12 App. Cas. 128. Cf. also *Sirdar Gurdyal Singh* v. *Raja of Faridkot* (1894), A. C. 670.

[4] *Schibsby* v. *Westenholz*, cited *supra*.

civilized States. And *thirdly*, there is the theory which merely regards the foreign judgment as evidence—though, no doubt, of high value—of the original cause of action, in a suit brought to enforce the latter. This theory is also recognised by English Courts, and it may, at the option of a plaintiff, be adopted in preference to the second theory, or *vice versâ*. It is based on the notion that the foreign judgment does *not* operate, like a domestic judgment, in extinguishing the original obligation by converting it into a debt of record of a higher nature, in accordance with the maxim *transit in rem judicatam*. As Bayley, J., observed in *Hall* v. *Odber*,[1] "it is only evidence of the debt"; and it follows from this principle that since the foreign judgment has not altered the rights of the parties, the plaintiff must be allowed an option, either to resort to the original ground of action, or to bring a suit on the judgment recovered, from which, as we have just seen, an implied contract to pay arises.[2] This is also the theory which, in practice, is acted upon by the French Courts. The law of France does not recognise a foreign judgment as possessing any binding authority outside the territory of the State in which it was passed. But, nevertheless, it regards the judgment as such weighty evidence that the findings of fact contained in it can only be rebutted by counter-evidence of the most cogent and convincing character. It is for this reason asserted by a French jurist, M. Massé,[3] that France practically accords as much respect to a foreign judgment as England, which is putting the claim

[1] (1809), 11 East, 118—124. Cf. also *Bank of Australasia* v. *Harding* (1850), 9 C. B. 661; *Bank of Australasia* v. *Nias* (1851), 16 Q. B. 717.

[2] Per Tindal, C.J., in *Smith* v. *Nicolls* (1839), 5 Bing. N. C. 208. In India it is doubtful whether, under the present Code of Civil Procedure (§ 13), the foreign judgment would not be a bar to the re-trial of questions arising out of the original cause of action, except as provided in § 5 of Act VII. of 1888.

[3] § 305.

on high ground, seeing that it has been acknowledged by a very eminent judge and jurist[1] that the Courts of England give as full effect to foreign sentences as is given to them in any part of the civilized world. It is not, however, *every* foreign judgment which can claim to be treated in accordance with one of the above theories. It must fulfil certain preliminary conditions, or it will be ignored altogether. What those conditions are must now be considered.

The foreign Court must have had jurisdiction over the defendant.

91. To entitle a foreign judgment, for example, to respect in another country the defendant must have been properly subject to the jurisdiction of the Court which passed it. In what circumstances an English Court will be disposed to concede that jurisdiction has been properly exercised, has thus been summed up by the late Lord Justice Fry in *Rousillon* v. *Rousillon* :—[2]

(i) Where the defendant is the subject of the foreign country in which the judgment has been obtained; or—

(ii) Where he was resident in the foreign country when the action began; or—

(iii) Where the defendant, in the character of plaintiff, has selected the *forum* in which he is afterwards sued; or—

(iv) Where he has voluntarily appeared; or—

(v) Where he has contracted to submit himself to the *forum* in which the judgment was obtained; or possibly, if *Becquet* v. *McCarthy*[3] be right, a case which was said by Lord Brougham[4] to have gone "to the verge of the law"—

(vi) Where the defendant has real estate within the foreign jurisdiction, in respect of which the cause of action arose while he was within that jurisdiction."

[1] Marshall, C.J., in 4 Cranch (U.S.) 270.

[2] (1880) 14 Ch. D. 371.

[3] (1831) 2 B. & Ad. 951.

[4] In *Don* v. *Lippmann* (1837), 5 Cl. & Fin. 21.

And with reference to ground iv., the authority for which is *De Cosse Brissac* v. *Rathbone*,[1] it is to be observed that a defendant will be held to have "voluntarily appeared" if, in fact, he appears and pleads, although his pleading may extend to both the jurisdiction of the Court and the merits of the case.[2] This is on the principle that if there exists no ground (such as above indicated) for imposing any duty on the defendant to obey the judgment of the foreign Court, his appearance must be attributed to his own voluntary act. For, as pointed out by Lord Selborne in the very recent case of *Sirdar Gurdyal Singh* v. *the Raja of Faridkot*,[3] he is under no obligation to appear by reason merely of the notice of the suits which he may have received, unless the Court which issued them had jurisdiction over him. By not appearing the defendant has shown that he declines the jurisdiction of the Court, and in such a case the facts upon which the jurisdiction is alleged to be founded are not to be assumed, but must be proved to the satisfaction of the executing Court by the party who claims that it has been validly exercised. It is not to be supported by fictions, but by facts.[4] The important ruling of the Privy Council, which has just been referred to, and which was passed by a particularly strong Board of the Judicial Committee, specially convened to hear the appeal, has also definitely settled another interesting question, which, previously to it, was still left in some doubt. The primary rule was, of course, well established that all jurisdiction was territorial and *extra territorium jus dicenti impune non paretur*.[5] Roman juris-

[1] (1861), 6 H. & N. 301. Cf. *Schibsby* v. *Westenholz* (cited *supra*), L. R. 6 Q. B. 162.

[2] *Boissière* v. *Brockner*, 6 Times L. R. 85; *Voinet* v. *Barrett* (1885), 54 L. J. Q. B. 521.

[3] (1894) A. C. 670.

[4] Bar, § 427, p. 924, Gillespie's translation.

[5] Dig. 2, 1, § 20.

CHAP. VII. prudence had also bequeathed to later systems of law the equally well established rule of jurisdiction, *actor sequitur rei forum*, *i.e.*, that the plaintiff must sue in the Court to which the defendant is subject at the time of suit—a rule which Sir Robert Phillimore (*rightly*, as Lord Selborne thinks) [1] pronounces to "lie at the root of all international, and most domestic, jurisprudence on this matter." [2] But with reference to the doctrine which Savigny had extracted from the Roman law, of an assumption of voluntary submission to the jurisdiction of the Court of the place of the fulfilment of an obligation,[3] it was supposed, but never *actually* decided in England, that "if at the time when the obligation was contracted the defendant was within the foreign country, but left it before the suit was instituted," he would be bound by a judgment obtained in that country concerning such an obligation.[4] In *Schibsby* v. *Westenholz* (cited *supra*), Blackburn, J., in delivering the opinion of the Court, remarked that he and his learned colleague "were inclined" to take this view; but he added, "though, before finally deciding this, he should like to hear the question argued." The question remained in this unsettled condition, till the recent decision of the Privy Council in the case above quoted—where it was fully argued—finally set it at rest with a negative answer. That was a case in which the defendant had been in the service of the Raja of Faridkot as his treasurer, and the claim was merely personal, for money alleged to be due, or recoverable in the nature of damages, from him. The Raja had instituted two suits in the Civil Court of his own State after the defendant had left his service and ceased to reside

1 In *Sirdar Gurdyal Singh* v. *Raja of Faridkot*, cited *supra*.

2 *Private Inter. Law*, Vol. IV., § 891.

3 *System d. heut. Röm. Rechts*, Vol. VIII., § 370, Guthrie's translation, pp. 160—4.

4 Cf. Phillimore, Vol. IV., § 934.

within his territorial jurisdiction, and had obtained *ex parte* judgments against him, upon which he subsequently sued in a British Indian Court. It was then pleaded for defendant that the Faridkot Court had no jurisdiction over him at the time of suit—a contention which was traversed on the ground that, as the cause of action on which each of the original claims was founded arose in the Faridkot State, the Civil Court of the State was a competent Court to hear and determine the same. The Indian Courts had differed on the question of jurisdiction, and this was the point which was mainly pressed for the defendant before their Lordships of the Privy Council, and eventually decided in his favour. Lord Selborne, in delivering the judgment of the Judicial Committee, disposed of the question in the following lucid manner. "Faridkot," said his Lordship, "was a native State, the Raja of which had been recognized by Her Majesty as having an independent civil, criminal, and fiscal jurisdiction. The judgments of its Courts were, and ought to be, regarded in Her Majesty's Courts of British India as foreign judgments. The Additional Commissioner of Lahore thought that no action could be brought in Her Majesty's Courts upon a judgment of a native State, but in that opinion their Lordships did not concur. The appellant was for five years, beginning in 1869, in the service of the late Raja of Faridkot as his treasurer, and the causes of action on which the suits in the Faridkot Court were brought arose within that State and out of that employment of the appellant by the late Raja. The claim made in each of the suits was merely personal, for money alleged to be due, or recoverable in the nature of damages, from the appellant. It was immaterial, in their Lordships' view, to the question of jurisdiction (which was the only question to be now decided) whether the case, as stated, ought to be regarded as one of contract or of tort. The appellant left the late

CHAP. VII.

Raja's service, and ceased to reside within his territorial jurisdiction, in 1874. He was from that time generally resident in another independent native State, that of Jhind, of which he was a native subject, and in which he was domiciled, and he never returned to Faridkot after he left it in 1874. He was in Jhind when he was served with certain processes of the Faridkot Court, as to which it was unnecessary for their Lordships to determine what the effect would have been if there had been jurisdiction. He disregarded them, and never appeared in either of the suits instituted by the Raja, or otherwise submitted himself to that jurisdiction. He was under no obligation to do so, by reason of the notice of the suits which he thus received or otherwise, unless that Court had lawful jurisdiction over him. In these circumstances there was, in their Lordships' opinion, nothing to take the case out of the general rule that the plaintiff must sue in the Court to which the defendant is subject at the time of suit (*Actor sequitur forum rei*), which was rightly stated by Sir Robert Phillimore[1] to 'lie at the root of all international and of most domestic jurisprudence on this matter.' All jurisdiction was properly territorial and *extra territorium jus dicenti, impune non paretur*. Territorial jurisdiction attached (with special exceptions) upon all persons either permanently or temporarily resident within the territory while they were within it, but it did not follow them after they had withdrawn from it and when they were living in another independent country. It existed always as to land within the territory, and it might be exercised over moveables within the territory, and in questions of *status* or succession governed by domicile it might exist as to persons domiciled or who, when living, were domiciled within the territory. As

[1] *International Law*, Vol. IV., § 891.

between different provinces under one sovereignty (*e.g.*, under the Roman Empire) the legislation of the Sovereign might distribute and regulate jurisdiction, but no territorial legislation could give jurisdiction which any foreign Court ought to recognise against foreigners who owed no allegiance nor obedience to the Power which so legislated. In a personal action to which none of these causes of jurisdiction applied, a decree pronounced *in absentem* by a foreign Court, to the jurisdiction of which the defendant had not in any way submitted himself, was by international law an absolute nullity. He was under no obligation of any kind to obey it, and it must be regarded as a mere nullity by the Courts of every nation, except (when authorized by special local legislation) in the country of the *forum* by which it was pronounced. Those were doctrines laid down by all the leading authorities on international law; among others, by Story[1] and by Chancellor Kent,[2] and no exception was made to them in favour of the exercise of jurisdiction against a defendant not otherwise subject to it by the Courts of the country in which the cause of action arose, or (in cases of contract) by the Courts of the *locus solutionis*. In those cases, as well as all others, when the action was personal, the Courts of the country in which a defendant resided had power, and they ought to be resorted to, to do justice. The conclusion of the learned judges in the Chief Court of the Punjaub was expressed in the following sentence of the judgment delivered by Sir Meredyth Plowden, in the first of the two actions:—'On the whole, I think it may be said that a State assuming to exercise jurisdiction over an absent foreigner, in respect of an obligation arising out of a contract made by the foreigner while resident in the State and to be fulfilled there, is not acting in contravention of the

1 *Conflict of Laws*, 2nd ed., §§ 546, 549, 553, 554, 556, 586.
2 *Commentaries*, Vol. I., p. 284, note *c*, 10th ed.

CHAP. VII.

general practice or the principles of international law, so that its judgment should not be binding merely on the ground of the absence of the defendant.' If that doctrine were accepted, its operation, in the enlargement of territorial jurisdiction, would be very important. No authority, of any relevancy, was cited at their Lordships' bar to support it, except *Becquet* v. *Macarthy*,[1] and a passage from the judgment delivered by Mr. Justice Blackburn in *Schibsby* v. *Westenholz*.[2] Of *Becquet* v. *Macarthy*, it was said by a great authority, in *Don* v. *Lippmann*,[3] that 'it had been supposed to go to the verge of the law,' and it was explained (as their Lordships thought correctly) on the ground that 'the defendant held a public office in the very colony in which he was originally sued.' He still held that office when he was sued; the cause of action arose out of or was connected with it, and though he was in fact temporarily absent, he might, as the holder of such an office, be regarded as constructively present in the place where his duties required his presence, and, therefore, amenable to the colonial jurisdiction. If the case could not be distinguished on that ground from that of any absent foreigner who at some previous time might have been in the employment of a colonial Government, it would, in their Lordships' opinion, have been wrongly decided; and it was evident that Lord Justice Fry, in *Rousillon* v. *Rousillon*,[4] took that view. The words of Mr. Justice Blackburn's judgment in *Schibsby* v. *Westenholz*[5] which were relied upon were these:—'If at the time when the obligation was contracted the defendants were within the foreign country, but left it before the suit was instituted, we should be inclined to think

[1] 2 Barn. & Ad. 951.
[2] L. R. 6 Q. B. 155.
[3] 5 Clark & Finnelly, 1.
[4] L. R. 14 Ch. Div. 351.
[5] L. R. 6 Q. B. 161.

the laws of that country bound them, though, before finally deciding this, we should like to hear the question argued.' Upon that sentence it was to be observed that beyond doubt in such a case the laws of the country in which an obligation was contracted might bind the parties, so far as the interpretation and effect of the obligation was concerned, in whatever *forum* the remedy might be sought. The learned judge had not to consider whether it was a legitimate consequence from that that they would be bound to submit, on the footing of contract or otherwise, to any assumption of jurisdiction over them in respect of such a contract by the tribunals of the country in which the contract was made at any subsequent time, although they might be foreigners resident abroad. That question was not argued, and did not arise in the case then before the Court, and, if that was what Mr. Justice Blackburn meant, their Lordships could not regard any mere inclination of opinion on a question of such large and general importance, on which the judges themselves would have desired to hear argument if it had required decision, as entitled to the same weight which might be due to a considered judgment of the same authority. Upon the question itself, which was determined in *Schibsby* v. *Westenholz*, Mr. Justice Blackburn had at the trial formed a different opinion from that at which he ultimately arrived; and their Lordships did not doubt that, if he had heard argument upon the question whether an obligation to accept the *forum loci contractûs*, as having by reason of the contract a conventional jurisdiction against the parties in a suit founded upon that contract for all future time, wherever they might be domiciled or resident, was generally to be implied, he would have come (as their Lordships did) to the conclusion that such obligation, unless expressed, could not be implied."

In connection, however, with the question of competency of the foreign Court, it is to be observed that the conduct of

CHAP. VII. a party may preclude him from raising the question.[1] Thus, as we have seen, a defendant by voluntarily appearing and taking the chance of a judgment in his favour has been precluded from afterwards objecting to the jurisdiction, though in a subsequent case (that of *Schibsby* v. *Westenholz*) the point was expressly left undecided; while, still later, the general proposition was apparently approved by Lord Justice Fry in *Rousillon* v. *Rousillon*.[2] So also, on the other hand, if a person, as plaintiff, selected the tribunal of a foreign country as the one in which he would sue, he cannot afterwards be heard to say that the judgment of that tribunal was not binding upon him.[3] And the doctrine of the *forum rei* as a sufficient ground of competency for a foreign judgment, upon which Lord Selborne, in *Sirdar Gurdyal Singh's Case*, lays such stress, is thus expanded by Blackburn, J. "If," said his Lordship, "the defendants had been at the time of the judgment subjects of the country whose judgment is sought to be enforced against them, we think that its laws would have bound them. Again, if the defendants had been at the time when the suit was commenced resident in the country, so as to have the benefit of its laws protecting them, or as it is sometimes expressed, owing temporary allegiance to that country, we think that its laws would have bound them."[4] It would appear, also, that the competency here spoken of is general *territorial* competency, and is not affected by any municipal regulation, whereby litigation is distributed among different Courts in the same State. Accordingly, if the foreign suit was not brought in the right court of a country territorially competent, it has been held that this was matter of defence which ought to have been pleaded in that court, and

[1] Cf. Bar, § 413, and note (22), p. 899, Gillespie's translation.
[2] 14 Ch. D. (1880), 351. Cf. Westlake, § 326, p. 348, 3rd ed.
[3] *Schibsby* v. *Westenholz*, L. R. 6 Q. B. 161.
[4] *Ibid.*

which the defendant is estopped from subsequently raising in a suit brought on the judgment recovered in another country.[1] On the other hand, a Court may be territorially competent but not internationally. Thus, to found jurisdiction in the latter sense, it is not enough that the defendant should possess moveable property within the State. That circumstance may indeed, according to the domestic legislation, give a claimant the right to attach such property there, *fundandæ jurisdictionis causâ*. But if the defendant is not himself subject to that jurisdiction upon any of the other grounds indicated above, the jurisdiction in the particular case will be limited to the extent of property attached, and will not be recognized outside the territorial limits of the State beyond that amount. Thus, where certain plaintiffs domiciled in Natal had attached property there belonging to the defendants, who were domiciled in the Cape Colony, in order to found jurisdiction, and had obtained judgment against the defendants in Natal, but the property attached proved quite insufficient to cover the judgment, and the plaintiff thereupon sued the defendants in the Supreme Court of the Cape Colony on the Natal judgment, it was held that the plaintiff could not succeed. "If it had been proved," said De Villiers, C.J., "that the defendants were residents of Natal at the time judgment was given, no difficulty would arise, because the court would be bound by the comity of the States to give effect to the judgment against persons domiciled in the State in which the judgment was given; but in the present case the defendants resided within this Colony, and judgment was given against them at Natal. If a person in Natal wishes to sue any person within this Colony, he must come into this Court to do so, and I cannot accede to the proposition that because there had been an attachment of the defendant's property in Natal, the

[1] *Vanquelin* v. *Bonard*, 15 C. B. N. S. (1863), 341, at pp. 350, 368, and 374; S. C. Law Jour. 33 C. P. 78, 84; *Henderson* v. *Henderson* (1844), 6 Q. B. 288.

CHAP. VII.

Court of Natal obtained jurisdiction over his property here. By the attachment of the property in Natal the Court obtained a jurisdiction in respect of that particular property, but the defendants not having appeared in that court at all, I do not think that this Court is bound to give effect to the judgment."[1]

Other conditions required to make a foreign judgment effective.

92. Among the other conditions[2] which a foreign judgment must fulfil to be entitled to recognition extraterritorially, it must (a) have been passed on the merits between the same parties or their representatives in interest, (b) it must be free from fraud,[3] and (c) not tainted with "a total disregard of the comity of nations,"[4] or inconsistent with the plain principles of "natural justice."[5] Where these conditions are all existing, the foreign judgment, if passed by a competent Court definitively, may not only be sued upon in England, but may also be pleaded as an *exceptio rei judicatæ* in bar of a second suit, where the plaintiff's claim has been judicially decided against him, or where judgment has been recovered and satisfied. If the foreign judgment has not, however, decided the very subject-matter which is litigated upon in a subsequent suit, it is plain the *res* is not adjudicated, and consequently the former judgment cannot be pleaded as a bar to the trial of the issues raised in the second suit. It would seem to be equally plain that, if, for instance, it should happen that by the law of a foreign country a plaintiff was entitled

[1] *Acutt, Blaine & Co.* v. *The Colonial Marine Assurance Co.*, 1 Juta, 406, cited in *Opinions of Grotius*, by D. P. De Bruyn, pp. 98, 99.

[2] *Vide* Sect. 14 of the Indian Code of Civil Procedure.

[3] Per Blackburn, J., in *Castrique* v. *Imrie* (1870), L. R. 4 H. L. 414; *Blake* v. *Smith* (1810), 8 Sim. 303; *Ochsenbein* v. *Papelier* (1873), L. R. 8 Ch. 695; *Abouloff* v. *Oppenheimer* (1882), 10 Q. B. D. 295; and cf. same principle applied to English judgments, *Innes* v. *Mitchell* (1857), 4 Dr. 102, note.

[4] Per Lord Chelmsford in *Liverpool Marine Credit Co.* v. *Hunter* (1868), L. R. 3 Ch. at p. 484.

[5] Per Lord Hatherley in same case.

to judgment simply on the non-appearance of a defendant who had been duly served, and without adducing any evidence whatever in support of his claim, or if the wrong-headedness of a foreign judge should induce him to so decide, the plaintiff would not be entitled in an English Court to sue upon a judgment so obtained. If, on no other ground, such a judgment of a foreign Court would, at all events, be so contrary to the fundamental principles of the law of England as, for this reason alone, to be incapable of receiving any effect in a British Court. Again, in regard to fraud, that is an element which would vitiate any obligation,[1] and that it can be pleaded against a foreign, as it can in the case of a domestic, judgment, is beyond all doubt; for, as Lord Coke says, "it avoids all judicial acts, ecclesiastical or temporal."[2] It has been so decided by the Court of Appeal in Chancery in the case of *Ochsenbein* v. *Papelier*,[3] where Lord Selborne disposed of the contrary contention in the following clear terms. "It has been suggested," said his Lordship, "that there may be a doubt about the power of a Court of law to give full effect to the allegations of fraud contained in those portions of the bill which relate to the foreign judgment. I should be sorry to think that anything should fall from this Court which might give the least colour to any doubt as to the power of a Court of law to take cognizance of fraud in obtaining judgments. . . . . I say, therefore, without hesitation, that, supposing the fraud to be one provable here, it could be pleaded at law, and would be a legal defence." The fraud, however, must be of a party seeking to enforce the judgment, and not of a mere stranger.[4] And lastly, as to the foreign judgment not being inconsistent with the

[1] Per Blackburn, J., in *Castrique* v. *Imrie*, cited *supra*.
[2] Per De Grey, C.J., citing Coke, in *Duchess of Kingston's Case*, 2 Sm. L. C. 760, 7th ed.
[3] L. R. 8 Ch. 695.
[4] Per Brett, J., in *Abouloff* v. *Oppenheimer* (1882), 10 Q. B. at p. 298.

principles of natural justice, this does not mean that the Court (other than a British Indian Court dealing with the judgment of a Court in a Native State) whose auxiliary aid is sought is to sit in appeal on the judgment of the foreign Court and to examine its findings of fact, but simply that there should not be that disregard of those general principles which commend themselves to all civilized nations alike as in accordance with the plain dictates of natural justice,[1]—as, for instance, that no judgment should be passed against a person who has had no notice in fact, either actual or constructive, of the pendency of legal proceedings against him, and, consequently, of being heard in his defence; or that, supposing such a case to be conceivable, a judge was so perverse as to hold that, although the defendant had made good his defence of payment, yet, as he was a rich man, to whom the amount was of no consequence, while the plaintiff was a poor man, to whom it would be of substantial assistance, and probably save him from starvation, it was right to reject the defence and decree the claim; or, again, that the judge was himself the plaintiff, or pecuniarily interested in the decision of the subject-matter of the suit. Such instances of an absolute disregard of justice may be hardly likely to occur in any country where a regular system of jurisprudence prevails. But the possibility of their occurrence cannot be ignored in a statement of general rules concerning the effect to be given to foreign judgments. Formerly, indeed, authorities were not wanting in English, as well as Scotch, case law to justify an examination into the *merits* of a foreign judgment when it formed the basis of a suit in England or in Scotland. Thus Lord Mansfield, in *Walker* v. *Wilter*,[2] said that "foreign judgments are a ground of action everywhere, *but they are*

[1] *Henderson* v. *Henderson* (1844), 6 Q. B. 298.
[2] 1 Doug. (1778), 6.

examinable;" and in *Tarleton* v. *Tarleton*,[1] Bayley, J., expressed the opinion that, "as between the parties to the suit, the justice of it (*i.e.*, the foreign judgment) might be again litigated, but as against a stranger it cannot." So in Scotland Lord Jeffrey held that a foreign judgment (in that case of the Court of Chancery of the State of New York) could be "impugned on the part of the defenders, not merely by proof of want of jurisdiction in the Court from which it issued, or of its having been pronounced in the absence of the defender, or of material irregularities and informalities in the course of the proceedings, but also by proof of its having proceeded on error of fact, or even on error of law, more especially when the law applicable to the case was not the proper law of the country where the suit was tried and determined."[2] This *dictum* was referred to with approval in *Whitehead* v. *Thompson*,[3] where it was laid down that a foreign judgment is examinable on grounds, clearly and relevantly stated, going to impeach its validity and its justice. But even so far back as 1679 there are indications of the more modern doctrine of the English Courts that the judgment of a competent Court of an ordinary European or American State cannot be questioned in England for error either in fact or in law. Thus in *Gold* v. *Canham*,[4] decided in that year, Lord Nottingham allowed one partner to charge another with money paid for a partnership debt under a foreign sentence, "*the justice whereof*," he said, "*is not examinable here*." And in *Henderson* v. *Henderson*, cited *supra*, Lord Denman, C.J., delivering the judgment of himself, Williams, Coleridge, and Wightman, JJ., accepted this doctrine as well-established. "Several pleas," he said, "were pleaded to show that the

[1] 4 M. & S. (1815), 23.
[2] *Southgate* v. *Montgomerie* (1837), 15 Ct. of Sess. Rep., 1st Ser., p. 507.
[3] 23 Ct. of Sess. Rep., 2nd Ser. (1861), p. 773.
[4] 2 Sw. 325; S. C. 1 Ca. in Ch. 311.

defendant had not had justice done him in the Court of Chancery at Newfoundland. This is never to be presumed, but the contrary principle holds, unless we see in the clearest light that the foreign law, or at least some part of the proceedings of the foreign Court, are repugnant to natural justice; and this has often been made the subject of inquiry into in our courts. *But it steers clear of an inquiry into the merits of the case upon the facts found*, for whatever constituted a defence in that court ought to have been pleaded there." So in the *Bank of Australasia* v. *Nias*,[1] Lord Campbell regarded it as "contrary to principle and expediency for the same questions to be again submitted to a jury in this country"; and in 1861 the Court of Exchequer held that this doctrine was no longer an open one.[2] Accordingly, in *Godard* v. *Gray*,[3] Blackburn, J., said: "The decisions seem to us to leave it no longer open to contend, unless in a court of error, that a foreign judgment can be impeached on the ground that it was erroneous on the merits, or to set up, as a defence to an action on it, that the tribunal mistook either the facts or the law. . . . The defendant can no more set up as an excuse that the judgment proceeded on a mistake as to English law than he could set up as an excuse that there had been a mistake as to the law of some third country incidentally involved, or as to any other question of fact." Here it is noteworthy the foreign Court made a mistake as to the English law applicable to the case, and yet the Queen's Bench (Hannen, J., dissenting) refused to admit the defence in a suit brought in England on the judgment. Again, in *Castrique* v. *Imrie*,[4] the same learned judge, after an exhaustive review of the older authorities, enunciated the

[1] 16 Q. B. (1851), 736.
[2] *De Cosse Brissac* v. *Rathbone*, 6 H. & N. 301.
[3] L. R. 6 Q. B. (1870), at p. 150.
[4] L. R. 4 E. & J. A. (1870), 434.

same doctrine, that the judgment of the foreign Court, if final, is examinable for no error or mistake, except a mistake by which it gave itself jurisdiction, when, by the principles of private international law, it would have had none. The only exception which later case law has engrafted upon this doctrine is where *both* parties *admit* that the foreign Court has wrongly interpreted its own law. In such a case it has been held that there was no rule of comity and no principle on which an English Court could be called upon to give effect to the foreign judgment.[1] So in Scotland, the older doctrine, if it has not been as completely abandoned as in England, has at least been so modified as to very closely assimilate to the later English view. Lord Fraser, for instance, has expressed his doubts as to the soundness of the *dictum* of Lord Jeffrey already quoted,[2] and has pronounced a judgment of a foreign Court of competent jurisdiction to be more than *primâ facie* evidence; "it is conclusive, and is given effect to." In a somewhat later decision by Lord McLaren, in the case of *Gudin*,[3] the law is perhaps more cautiously laid down to the effect that, although a decree or judgment of the Superior Courts of England when founded on for execution in a Scotch Court, is examinable, this is not to be understood to mean that there is to be a re-trial of the cause on issues of fact or law. The Scotch Court, according to this latter view, will not refuse to give effect to the foreign judgment merely because, on a balance of evidence, it might itself have come to a different conclusion. And the examination of the foreign judgment at all is confined to cases where it is sought to be enforced in a Scotch Court. Where the foreign judgment, however, is only pleaded in bar as *res judicata*, in answer to a fresh demand by the same

[1] *Meyer* v. *Ralli* (1876), L. R. 1 C. P. D. 358.
[2] *Pattison* v. *M'Vicar* (1886), 13 Ct. of Sess. Rep., 4th Ser., p. 555.
[3] 14 Ct. of Sess. Rep., 4th Ser. (8 Decr. 1886), 216.

pursuer, who has failed to establish his claim in a foreign Court, it cannot be examined.[1] This is explained by Erskine,[2] on the ground that the defender, in whose favour the decree was given, does not in such case apply to the Court for its aid, but, on the contrary, rests entirely on the sentence recovered by him in a foreign Court confessedly competent in the cause; and so in effect excepts to the jurisdiction of the judge before whom he is called as having no authority over that Court, nor any right of reviewing its sentences. With respect, however, to judgments of the Supreme Courts of England, Ireland, or Scotland, it is enacted by the Judgments Extension Act of 1868 (31 & 32 Vict. c. 54), that those of one Supreme Court will have the effect of judgments of the Supreme Courts of the other two territories if duly registered there, as directed by the Act. In British India, up to 1888, the Courts adopted the English doctrine. But in that year the Legislature deemed it necessary to authorize Courts in British India to examine the merits of any judgment of any foreign Court in Asia or Africa (excepting Courts of Record established by letters patent of Her Majesty, or any predecessor of Her Majesty, or a Supreme Consular Court established by an Order of Her Majesty in Council), when pleaded before them in bar of a fresh suit as a *res judicata*.[3] This step was taken with reference to the very different character of Courts in such States, as compared with those existing in European countries; for it was felt that, however great may have been the efforts on the part of several of the Sovereign Princes in India to place their Courts on a sound basis, the time had hardly come when

[1] This was also the earlier theory of the English Courts, as indicated in *Phillips* v. *Hunter* (1795), 2 H. Bl. 410.

[2] Vol. IV. 3, 4. Cf. also per Lord Braxfield, L.J.C., in *Watson's Case:* "A *res judicata* is good all the world over. The Courts here would have no right to review this final judgment." 8 Bell's *Cases*, 107.

[3] *Vide* Sect. 5 of Act VII. of 1888.

a principle applicable to Courts in European countries, presided over by trained lawyers, could be safely extended indiscriminately to all the Courts of the independent Native States whose territories adjoin those of the British Crown. Under the existing law, the Governor-General in Council, as above mentioned, can declare Courts, in certain Native States, to be entitled to have their decrees executed in British India as if they had been passed by a British Indian Court; and this provision affords an adequate means of recognizing the confidence which may be justly shown by British Courts in the decisions of the judicial tribunals in the more advanced and better administered Native States. But to treat the judicial administration in *all* Native States on the same footing, and as entitled to the same respect, would be as impolitic as it would be unwise; and the amended law, if properly worked, will henceforth enable Courts in British India to avoid lending themselves blindly to perpetuate injustice by enforcing judgments of Native and African States, without reference to what the true merits of each case might require. Nor need the Native States feel themselves aggrieved by the recent legislation, seeing that France still refuses (except where a treaty provides otherwise), at least in theory, to execute *any* foreign judgment until it has been confirmed by a French Court, and that the same practice pravails in Belgium and the Netherlands; while other States, like Sweden and Norway, yield no recognition whatever to foreign judgments as such, but relegate the plaintiff in every case to his original cause of action. It is, perhaps, necessary to add the caution that in applying the above principles as to a plea of *res judicata*, based on a foreign judgment, it does not at all follow that, because a plaintiff has been refused a certain relief abroad—as, for instance, rescission of contract—he may not be still entitled to sue for other relief in another country, *i.e.*, for damages, on the same facts.[1] And in dealing with a plea of *res judicata*, an Indian Court will bear in mind the conditions required by sect. 13 of the Code of Civil Procedure of 1882; while an English Court will, in like manner, pay due regard to what is said by Wigram, J., in *Henderson* v. *Henderson*,[2] as to when this plea applies in personal actions, read in connection with the later exposition by Lord Westbury, which somewhat qualifies the former, in *Hunter* v. *Stewart*.[3]

Foreign judgments *in rem* held conclusive all the world over, if passed by competent Court and untainted by fraud.

93. The same principles which have been enunciated above as to *res judicata* in the case of personal actions apply with even greater force to a foreign judgment *in rem*. In the case of a foreign judgment *in personam* the plea, as we have seen, can only be effective if the parties in the second action are the same or their representatives in interest. Where they are not so, the rule of law *res inter alios acta* operates, and the former judgment is not only not binding, but is even not admissible, in evidence, except under very special circumstances, against strangers. But a judgment *in rem* stands on a different footing in this respect. The effect of it, as pointed out in a preceding paragraph,[4] is to change or determine the ownership of a thing, whether moveable or immoveable, and by thus disposing of the thing itself general convenience has induced the doctrine that it should be binding all the world over. Thus a condemnation in a Prize Court not merely declares the vessel prize, but vests it in the captors. The *status* of the thing being thus altered, the sentence altering it, whether from a Court of exclusive jurisdiction or not, ought to be respected everywhere, or

[1] *Callandar* v. *Dittrich* (1842), 4 M. & Gr. 68; Westlake, § 336, p. 356, 3rd ed.

[2] 3 Ha. (1843), 115.

[3] (1861), 31 L. J. Ch. 346.

[4] *Vide* § 51, p. 86.

the greatest confusion would arise.[1] But to produce this effect the judgment must, of course, be that of a competent Court. Thus Lord Stowell designated the assumed exercise of jurisdiction by a Prize Court of a *belligerent* Power sitting in a *neutral* country as a "licentious attempt to exercise the rights of war within the bosom of a neutral country."[2] The true criterion for determining the international validity of a judgment *in rem* is, however, more fully stated by Blackburn, J., in delivering the opinion of the judges in *Castrique* v. *Imrie*.[3] "We may observe," he says, "that the words as to an action being *in rem* or *in personam*, and the common statement that the one is binding on third persons and the other not, are apt to be used by English lawyers without attaching any very definite meaning to those phrases. We apprehend the true principle to be that indicated in the last few words quoted from Story.[4] We think the inquiry is, first: whether the subject-matter was so situated as to be within the lawful control of the State under the authority of which the Court sits; and, secondly, whether the sovereign authority of that State has conferred on the Court jurisdiction to decide as to the disposition of the thing, and the Court has acted within its jurisdiction. *If these conditions are fulfilled, the adjudication is conclusive against all the world.*" This conclusiveness extends to every fact which the foreign Court has found, either as part of its actual adjudication or as one of the stated grounds of its decision.[5] Since, however, all judicial acts may be avoided or impeached for fraud, it is clear that a foreign judgment *in rem* may also be

[1] Phillimore, Vol. IV., § 950.

[2] *The Flad Oyen*, 1 Rob. Adm. 336.

[3] L. R. 4 E. & I. A. (1870), 429.

[4] Cf. *Conflict of Laws*, § 586.

[5] *Hobbs* v. *Henning*, 17 C. B. N. S. at p. 825; S. C. 34 L. J. C. P. 117; *Fisher* v. *Ogle*, 1 Camp. 418; *Dagleish* v. *Hodgson* (1831), 7 Bing, 504.

so,[1] provided that the fraud alleged is not something which might have been raised as a defence in the foreign Court upon the facts which were then before it.[2]

Plea of *lis alibi pendens* where the other action is in a foreign Court.

94. The mere pendency of proceedings in a foreign Court will not, however, prevent an English Court from exercising jurisdiction about the same matter at the instance of the same plaintiff. The doctrine of *lis alibi pendens*, which affords a good defence where two Courts have concurrent jurisdiction within the same dominions,[3] subject, of course, to any domestic legislation defining the relation between such Courts, has no application where the other action is pending in a foreign Court. Indeed, to admit the plea in the latter case would be often attended with great injustice to the plaintiff, for it would enable the defendant to gain time to remove his assets from one jurisdiction to another, and the decree which the plaintiff might eventually obtain in one State would become practically unfructuous. Seeing, moreover, that the plaintiff cannot escape the necessity of a double action, inasmuch as he would not be permitted in England to enforce his foreign judgment by prompt execution, but would be compelled to bring a fresh suit upon it, he ought not, in fairness, to be denied the right to proceed with his foreign suit concurrently with a similar action in an English Court, in order to obtain speedy satisfaction of his claim. A certain inconvenience may no doubt be felt by a defendant in having to defend a multiplicity of actions concerning the same matter. But the answer to this objection is given by Camden, J., in *Bayley* v. *Edwards*[4]:—"As to the incon-

[1] *Shand* v. *Du Boisson* (1874), L. R. 18 Eq. 283; *Messina* v. *Petrocochino* (1872), L. R. 4 P. C. 144, 157.

[2] *Castrique* v. *Behrens* (1861), 30 L. J. Q. B. 163.

[3] *Ostell* v. *Lepage* (1851), 5 De G. & S. 95, 105; and Section 12 of Act XIV. of 1882 (the Code of Civil Procedure for India).

[4] 3 Sw. (1792), 711.

venience," he said, "considering the difficulties of administering justice between parties occasionally living under separate jurisdictions, I think the parties ought to be amenable to every Court possible, when they are travelling from country to country; and we must then endeavour to correct the mischief of these double suits as much as we can by allowing in each country the benefit of all the other proceedings in the other part of the king's dominions." The learned judge was here dealing with a Jamaica case. The question, rather, is one of the balance of convenience, and it is now well established that the mere existence of a *lis alibi pendens* abroad at the date of the commencement of a suit in England for the same matter will afford no defence to the prosecution of the latter.[1] It must be shown that there is vexation actually caused to the defendant, and that without any necessity for it, before an English Court will interfere by putting the plaintiff to an election between the English and the foreign suit. The principles by which the Court ought to be guided in applications of this nature were fully examined and discussed in the case of *McHenry* v. *Lewis*,[2] and the decision in that case was referred to by Lord Justice Lindley in a subsequent case as a "most valuable" one. "As I understand it," said the Lord Justice, "it comes to this: that where the plaintiff is suing in this country and also abroad in respect of the same matter, and a motion is made to compel the plaintiff to elect, it is not sufficient for the person so moving to point out that there are two proceedings being taken with reference to the same matter; he must go a step further, and show that there is vexation in point of fact; that is to say, that there is no necessity for harassing

[1] *Cox* v. *Mitchell* (1859), 7 C. B. N. S. 55; *Scott* v. *Seymour* (1862), 1 H. & C. 219, 229; *The Mali Ivo* (1869), L. R. 2 A. & E. 356; *The Catterina Chiazzare* (1876), L. R. 1 P. D. 368; *Thornton* v. *Thornton* (1886), 11 P. D. 176; *Mutrie* v. *Binney* (1887), 35 Ch. D. 614.

[2] 22 Ch. D. (1882), 397, confirming 21 Ch. D. (1882), 202.

CHAP. VII. the defendant by double litigation. Moreover, I think the Court ought to be very cautious before it interferes in cases of that kind, and for this reason: the Court here is not, and cannot be, alive to all the advantages which a person may expect to derive from suing in the foreign Court."[1] And it appears that the same principles will be applied whether the earlier proceedings were begun in England or abroad. Thus, in *Hymen* v. *Hehn*,[2] where the defendant in England took proceedings abroad, it was held that a special case of vexation must be made out in order to restrain him. The double proceedings will be more readily interfered with where the English Court is familiar with the procedure of the competing Court, as, for example, if the other action is pending in Scotland, Ireland, or in a British dependency, where similar remedies are afforded as are available in England, and where execution on the English judgment can easily be done, than where the action is pending in a country politically foreign.[3] The Scotch Courts follow in this matter very much the same rule as the English. Thus, in the case of *Cochrane* v. *Paul*,[4] Lord Neaves expressed it in these terms. "There seems," he said, "no incompetency in a creditor bringing several suits against his debtor in several countries for the same debt, if there is jurisdiction in all, though there is always an equitable power and duty of control in each tribunal to see that there is not on the whole an improper and oppressive accumulation of litigation or diligence." Whether, supposing both actions to proceed simultaneously, an earlier judgment obtained in the foreign suit can be pleaded in the English suit as *res judicata*, is a question which can scarcely be said to be settled. In *The Delta*[5] case

[1] *Peruvian Guano Co.* v. *Bockwoldt* (1883), 23 Ch. D. 225.
[2] 24 Ch. D. (1883), 531.
[3] *McHenry* v. *Lewis*, cited *supra*.
[4] 20 Ct. of Sess. Rep., 2nd Ser. (1857), p. 178.
[5] 1 P. D. (1876), 393.

the question was answered in the negative; but in a more recent case, Pearson, J., was not prepared to say, without a closer examination of the rules of Court, that a defendant was not now at liberty to set up as *res judicata* a decision on the points at issue by a Court of competent jurisdiction during the process of the action.[1] This doubt may be justified with reference to the rule of Court permitting a defendant to plead a defence arising since action brought, subject only to a question of costs. But if the jurisdiction of an English Court to deal with a suit is not ousted by a *lis pendens* relating to the same matter in a foreign Court, it does not appear to be a very sound doctrine to hold that this jurisdiction is immediately taken away if the foreign Court happens to decide before the English Court does so. A jurisdiction once legally vested in a Court should not be liable to be divested by something which is subsequently done by a foreign Court under a different sovereign authority. In accordance with the maxim, *Judex tenetur impertiri judicium suum*, a judge who has jurisdiction is bound to give justice to those who ask for it. And the only ground on which the contrary view could be supported—namely, to avoid the possibility of conflicting decisions in regard to the same subject-matter—would, at all events, have no weight in a country like France, Belgium, or British India, where the merits of the foreign judgment are open to review.[2] In this matter, however, as in all questions properly dealing with the procedure of actions, the precise course to be taken must be determined according to the law of each court.[3] And it is with distinct reference to the rules framed under the Judicature Acts that Pearson, J., expressed his doubts as to whether the doctrine laid down

[1] *Houston* v. *Sligo* (1885), 29 Ch. D. 454.

[2] Cf. *Cours de Droit International Privé*, par Ch. Brocher, III., § 21, p. 112. (1885.)

[3] Bar, § 473, p. 1008, Gillespie's translation.

CHAP. VII.

in *The Delta* on the point here discussed would now hold good.

We have thus gone through the various topics in which the conflict of laws appertaining to different independent States comes most conspicuously into play. And although the positivism of the English school of jurisprudence has given it a character which is markedly at variance with the jurisprudence of the European Continent, the tendency of the more recent literature and case law is unquestionably to deal with questions on which the rights of foreigners depend, or in regard to which foreign laws may justly claim to have effective operation, in a spirit of larger toleration, and with due respect to principles of law which have gained general recognition amongst civilised nations. We have endeavoured in the foregoing chapters to deal with the subject of private international law in a manner which would simplify its study, and to indicate its leading principles not only from the point of view of general European jurisprudence, but more particularly as accepted by English judges and text-writers. Fortunately the case law available is abundant, and expositions by such eminent judges as Lords Brougham, Eldon, Stowell, Westbury, Chelmsford, Hatherley, Blackburn, and Selborne—to mention here only a few of the distinguished men whose decisions have been constantly quoted in the preceding pages—serve as beacon lights to illuminate the path of the diligent student, and prove that the principles which determine the law applicable to the reciprocal relations between subjects of different States are not propounded arbitrarily and at haphazard, but in accordance with the dictates of sound reason and in furtherance of justice. The incessant development of human activity in territories subject to diverse sovereignties, and the ever increasing relations between strangers—who constitute at the present time an important section of the actual population of each State—and citizens, give an importance to the subject of the present treatise which of itself necessitates the acceptance of certain uniform principles, and which finds a practical expression in international conventions like that of Paris of 1883 and of Berne of 1885, and in the unmitigating efforts of congresses held under the auspices and guidance of such men as Parodo, Lieber, Bluntschli, Field, Beach-Lawrence, Lorimer, Mancini, Sclopis, Woolsey, Asser, Robin, Jacquemyns, Alphonse, Rivier, Massé, and Westlake. Some of these great workers, alas! have gone away from us. But the spirit they evoked survives, and there is a feeling abroad in each civilised State that it is not only an independent organism, a *persona* which desires above all to maintain autonomy and liberty, but that it has a mission also to fulfil extraterritorially, which makes it impossible for it to restrict its activity within its own limits of sovereignty—a feeling, in short, that each State is but a member of a great family of nations, and that there is, consequently, a need of a common law and a true community of rights.[1] The stranger, as Laboulaye eloquently says, is no longer an enemy as in ancient times, a serf in the Middle Ages, and a waif in the last century; he is now a guest who enjoys all the civil rights which are accorded to a friend. But where there is a community of rights there must be a common law—*ubi societas, ibi jus.* And it is to endeavour to ascertain the principles on which this common law may be based, and to set them forth with special reference to the requirements of students in this department of legal study, that is the object of the present treatise. In this department the student must

[1] Cf. *Diritto Internazionale Privato,* par Pasquale Fiore, terza edizione. Prefazione, p. 5. (1888.)

CHAP. VII.

forget the exclusiveness of his national teaching, and he must be prepared to find many departures from that fundamental maxim of a feudal system—*leges non valent extra-territorium.*[1] At the present day laws not only do operate outside their own sovereign limits, but furnish, as we have seen, the only rule for the determination of many important legal questions between opposing litigants. To understand when they must be admitted to do so, and how they are to be judicially ascertained, constitute the teaching of that branch of jurisprudence which deals with the so-called *comitas nationum*, and is designated private international law. No subject can offer a more interesting course of study to the student of law than the prosecution of this double inquiry; none opens out to him a larger field for instructive investigation; and none possesses a richer and more comprehensive literature. In entering upon it the student leaves the dry bones of any one system of positive law behind him, and at every step forward he feels the freshness and freedom of the inquiry which lies before him. His view is no longer confined to one narrow groove, marked by insular prejudices and characteristics. But it expands with cosmopolitan fulness until it embraces every system of law which can claim recognition from a civilised State. The Christian, the Muhammadan, the Hindu, and the Confucian stand here on the same platform of a common humanity; and each can claim that his law, so long as it is not opposed to certain generally accepted principles of morality, shall be recognised whenever a proper case for its recognition can be shown to exist. It is not the religion of a State, but its degree of

[1] In saying this, it is not forgotten that it is to the Italian jurists of the thirteenth century—who, following in the footsteps of Baldus and Bartolus, established the doctrine that personal laws extend their empire and authority so as to attach to the person everywhere—that we thus owe the first indications of the modern theory as to the extraterritoriality of certain laws. Cf. Fiore, I. § 27, p. 49.

civilisation; not the creed it professes, but the character of its laws and the constitution of its courts which gives or give it a title to be considered a member of the family of nations. Once admitted into that family, its subjects are equally entitled to have their laws respected internationally, whether their religion be monotheistic or polytheistic, or whether the founder of that religion be a Moses, a Muhammad, a Buddha, or Christ.

INDEX.

Abandonment of Domicil, what necessary to constitute, 44.

Absence, temporary, will not destroy domicil, 36.

Act, capacity to, 53.

Action,
  parties to, when determined by the *lex fori*, 192.
  jurisdiction in entertaining, 224.

Actor sequitur Forum Rei, 106, 226, 228.

Agency,
  form of, depends on the *lex loci actûs* or residence of the agent, 142.
  so, relation between principal and agent, 142.
  relation between third persons and principal governed by the *lex loci actûs*, 143.
  agent has *primâ facie* no authority to bind foreign principal, 144.
  provisions of the Factors Act, 1889...144.
  law of the flag, 145.
  ratification of unauthorized acts of agents, 146.
  effect of ratification, 146.

Agent. See *Agency*.

Aliens,
  who are, 21.
  acquisition of British nationality by, 21.
  status of, 26.
  equal in sight of law with native subject, 48.
  have right to trade names, 182.

Allegiance, indissoluble, not now recognized except in Russia, 29.

Ancient Times, private international law in, 3—10.

Anglo-Indian domicile 38.

ANGLO-TURKISH domicil 39.

ASSIGNMENTS, general and particular (*q. v.*)

AUXILIARY PROCEEDINGS. See *Procedure.*

BANCROFT TREATIES, 31.

BANKRUPTCY,
effect of, on capacity, 52.
effect of, on personal estate of the debtor, 91 *et seq.*
jurisdiction in, based on domicil or residence, 91.
English bankruptcy carries all moveables and immoveables within the British dominions, 93.
title to immoveables of trustee in, perfected by compliance with the *lex sitûs*, 93.
foreign bankruptcy confers title to English moveables and immoveables, but title to latter to be perfected by English law, 94.
passes *choses in action*, 94.

BARRISTER, his right to sue for fees, governed by law affecting his bar, 107.

BILLS OF EXCHANGE, principles of private international law applied to, 117—124.

BUSINESS,
places of, may be deemed to be domicil of juristic persons, 44.
and also of other persons, 35.

CAPACITY,
effect of bankruptcy on, 52.
to act, depends on *lex domicilii*, 53—57.
but sometimes on *lex loci actûs*, 56.
of juristic persons, 74.
of corporations to acquire land depends on the *lex sitûs*, 77.
See *Marriage; Contracts; Wills.*

CESSION OF TERRITORY, exercise of option on, 19.

CHANGE OF DOMICIL, effect on right of succession to personal estate, 87—90.

CHOSES IN ACTION,
former law as to assignability of, 91.
pass on bankruptcy, 94.
assignment of, 95.

CIVIL PROCEDURE CODE OF INDIA, 79, 222, 240.
CIVIL STATUS, depends on *lex domicilii*, 47. See *Domicil.*
COLLISIONS AT SEA, 151.
COLONIES, naturalisation in, 24.
CONDITIONS required to make foreign judgments effective, 234.
CONSTRUCTION. See *Contracts; Wills; Matrimonial Domicil.*
CONSULAR Office, does not create domicil, 38.
CONTRACTS,
corporations may sue on, 75.
when contract obligations descend to heirs, 98.
theories as to law, applicable to, 100.
forum of debtor gives jurisdiction in, 106.
preliminary rules applicable to, 111.
contracts contrary to international comity, not enforceable, 111.
illegal by, *lex fori*, not enforceable, 111.
impossible, not enforceable, 111.
illegal by *lex loci solutionis*, not enforceable, 112.
revenue and penal laws of other countries ignored, 113.
unless the contract is rendered void for non-compliance, 114.
contracts time-barred by English law, will not be enforced, 114.
law governing the intrinsic validity and effect of contracts, 114 *et seq.*
validity with reference to making of contracts depends on the *lex loci actûs*, 115.
performance depends on the *lex loci solutionis*, 115.
question of interest, 116.
currency, 116.
bills of exchange, 117—124.
quasi contracts (*q. v.*)
law applicable to form of, *lex loci contractûs*, 126.
except as regards contract of immoveables, 128.
proof of, governed by *lex fori*, 129, 132.
remedy for breach of, governed by *lex fori*, 130.
construction of, governed by intention of the parties or by the *lex loci*, 136.
marriage contracts by the law of the matrimonial domicil, 137.
contracts, affected by commercial customs, 141.

Convention of Berne, 166.
given effect by 49 & 50 Vict. c. 33...168.

Convention of Paris, 175, 177.

Copyright,
what is, 164.
rules of international copyright founded on reciprocity, 164.
difference of, between published and unpublished writings at common law, 165.
history of international copyright, 166.
conditions for Order in Council to give effect to Convention of Berne, 168.
rules governing copyright of foreign authors, 168—170.
and those of authors whose countries have not joined the Convention of Berne, 170.
no copyright in works not published first in England, 171.
copyright, if work published first in England, provided author resident in England at the time, 171.
secus, if author not resident in England, 171.
possible exception in case of colonial residence, 172.
American law respecting, 172.

Corporations,
domicil of, 44.
capacity of, to act, 74.
may sue on contracts, 75.
nature of its constitution depends on *lex domicilii*, 75.
capacity to acquire land depends on *lex sitûs*, 77.
liability to income tax, 77.
Rules of Supreme Court respecting, 77.

Currency, 116.

Denization, 25.

Divorce,
exercise of "option" on, 20.
domicil of wife, in case of, 40.
jurisdiction in, founded on domicil, 66.
but sometimes on mere residence, 67.
sufficiency of grounds of, regulated by the *lex fori*, 68.

Domicil,
distinguished from nationality, 34.
what constitutes voluntary, 35.
of necessity, 38.
Anglo-Indian, 38.
Anglo-Turkish, 39.
of married women, 40.
of infants, 40.
of orphans, 40.
of origin, 43.
of juristic persons, 44.
determines civil status, 50.
jurisdiction in divorce, &c. See *Divorce; Wills; Jurisdiction; Foreign Judgments.*
law of. See *Lex domicilii.*

Evidence regulated by the *lex fori*, 195.

Exile involuntary, effect on domicil, 37.

Expatriation, right of, 29.

Extra Territorium Jus dicenti impune non paretur, 225, 228.

Factors Act, 1889...144.

Flag, law of, 145.
does not protect liability in torts, 157.

Foreign Authors. See *Copyright.*

Foreign Courts. See *Foreign Judgments; Jurisdiction.*

Foreign Judgments,
how treated internationally, 219.
current theories: (1) its adoption as domestic, 220.
(2) as a ground of action, 222.
(3) as evidence of original liability, 223.
when given effect to in England: the foreign Court must have had jurisdiction, 224 *et seq.*
other conditions necessary to make foreign judgment a *res judicata:*
it must have gone on the merits of the case, 234—5.
it must be free from fraud, 234, 235.
it must not totally disregard "the comity of nations," 234.
it must be consistent with natural justice, 234, 236.

FOREIGN JUDGMENTS—*continued.*
merits of, not examinable, 238 *et seq.*
except in India, 240
and in some other countries, 240.
mistake of law in, admitted by both parties, vitiates, 239.
judgment of native Indian Courts, how treated, 241.
in rem, its effect, 242.
its binding character all over the world, if passed by a competent Court, 243.
when avoided by fraud, 244.
when it will end proceedings respecting the same subject-matter, 247.

FOREIGN LAW, proof of, 216, 217.

FOREIGN LIMITATION LAW, not enforced if remedy merely barred, 114.

FOREIGN PENAL LAWS, not enforced extra-territorially, 114.

FOREIGN REVENUE LAWS, not generally protected extra-territorially, 113.

FOREIGN SOVEREIGNS,
position of, in monarchical States, 78.
rules of Indian law respecting native Indian princes, 79.

FORMALITIES OF CONTRACT, by what law governed, 127.

FRAUD
vitiates a foreign judgment *in personam*, 235.
when, avoids a foreign judgment *in rem*, 244—5.

FRENCH LAW governs all French subjects, in a French court, though domiciled abroad, 50.

GENERAL ASSIGNMENTS, validity of, determined by *lex domicilii*, 86.

HEIRS, transmission of liability on contracts to, how regulated, 98.

IMMATERIAL RIGHTS. See *Copyright; Patent; Trade Mark; Industrial Designs; Trade Name.*
how different from other *jura incorporales*, 163.
assignment of, 185.

IMMOVEABLES. See *Lex sitûs.*

INCAPACITY. See *Capacity.*

INCOME TAX, payable by foreign corporations only on English profits, 77.

INDUSTRIAL DESIGNS, 177.

INFANTS,
domicile of, 40.
exercise of "option" by, 20.

INTERCHANGE OF TRAFFIC, basis of international law, 1.

INTEREST, 116.

INTERNATIONAL COPYRIGHT ACT, 1886...90.

JUDEX TENETUR IMPERTIRI JUDICIUM SUUM, 246.

JUDGMENT,
in rem binds moveables, 86.
mode of enforcing, depends on *lex fori*, 205.
exception thereto, 207.
foreign. See *Foreign Judgments.*

JUDICATURE ACT, 1873, provisions of, as to assignability of choses in action, 91, 92.

JUDICIAL SEPARATION, 68.

JURISDICTION,
in divorce based on domicile, 66.
in bankruptcy based on domicile or residence, 91.
service out of, 213.
in Indian law, 215.
when English Courts will recognise jurisdiction of foreign Courts, 224.
what is voluntary submission to found jurisdiction, 225 *et seq.*
mere possession of moveable property does not found, 233.

JURISTIC PERSONS,
capacity to act, 74.
domicile, 44.
in Indian law, 45.

JUS COGENS in copyrights, 163.
exigendi, 96.
sanguinis, 16.
soli, 16.

LEGAL PERSONALITY consists of political status and civil status (*q. v.*).

LEGES NON VALENT EXTRA TERRITORIUM, 250.

LEGITIMACY,
depends on *lex domicilii*, 69.
right of illegitimate children, when recognised in English law, 71.

LEGITIMATIO PER SUBSEQUENS MATRIMONIUM, 71.

LEX DOMICILII,
determines capacity to act, 53.
essentials of marriage, 57.
legitimacy, 69.
legitimation, 71.
constitution of corporations, 75.
juridical capacity of corporations, 75.
validity of general assignments of moveables, 86.
succession at death, 86.
assignment at marriage, 87.
validity of wills, 88.
exceptions, 89.
effect of bankruptcy on moveables, 91.
applied to wills of foreigners, 130.

LEX FORI,
determines grounds of divorce, 68.
contracts illegal by, not enforced, 111.
determines period of limitation of actions, 114.
priorities, 209.
proof of contracts, 129, 132.
remedy on breach of contracts, 130.
See *Procedure*.

LEX LOCI ACTÛS OR CONTRACTÛS,
sometimes determines capacity to act, 56.
form of marriage governed by, 58.
application of, to contracts, 131.
when affects validity of contracts, 115,
form of contracts, 128.
determines construction of contract, 136.
form of agency, 142.
relation between principal and agent, 143.
third parties, 144.

LEX LOCI CELEBRATIONIS, 58, 97.

LEX LOCI SOLUTIONIS,
applied to contracts, 102, 103.
contracts illegal by, not enforced, 112.
when affects validity of contracts, 115,

Lex Sitûs,
governs effect of marriage on immoveables, 62.
exception in S. Africa, 63.
capacity of corporations to acquire lands, 77.
disposition of immoveables, 82.
moveables in particular assignments, 84.
ships in particular assignments, 90.
as affecting assignment of land on bankruptcy, 93.

Limitation of Actions,
period of, 196.
exception, 199, 201.

Lis alibi pendens, when plea of, effective in staying proceedings, 244.

Locus regit Actum, 53, 84, 94, 127, 133.

Maritime Law, 158.

Marriage,
essentials of, depend on *lex domicilii*, 57.
form of, depends on *lex loci actûs*, 58.
must be monogamous, 60.
except in India, 61.
effect of, on property of spouses, 62.
immoveables, 63.
personal relation of the spouses, 65.

Marriage Settlements, effect and validity of, governed by the law of the matrimonial domicil, 63.

Married Women, domicil of, 40.

Matrimonial Domicil,
what, 63.
governs construction of marriage contracts, 137.

Maxims,
actor sequitur forum rei, 106, 226, 228.
extra territorium, jus dicenti impune non paretur, 225, 228.
judex tenetur impertiri judicium suum, 246.
leges non valent extra territorium, 250.
locus regit actum, 53, 84, 94, 127, 133.
mobilia sequuntur personam, 81, 84, 91, 97.
mobilia ossibus inhærent, 81, 84, 91, 97.
nemo potest exuere patriam, 29.
omnis ratihabitio retrotrahitur et mandato priori æquiparatur, 146.
qui facit per alium, facit per se, 143.
ubi societas, ibi jus, 249.

MELCHA, position of, under Hindu law, 3.

MERITS,
of foreign judgment not examinable, 236.
except of foreign Asian or African Court in British Indian court, 240.

MIDDLE AGES,
private international law in, 4—10.
achievement of the jurists of, 9.

MINOR, domicil of, 40.

MISTAKE OF LAW, 239.

MOBILIA OSSIBUS INHÆRENT, 9, 81, 84, 91, 97.

MOBILIA SEQUUNTUR PERSONAM, 9, 81, 84, 91, 97.

MORAL SENSE, laws of one nation opposed to, of another nation, not enforced, 51.

MORATORIUM, effect of foreign provisions relating to, 120.

MOVEABLES,
general assignment of, governed by *lex domicilii*, 86.
particular assignment of, governed by *lex sitûs*, 84.
bound by judgment in law of Court of *situs*, 86.
effect of bankruptcy on, 91.

NATIONALITY OR POLITICAL STATUS,
theories for determining, 16.
how determined in Rome, 16.
England, 16, 19.
America, 17.
France, 17.
Germany, 18.
Italy, 18.
how acquired in England, 19.
how formally determined, 27.
plurality of, 28.
cesser of one, depends on acquisition of another, 31.
idea of, 32.
questions to which applicable, 33.
distinguished from domicil, 34.

NATIVE COURTS OF INDIAN STATES, how their judgment is treated, 241 *et seq.*

NATIVE PRINCES OF INDIA, rules applicable to, 79.

NATURAL JUSTICE, what, 236.

NATURALISATION,
how affected, 21.
effect of, 23.
in the Colonies, 24.

NEMO POTEST PATRIUM EXUERE, 29.

NINETEENTH CENTURY, history of private international law in, 10—14.

OBLIGATIONS. See *Contracts; Torts; Wills.*

OFFICIAL RESIDENCE, effect of, in constituting domicil, 38.

OMNIS RATIHABITIO RETROTRAHITUR, ETC., 146.

"OPTION,"
what is, 19.
on cession of territory, 19.
on divorce, 20.
on widowhood, 20.
by infants, 20.

ORIGIN, domicil of, 43.

ORPHANS, domicil of, 40.

PARLIAMENTARY RESIDENCE, no proof of domicil, 38.

PARTICULAR assignment of moveables, 84.

PARTIES TO ACTION, how far determined by the *lex fori*, 192—194.

PATENT RIGHTS,
what are, 173.
international aspect of, 173.
rules of, 173.
Convention of Paris regarding, 175.
effect of 46 & 47 Vict. c. 57 on, 175.

PENAL LAWS, foreign, not enforced extra-territorially, 52.

PERSONAL LAW, scope and operation of, 5.

PERSONS, capacity, state and condition of, governed by what law, 50.

POLITICAL refugees do not lose domicil of origin, if absence involuntary, 37.

POLITICAL STATUS. See *Nationality*.

PRINCIPAL. See *Agency*.
foreign principal, 144.

PRIORITY, determined by the *lex fori*, 209.

PRIVATE INTERNATIONAL LAW,
basis of, 1.
meaning of, 1, 2.
development of, 2—14.
in ancient times: among the Hebrews, 3.
the Romans, 4.
in the middle ages: early portion, 4.
later portion, 6—10.
during the nineteenth century, 10—14.

PROCEDURE,
nature of the inquiry respecting the law applicable to, 188.
difficulty in distinguishing between question of essentials and of procedure in obligations, 190.
lex fori on parties to an action, 192.
governs evidence, 195.
limitation of actions, 196.
probably different in India, 198.
and on the Continent, 198.
may be excluded if right extinguished, 201.
mode of enforcing mode of judgment, 205.
exceptions, 207.
right of set-off, 208.
priorities, 209.
law applicable to auxiliary proceedings taken in aid of a suit extra-territorially, 210 *et seq.*
form of oath and mode of recording evidence governed by the law of the place where judicial act is done, 212.
probative value of such evidence determined by the *forum*, 212.
rules of English law as to service out of the jurisdiction, 213.
Indian law as to service out of the jurisdiction, 215.
proof of foreign law, 216, 217.
res judicata. See *Foreign Judgments*.
lis alibi pendens (*q. v.*).

PROFESSIONES JURIS, 5.

QUASI CONTRACTS,
examples of, 125.
law applicable to, 125—127.

QUI FACIT PER ALIUM, FACIT PER SE, 143.

RATIFICATION, 146.

RECUPERATIO, the first outline of a system of international justice, 4.

RELEGATIO, if perpetual, gave necessary domicil, 37.

RESIDENCE,
what necessary to constitute domicil, 35.
occasioned by parliamentary duties, creates a domicil, 38.
of officials, effect of, 38.

RES JUDICATA. See *Foreign Judgments.*

RESTITUTION OF CONJUGAL RIGHTS, 68.

REVENUE LAWS, foreign, not enforced, 113.

RULE OF THE ROAD, 158.

SET-OFF, right of, 208.

SHIPS, validity of disposition of, depends on *lex sitûs*, 90.

SLAVES, contract relating to, when may be enforced, 51.

SOVEREIGN,
position of, in monarchical States, 78.
suits by or against, 79.

STATUS,
what is meant by, in legal sense, 47.
political, as distinguished from civil, 15, 16, 48.
law of domicil governs, 50.

STATUTE THEORY, 6.
its origin, 7.
its principles, 8.

STATUTES,
22 Hen. VIII. c. 8......25.
12 & 13 Will. III. c. 2......25.
8 Anne, c. 19......164.
4 Geo. II. c. 21......73.
53 Geo. III. c. 159......156.
54 Geo. III. c. 136......167.
5 Geo. IV. c. 113......112.
1 Will. IV. c. 22......211.
1 & 2 Vict. c. 59......167.
3 & 4 Vict. c. 105......211.
6 & 7 Vict. c. 98......112.
7 & 8 Vict. c. 12......167, 169
15 & 16 Vict. c. 12......168.
17 & 18 Vict. c. 104......160.
22 & 23 Vict. c. 63......218.
24 & 25 Vict. c. 11......218.
24 & 25 Vict. c. 114......26, 89
24 & 25 Vict. c. 121......41.
25 & 26 Vict. c. 63......155.
31 & 32 Vict. c. 54......240.
33 & 34 Vict. c. 14......16.
35 & 36 Vict. c. 39......31.
38 & 39 Vict. c. 12......168.
44 & 45 Vict. c. 21......65.
45 & 46 Vict. c. 61......117.
46 & 47 Vict. c. 52......93.
c. 57......175, 183.
49 & 50 Vict. c. 33......90, 168.
50 & 51 Vict. c. 28......186.
52 & 53 Vict. c. 45......144.

STUDENT, residence as, does not constitute domicil, 36.

THINGS, law of, 80 *et seq.*
rights to, different theories respecting, 80.
See *Contracts; Moveables; Immoveables; Wills.*

TORTS,
law applicable to, 149.
must be suable by *lex loci actûs*, 149.
and also by the *lex fori*, 151.
effect of Merchant Shipping Act as to torts at sea, 157.

TRADE MARKS, 177.
infringement of, punished criminally, 186.

TRADE NAMES, 178.
aliens have a right to, 182.

UBI SOCIETAS, IBI JUS, 249.

WIDOWS, exercise of "option" by, 20.

WILLS,
validity of, 87.
in English law, 88.
of foreigners, 134.
of British subjects, 136.
construction of, 137—9.